UC

THE TOWN LABOURER AND THE INDUSTRIAL REVOLUTION

THE TOWN LABOURER AND THE INDUSTRIAL REVOLUTION

Malcolm I. Thomis

B.T. Batsford Ltd, London and Sydney

For Jacqueline

First published 1974

ISBN 0 7134 2832 5
ISBN 0 7134 2833 3

Printed in Great Britain by
Bristol Typesetting Co Ltd
Barton Manor - St Philips
Bristol

for the publishers B.T. Batsford Ltd,
4 Fitzhardinge Street, London W1H 0AH
and 23 Cross Street, Brookvale, NSW 2100, Australia

Contents

Acknowledgments

This text, being largely of an historiographical kind, derives mainly from the ideas and writing of others, and those familiar with the literature of the period will have no difficulty in recognising the work of the masters. This I have endeavoured to identify by quotation marks or at least a footnote acknowledgment; where a word formation or trick of thought betrays another mind whose presence remains unacknowledged I can only apologise and offer a tribute to those historians whose ideas have become so much a part of the common stock that we each of us look upon them as our own.

My other debt is to Margaret Hendry of Stirling University who typed my manuscript very speedily but who is not responsible for any of its faults.

1 *The Town Labourer: Historians and Social Critics*

'Hence it was that amid all the conquests over nature that gave its triumph to the Industrial Revolution, the soul of man was passing into a colder exile . . .'

— *The Town Labourer*, p. 311.

There is an Industrial Revolution that is familiar to almost all who know of the Industrial Revolution. It is that which has been described in the books of J. L. and Barbara Hammond, especially *The Town Labourer,* which is the most powerful presentation of a particular view that has been for over a half a century, almost universally held outside academic circles and very popular within them.[1]

The story of *The Town Labourer* concerns the emergence during the Industrial Revolution, as a result of scientific discovery and invention, of a new power capable of transforming men's lives for the better. But this transformation was not allowed to happen. Instead, capitalists acquired control, as a result of which the progress of industry benefited a tiny minority, who grew rich, and led to the immiseration of the great majority, who passed into another of history's Dark Ages, the Age of the Industrial Revolution. For the happiness which should have resulted from increased knowledge and the creation of wealth was substituted mass degradation, and until capitalism could be controlled the freedom and contentment of men were in jeopardy. Inside the factory there developed a régime of inhuman discipline which destroyed any dignity the workman previously possessed, a systemisation and institutionalisation of the evils of child labour accompanied by brutality and contempt for human life, with workmen and their children abandoned by the state to the whims of employers, victims of what is described as 'a class conflict of a most cruel and exhausting kind'. This took place within towns which 'represented nothing but the avarice of the jerry-builder catering for the avarice of the capitalist', which allowed man to survive, but provided for none of his needs beyond bare survival, and condemned him to becoming brutalised. In this life he could expect no protection from the law, an instrument not of justice but of repression, used to enforce that concept of society to which its governors subscribed; under the impact of the French and Industrial Revolutions order meant discipline and government meant force. The workforce of industrial England, and it is to England only that this book refers, were denied any share in the increased wealth that their efforts produced by a systematic war on trade unions, which robbed them of the opportunity to organise in self-defence, and in their poverty they were compelled to turn to their children as breadwinners for the family. The inhumanity displayed by society towards child labour in factories was paralleled by the neglect of those who worked in mines and as chimney-sweeps. It was not that men were consciously heartless and cruel, rather that prevailing philosophies of the age, the ideas of Malthus, Ricardo, McCulloch and Adam Smith, used selectively, rationalised poverty, neglect, and the need for the individual to provide for his own survival: 'if society took care of the interests of property, the deserving poor would become rich'; if they remained poor they deserved to remain poor. And if the conscience of the rich should be troubled, there was absolution in the teachings of Hannah More and William Wilberforce, who threw the whole force of the Evangelical Revival behind the demand for obedience from the working classes and offered them faith as their only hope of alleviation. Abandoned by those who might have given them help, the working classes began to move slowly towards finding their own salvation, in trade unionism, a school of heroism and public spirit, in Methodism, which extended a rival philosophy but in effect encouraged them to learn the techniques of industrial and political organisation, and in the birth of a social and political consciousness, which would lead on to the political campaigns of the future, such as Chartism and the Labour Party.

The Town Labourer is a passionate and committed book, the classic presentation of what has come to be known as the pessimist case on the Industrial Revolution, the grand denunciation featuring all the villains unequivocally denounced, the capitalist owners of factories and mines, the politicians such as Pitt and Wilberforce who collaborated with them. It is the popular view of the Industrial Revolution with all the eloquence and all the embellishments, not necessarily the view of the majority of academic historians but the Industrial Revolution of popular tradition, which has supplied sustenance to a wealth of ideologies and philosophies of life. It is what people know of the Industrial Revolution even if they have never read a history book.

The Town Labourer is a series of moral judgments, and historians have never been united on this issue. With reservations about their power and right to distinguish good from evil, they nonetheless do make moral judgments much of the time. Arnold Toynbee's belief that the effects of the Industrial Revolution were 'terrible' echoed Southey's contemporary comment on the 'evil' that had descended upon society.[2] In later times the 1834 Poor Law, for example, has evoked a torrent of condemnation to rival the outrage of Cole and Postgate at 'how dreadful a principle this was'.[3] Some historians wish only to describe; others feel that judgments are inescapable. E. H. Carr refuses to allow moral judgments on individuals, in part because of the futility of the exercise, but insists that they be passed upon the societies that created them, whilst E. P. Thompson expects his historian to be 'concerned with making some judgment of value upon the whole process entailed in the Industrial Revolution of which we ourselves are an end product.'[4] It would be foolish to suppose that any one school of thought monopolises wisdom on this subject, that, for instance, the distinction between the moral judges and the abstainers is the difference between the bad and the good historians. The individual chooses his own approach. It has been said of R. H. Tawney that he owes his great influence as much to the appeal of his politics and ethics as to his obvious professional qualities as a historian; without moral judgments his work would cease to exist and without his work historical writing would be much impoverished.[5]

Most would now accept the need to avoid judgments on the private morality of individuals where that had no general implication for the conduct of public affairs, no wider historical significance. In the bigger area where moral judgments are frequently involved, in the assessment of societies or civilisations, the magnitude of the subject often seems to obscure the nature of the verdict offered; the enormity of the historian's offence, if such it be, is in inverse proportion to the size of the crime he chooses to commit. Where the bigger issue is at stake the rule seems to be that historians should not make moral judgments without being aware of what they are doing and without admitting their awareness. *The Town Labourer* is concerned essentially with this matter of examining the quality of a new civilisation which the authors believe to have developed in consequence of industrialisation and of showing how that civilisation or society differed from what preceded it; this is a perfectly acceptable job for historians to do. It is also concerned with showing not only that the new society differed from its predecessor but that it was in a number of ways inferior to it. In other words, the authors apply a moral judgment to the society of newly industrialised England and assess it according to certain criteria, which are either personal criteria that relate only to them or universally acceptable ones by which societies as a whole can always be judged. Not only this, the authors are also concerned to examine how far and in what ways this society fell short of some ideal upheld by themselves, for it is this ideal rather than some universally acceptable standard that is the source of the criteria that they are applying. This is arguably a dubious purpose for a historian to engage in, though it is one shared by a multitude of historians of all persuasions. With the Hammonds it is at least clear and explicit; with others it is often implicitly present even when explicitly denied.

What in fact happens is that historians succumb to the temptation to argue on behalf of a hypothetical alternative; instead of explaining what things were like and why – their proper province – they explain what things could, or even should, have been like if affairs had been better conducted. They prescribe the course that history should have followed instead of the one that actually was followed, leaving themselves open to the charge that their preferences cause them to fail to see what a more objective observer would record. For example, it has been said of the Hammonds that for them the economic progress of the years of industrialisation was vitiated by inequitable distribution of wealth and consequent social divisions; in emphasising the inequalities within society, which in their view made it a defective society, they neglected to record the true achievement of economic growth that was taking place. The converse of their position is the argument that things were far from being as bad as the Hammonds, with their ideal in mind, believed, and were so good, in fact, that they constituted a successful demonstration of a rival ideal, that of a free enterprise economy and society.[6] But the changes of this period must not be judged in terms of their realisation of any particular ideal, whether individualist or collectivist or perhaps based on an interpretation of Christianity. There is a celebrated judgment which condemns the 'attainment of material riches as the supreme object of human endeavour and the final criterion of human happiness' and this distributes criticism alike upon the wealthy who make riches their goal and their opponents whose sole virtue is perhaps the transitory poverty from which they seek to escape.[7]

It is important then to identify the ideal which the Hammonds have in mind, or at least to identify and isolate the assumptions and beliefs through which the ideal is implied. Some of the principal ones are these: that the happiness of the many is more important than the profit of the few; that the benefits arising from mechanisation and technological change should be directed towards public not private advantage; that power within society should be controlled on behalf of the entire community and not entrusted to a few irresponsible individuals; that human life and dignity are matters of great importance; that the working classes should not exist merely for the service and profit of other classes; that education is preferable to indoctrination. All these propositions, which occur in *The Town Labourer,* involve a statement of preference between x and y, a moral choice illustrating the historian's dilemma, albeit expressed in more sophisticated language, contained in the satirical distinction between 'good kings' and 'bad kings'. There are 'good' principles and 'bad' principles in the organisation of society, and any society which rejects the 'good' ones will be found wanting when judgment is passed. The rival principles are explicitly summed up by the Hammonds in their statement of the two contrasting ideals or philosophies of society which they believe to have been in conflict during the period they are describing. One they name as individualism, which demands that genius and industry shall be free, that the individual by exercising ability and virtue shall be allowed to improve his status and rise to the very top of society; within this system, they say, the ideal working man aspires to become an employer. The other they describe as a collectivist or socialist philosophy, involving corporate ideas and the demand for a better standard for a whole race of men and women; within this system the ideal working man tries to raise the status of his entire class, not simply that of himself.[8] Of these two, the Hammonds very clearly reject the first and subscribe to the second, and the fact that one is thought preferable to the other pervades their entire work. They extend the historian's function of describing and explaining the situation under investigation and add to it that of the social critic, for not only is industrial society described and explained; it is also subjected to scathing attack for its deficiencies and failure to measure up to the standards applied by the investigators.

The Hammonds' posing of the problem of social organisation in terms of the two conflicting ideals is by no means unique; indeed W. B. Gallie, in a philosopher's study of history, suggests that the concept of social justice admits of only two rival descriptions, the individualist and collectivist ideals, which are those identified by the Hammonds.[9] In very recent times the early nineteenth century arguments between the free market advocates and the interventionists of the 'new moral order' have been represented as the 'alternative and irreconcilable views of human order – one based on mutuality, the other on competition', an historical confrontation of such universal significance that it almost predetermined the alignment of later historians on the two sides.[10] Tawney was one such historian; he attempted to do justice to the achievements of the liberal movement in British affairs, which reached its climax in the years 1832-70, whilst at the same time noting its limitations: a reverence for birth and wealth, especially the latter, which made real equality of opportunity unattainable, and a greater concern for the amassing of wealth than for its equitable distribution; a civilisation that would be enjoyed only by escape from the ranks of the masses and not by membership of them. And against what he called this 'social counterpart of natural selection through the struggle for existence' he posed the collectivist approach which would be directed towards a higher good, a 'new moral order' for the future, a mere hypothetical alternative as far as the past was concerned.[11]

It is common now to recognise that the rapid economic growth of the late eighteenth and early nineteenth centuries took place at some 'social cost', that developments in the social sphere did not keep pace with developments in the economic. This happened because the Industrial Revolution was carried out in an unplanned, uncontrolled way, without central direction, and financed on a capitalist, free enterprise basis. The result of this was that the profit motive was uppermost in determining expansion and expenditure, and those aspects of life which were not immediately necessary for the realisation of profit were neglected and received only belated attention. It is the assumption of the Hammonds that if the Industrial Revolution had taken place in other ways, for instance, as a result of some centrally planned process which was concerned less with the profit motive and more with the well-being of the work-force participating in the industrial changes, the order of priorities could and would have been different, that health, housing, sanitation, and the provision of municipal amenities, for instance, would have come much earlier and would not have been subordinated to the central profit motive that controlled the course of events as they did in fact develop. It is possible to devise any number of ideal programmes which would have been superior to the actual programme followed, but this is the characteristic of the ideal, that it is superior to the actual for the idealist who holds it. The actual will always, and by definition, be found unsatisfactory and wanting, when measured against the ideal, and some historians have assumed the function of judging a series of developments or a society against the ideal to which they subscribe. Others have renounced this kind of exercise as a proper one for professional historians, whose task is to examine and explain what actually happened rather than to say what should have happened. The problems and complications involved in this are sufficiently numerous in themselves without any need to become involved in what might have been, had history taken other, and better, courses.

The Industrial Revolution was, objectively, a capitalist, free enterprise exercise, whether an individual might find this a cause for satisfaction or regret, and it is this capitalist, free enterprise exercise which has to be explained and the consequences of which have to be examined. The history of such an operation need be neither a justification and glorification of capitalism and all its achievements nor a condemnation of the evils that resulted from this kind of arrangement of affairs. The pattern of society that free enterprise produced was not necessarily superior to that which would have been produced by an alternative economic system; nor can anyone say with assurance that it was necessarily worse, though it will always seem worse than the ideal system that was not chosen.

The actual, because it was not the ideal, will inevitably be a matter for strong criticism. The actual social philosophy of the rulers of early nineteenth century Britain was not one with which the Hammonds had any sympathy, and so they were in almost perpetual disagreement with what governments were doing in this period. They believed that prevailing attitudes produced a very general reluctance amongst governments to assume central power and direction over the many problems which industrialisation was throwing up, problems such as factory reform, the new towns, and public health, on all of which official action was tardy and ineffective. They believed too that the prevailing attitudes under which a free enterprise Industrial Revolution progressed ensured that the profit motive would always predominate, that social amenities would inevitably be neglected, that solutions offered to social problems would always be the cheap ones, that the economic case for mechanisation and technological change would inevitably override social considerations, that the very inspiration and motivation behind economic growth created an *a priori* case for assuming that it was not accompanied by rising living standards for the workers. Perhaps too their belief in the missed opportunity of central direction caused them to underestimate the problems involved in the transformation of the economy and society on the facile assumption that all would have been well and easy had the alternative route been taken. All these assumptions pervade their work, and if their work is to be re-examined they must at least be queried.

The alternative society has been as much the preserve of the contemporary social critic, an Owen, a Shelley, or an Oastler, as of the historian, and the Hammonds became part of a well-established tradition of writers who performed both roles. Toynbee had been outraged at the social evils consequent upon the industrialisation process, and this sense of outrage was to characterise the work of a whole school of later Socialist historians, including the Webbs, the Hammonds, the Coles, and Tawney, followed in recent years by E. J. Hobsbawm, Christopher Hill, and E. P. Thompson. With the Webbs and Tawney in particular, the past was being explored to explain the need and justification for social and political programmes they were themselves advocating, and arguably this practical concern was a corrupting influence on their history. Beatrice Webb examined and participated in, though not always at first hand, 'the working-class revolt against the misery and humiliation brought about by the Industrial Revolution', 'the gigantic cruel experiment which . . . was proving a calamitous failure', and she pursued her historical and sociological enquiries with what she called a 'ceaseless questioning of social facts'.[12] History which appears to be directed to a modern political purpose, to help ensure, for instance, that battles lost in nineteenth-century England might yet be won in the industrialising countries of modern Africa and Asia, will always arouse suspicions, as too will history that appears to be written to expound a social philosophy.[13] But this is not to discount its value, only to identify it as a particular genus which has loomed large in historical writing on the Industrial Revolution. For the social critics have not been alone in approaching the past with something more than pure academic intent. The desire to demonstrate the virtues and value of a 'free society' is at least as questionable as the desire to demonstrate its vices.[14]

It is a natural characteristic of the historian writing as a social critic that he displays a warmth, a sympathy, and a humanity that are sometimes felt to be undesirable in a historian, and these qualities are certainly abundantly present in the writing of the Hammonds to the extent that their work has been described as sentimental. On this charge they are acquitted by one eminent scholar who argues that there is no sentimentality in directing concern upon those who bore the burden of industrialisation and points rather to the positive achievement of writers who opened up an entire new field of study, the lives of ordinary people, which they are said to have investigated with remarkable 'historical imagination'. History could never be the same after their contribution.[15] Any lack of this warmth and sympathy possessed by the Hammonds is in fact seen as a failing, both in the characters of those who made history and those who interpret it. The unconcern shown by the Methodists for the fate of factory children is held to be one of the worst counts against them, whilst T. S. Ashton's reference to the 'depressing story of pauper children' is also thought to betray an insufficient emotion for the nature of the subject.[16] On the debit side it has been argued that their excessive sympathy for the plight of the working classes caused them to single out for mention only the depressing features of industrial society, to ignore the encouraging ones, and to present altogether too gloomy an account.[17] On occasion they even resort to mild trickery to lay on the gloom thick and heavy, as, for instance, when they talk of children in bibs undergoing punishment; now 'bibs' is a more suggestive but more misleading term than 'pinafores', which, they explain earlier, is what the word really meant.[18]

Not only did they present the Industrial Revolution in the worst possible light, which was bad enough, argue the critics, but they also managed to turn their account into an historical best-seller, which was unforgivable. So disturbed were they at the plight of the working classes that they failed to report, what Ashton later recorded as one of the substantial gains of industrialisation, 'the emergence of a self-respecting class of wage-earners', though they had already written their answer to that point when they commented in 1917 that before the working classes could emerge they had to overcome all the obstacles that were put in their way by a class holding the power that law, custom, education and wealth could create.[19] In other words, the Industrial Revolution was not a benevolent movement which encouraged working-class independence so much as a development which they survived against all the odds. It was a struggle successfully accomplished rather than a blessing to be enjoyed.

Those who are somewhat critical of the Hammond's emotional involvement in their subject are similarly critical of the kind of sources that they employed for their study, though both problems have a common origin. They were interested, it has been said, in inequality and unemployment and not in economic growth, and their criteria were human not economic;[20] it could alternatively be said that they were profoundly interested in people and only marginally interested in statistics, which inevitably limits their appeal to modern schools of economic historians. They knew nothing of the business records which have revealed the enormous leap forward in economic growth during the Industrial Revolution and knew only the reports of the many commissions of enquiry into what was wrong with the country and the correspondence that came in to the government from all and sundry on all kinds of issues, but particularly on law-breaking, actual or potential, of various kinds. They knew well the letters that arrived from magistrates, provincial solicitors, employers, informers, and the like and the replies that went out from the Home Office as its officials attempted to separate the wheat from the chaff and identify any useful information that was emerging. From all this material they formed an impression of an oppressive system of spies, informers, harsh employers, and panicky rulers, who were holding down a society allegedly about to erupt. They reacted violently against the view that the threat of revolution justified the means by which Britain was governed in these years, which they believed to be a myth deliberately fostered as a rationalisation for the oppressive policies of governments and employers. It is possible, as has been argued recently, that they underestimated the revolution menace, but their view that it was all part of a government conspiracy helped to strengthen their belief in the evil practices of governments and the leaders of society during these years.[21]

Another limitation that the Hammonds have as far as modern scholars are concerned is their deficiency in the field of economic history. There are many issues which are not particularly central to their thesis, but on which they touch in passing, where their somewhat crude views have failed to stand the test of time, however well they might have served as summaries of contemporary opinions. On questions like population growth, labour migration, and the origins of industrial capital they make no appreciable contribution to the detailed and scholarly investigations that have been undertaken in the last 50 years, though neither their reputation nor the validity of their thesis rests upon these aspects of their case. Their view that the Corn Laws formed an important element in the misery of the time was part of a long, popular tradition which could for a long time be assumed to be correct but is now accepted much less readily. Similarly, their assertion that the slave labour of the pauper apprentices formed the basis of the new industries and carried the mills through the first stages of industrialisation is an assumption or statement of faith rather than a conclusion reached as a result of an investigation of the situation.[22]

The new emphasis of those who have attempted to revise these judgments might almost seem to have arisen in response to the expressed regrets of Sir John Clapham that social historians were making insufficient use of the work of statisticians.[23] Clapham himself attempted to redress the balance of opinion on the social consequences of industrialisation by utilising data on wages and prices, and others have followed where he led. Professor Postan has noted the increasing role of economists in economic history as they have extended their enquiries on economic growth into past centuries, taking with them their own 'climate' and techniques not necessarily well-suited to the subject matter they are beginning to handle.[24] Perhaps the most disturbing aspect of the arrival of the historians with the strong orientation towards economics has been an over-ready acceptance of the 'virtues of economic growth', a new central purpose or mission for industrialising nations to accomplish, a new panacea for the problems of society, to the pursuit of which all other activities come to acquire a subordinate or peripheral role and the realisation of which is offered as a justification of almost any act of social policy which accompanied its achievement. It has been said of these 'anti-catastrophic empiricists' that they, unlike the Hammonds, have neglected to place the economic growth of the period of Industrial Revolution within its proper political and social setting, ignoring the ideological climate in which industrialisation grew, and that this has encouraged them towards a renewed confusion of history with their own ideological views; that their sympathy for the capitalist entrepreneur has produced another dose of that mixture of 'history and apologetics' which the Hammonds on earlier occasions were guilty of concocting.[25]

Statements of faith are, of course, of the very essence of historical writing in what has been called the Whig tradition of British historiography, and the Hammonds fit very squarely inside this tradition. It is one that has its good men and its bad men, its good causes and its bad causes, with good being determined as much by eventual success as by moral consideration. The Hammonds combined both the moral standpoint and the Whig tradition, for most of their morally desirable causes eventually became successful ones, and they were able to rejoice in the eventual emergence of parliamentary democracy, of government responsibility in large measure for social welfare, of working-class institutions such as the trade unions and the Labour Party, and of equal opportunity through a free national education system. Their heroes are people who advocated and pursued these and similar causes, their villains those who opposed them or failed to make any contribution to their evolution. The problems of society are solved by good men and perpetuated by bad ones, and it is possible to identify in all spheres of human activity, whether in politics, labour disputes, or the building of drains, those who have worked for 'progress' and those who have resisted it.

This tendency to see history in such black and white terms has been increasingly resisted in modern times with the result that history books are now populated by grey men and the problems and failings of society are much less attributed to human weakness. So many of the issues which provoked moral outrage and disgust in the Hammonds at the failure of governments and employers to rectify intolerable situations are now seen as the almost inescapable complications that attended a process of rapid change, the fault of no-one in particular, which would rectify themselves in time, self-curing matters rather than issues that demanded mighty campaigns and mighty campaigners. The problems associated with the administration of justice and the maintenance of law and order, factory conditions during the early stages of industrialisation, the increased population and the new towns in which the extra people lived, are all seen as matters too unexpected, too large, and too complicated for immediate solution. They just happened, without anyone planning them, and eventually they would be attended to without the need for anyone to become particularly excited about them. The calculated oppression of a central government which operated its régime of terror by means of a spy system and a standing army in place of a police force dissolves into a blundering, well-intentioned incompetence as authorities sought to cope with huge numbers of tightly-packed people by means of administrative machinery out of date and inefficient for its new purposes. The calculated oppression of the early factory masters dissolves itself into the fumbling efforts of novice operators striving to recruit a labour force and teach themselves elementary techniques of management as yet unknown. This kind of interpretation of history, a philosophy of history almost, has been labelled 'Tory'; it is a highly mechanistic view of government, society, and the processes of change, and it allows little significance to the people who were so important to the Hammonds as perpetrators of outrageous deeds, as sufferers, and as reformers. It is entirely contrary to the approach which they adopted and it appears at almost every stage of the argument where their views are being re-examined.

Closely akin to this kind of approach is the attack delivered upon those who suggest that the governments of these years should somehow have converted Britain into a welfare state overnight: such people have too high an expectation of what was possible within the time-span under consideration. The social problems resulting from industrialisation took time to diagnose and time to cure because society lacked the professional skills and administrative machinery necessary to undertake the immense task facing society. It was not that governments lacked the will to improve but rather that they were confronted with almost insuperable difficulties, lacking, for instance, the essential bureaucratic machinery to implement policies even when they had been decided upon. In the circumstances it would be unrealistic to have expected more; governments should be praised for the amount they managed to achieve so quickly rather than condemned for what they were not able to accomplish.[27]

Again, part of the problem is that of wishing to measure achievement against the hypothetical alternative rather than in terms of what was currently possible at a particular moment in time. In this case the alternative is that suggested by the modern bureaucratic state which exercises very wide powers in all welfare areas, but it is little help to an understanding of the problems of the early nineteenth century to suggest that they would have been better solved by a government from the middle of the twentieth century. Nor is it universally conceded that such efforts as central governments did make towards regulating social and economic conditions were necessarily conducive to the solution of those problems towards which they were directed. The Factory Acts, for instance, have been suggested as an actual impediment to the improvement of factory conditions, which might have been better left to the discretion of the factory owner than tackled by an interfering government which knew too little of the affairs which it sought to regulate.[28]

But the desire to regulate took a long time to grow and what the Hammonds were in fact doing in *The Town Labourer* was lamenting the disappearance of paternalism as a motivating sentiment in government policies and describing the evils which they believe resulted from this changing attitude and would continue until the state resumed responsibility, in greater measure than ever before, for solving the problems arising out of industrialisation. Almost their central theme is the clash between liberal individualism, the ideal which triumphed in the period they are describing, of which they are highly critical, and collectivism, the ideal that they advocate, which will, they believe, offer solutions to the problems neglected by individualism. Like later scholars they show that the late, eighteenth and early nineteenth centuries saw the dismantling of centuries of protective, paternalistic control of trade and industry, of apprenticeship laws, wage controls, and bread assizes, as a free market economy was established according to the teachings of the political economists. The notion of a state as 'an association for mutal aid had', they argued, 'almost vanished from the mind of a generation that believed that the degradation of the working class had begun with Speenhamland and would cease with the austerity of the New Poor Law'. In the words of Brougham, society should protect the individual against only those evils that the prudent man could not foresee; for the rest it was up to him to make whatever provision he could. And in the name of this liberty or freedom for the individual, argue the Hammonds, the factory children became 'a pitiless indictment of those rulers who, in the days of their material power, had abandoned the weak to the rapacity of the strong'.[29] That this was an unsatisfactory situation was a view shared by some contemporaries and many later commentators. Robert Owen, for instance, was not content to see industrialisation continue on its unregulated way and argued that it would produce permanent evils unless subjected to the interference and direction of the law.[30] The Hammonds believed that this was becoming the central question of the whole industrialisation process, whether and when the capitalist's claim to uncontrolled exercise of his power should be withstood, for it was necessary somehow to bring into 'harmony and discipline those rude forces that either destroy a civilisation or give it new power.'[31]

It has been said of the Hammonds that they were liberals, yet their principal criticism of the governments of these years concerned their failure to govern: the paradox disappears if it can be agreed that the whole hypothetical alternative which they advocated was a rejection of liberalism and committed them very deeply to a collectivist philosophy.[32] Specifically on the issue of liberalism, they outlined the liberal belief that in a society where industry and determination could raise a person from poverty to riches injustice would always be kept within tolerable limits.[33] Their works are both an implicit and explicit rejection of this faith and a forcible argument for the need for state intervention to supply that justice that they believed to be lacking in the liberal state of the nineteenth century.

In the absence of state intervention the society which they describe is the familiar one of the 'Two Nations', the rich and the poor, the governors and the governed, a society of class struggle between the ruling class and the working class. 'The fierce struggle', they write, 'that is the subject of this book looks . . . like a class conflict of a most cruel and exhausting kind'. Measures were taken 'by the ruling class against the working class'; England was in the hands of 'an oligarchy free from misgiving about its capacity for government', assisted by Methodists and other Evangelicals who supported the political régime by propagating a religious faith 'ideal for the working classes in reconciling people to hardship'. By 1830, they argued, almost no aspect of life, society, or politics looked the same to the two worlds, and it was from the discontented world of the working classes that ideas and movements would develop that would transform society and bring it, if not up to the ideal of the Hammonds' hypothetical alternative, at least a little way along the path towards it.[34]

This birth of a working-class social and political consciousness, a more moderately argued claim than some that have since been made on this subject, is almost an epilogue to the story that the Hammonds had to tell rather than a central theme of the story. It is both a conclusion and a starting point, a verdict on developments to this point and a forecast of a role still to be played, and though the Hammonds made little attempt at systematic analysis of working-class techniques of protest and organisation, they touched upon food-rioting and machine-breaking as matters of more than law and order significance, they looked backwards with the hand-loom-weavers to solutions that could obtain only in a traditional setting, and forwards with the parliamentary reformers and trade unionists who would seek to accept the new system and exploit it to their own advantage. They looked to influences such as education and religion which would at the same time reconcile the working classes to industrialisation and accommodate them within it, whilst supplying them with the means to ensure them more than a passive role. And from the very success of some groups in adjusting and exploiting would develop a sectional selfishness that would undermine that sense of working-class unity and solidarity earlier identified as the product of the industrialisation process. The controversies concerning 'the making of the English working class' have in fact become one of the principal disputes arising from the study of the social consequences of industrialisation which the Hammonds helped to pioneer.

Another is the standard-of-living debate, for their whole study of *The Town Labourer* is about living standards. Whilst they make precise claims about wages and prices which have not always stood the test of empirical investigation, since they arose from what have been described as 'psychological intuitions and emotional sympathies' rather than detailed scholarship, they make more general claims about the quality of life and the nature of the new civilisation which form their main thesis and remain a central theme of present-day arguments.[35] Just as Toynbee had argued that free competition produced wealth without well-being and Tawney was later to argue that the way in which income was produced was as important as the amount of that income, so were the Hammonds concerned to investigate the many aspects of life which are immeasurable but nonetheless vital to any overall assessment.[36] Toynbee had confidently asserted that 'we all know the horrors that ensued in England before it (the Industrial Revolution) was restrained by legislation and combination', and the Hammonds, sharing his general view, spelt out those 'horrors' in more detail.[37] Today the horrors themselves are not something that 'we all know' but matters of debate and controversy which, with the passage of time, have taken on new appearances which make their evaluation a more difficult exercise. Yet they are the base on which the Hammonds constructed their mighty edifice, and if the foundation crumbles the whole building goes with it. The object of this essay is to enquire whether the construction stands or falls.

Unlike a recent book on the Swing Riots, which re-covered the ground of *The Village Labourer* and which, in the words of its authors, 'supersedes the Hammonds', in every aspect except one', this book does not aim to supersede the Hammonds in any way at all.[38] *The Town Labourer* remains for all time the classic statement of a particular view of the Industrial Revolution and its social consequences. This book aims simply to look again at some of the topics discussed by the Hammonds in the light of some of the work done over the half century that has elapsed since they produced their first edition of *The Town Labourer*.

2 *Law and Order in Industrial England*

'. . . the law . . . an instrument not of justice but of repression.'
—*The Town Labourer*, p. 72.

The problem of law and order in industrialising England is one that exemplifies clearly the conflicting views that have arisen as historians have attempted to interpret this age. That there was a problem was a matter of no doubt amongst contemporaries; nor has it been amongst the historians. The controversy arises over the causes of this situation and what it illustrates. The Hammonds rightly stressed both the French and Industrial Revolutions; the one had transformed the minds of the ruling classes; the other had 'convulsed the world of the working classes', and to the rich the masses seemed ripe for rebellion.[1] From the social and economic consequences of industrialisation and from the political inspiration and apprehension derived from the example of successful revolution in France, a conflict was born which was arguably to determine the whole course of nineteenth century British history and was certainly to pose in an acute form the law and order issue of the first half of that century. Whether the instigation of the troubles was working-class villainy on the one hand or the malevolence of the propertied classes on the other was a matter of viewpoint, and the Hammonds clearly supported the second view.

This kind of analysis is accurate enough as far as it goes. The old causes of public disorder, food shortages and religious intolerance, persisted but were supplemented in the nineteenth century by industrial and political protest on a totally new scale which seemed to threaten a complete breakdown of the machinery of law and order. The machine-breaking violence of 1811–16, the Reform Bill riots of 1831, and the Chartist riots of 1839 and 1842, to name but a few outstanding examples were quite unprecedented in scale and even in kind. Incendiary riots involving attacks on shopkeepers, the destruction of industrial property, assaults on private houses, and clashes with the army were increasingly a feature of the national scene, sufficiently so to prompt Sir James Graham, in common with predecessors in the office of Home Secretary, to suppose in July 1842 that treason was stalking abroad in the shape of a 'mad insurrection of the working classes'.[2] This kind of opinion was expressed almost universally amongst men of property for almost half a century. Graham himself moved from description to a first stage of analysis by suggesting that there was 'something inherent in an industrial society which disposed men to riot'.[3] Many, such as the Hammonds, have since been more than willing to spell out that certain 'something', and few would deny that the social and economic injustices of the new society were an important element in the problem.

So far the analysis is acceptable, but it is also necessary to understand what it was about the nature of industrial society, apart from the exploitation element, that caused its members to be a greater threat to public order than previously and why the governmental and administrative machine was quite unable to cope with the extra strains that were imposed upon it. And again there arises the conflict of interpretation: on the one hand the view that evil men were employing existing agencies of government oppressively and failing to modernise or humanise them, on the other hand the view that events were occurring too quickly for the government to have any chance of coping, being forced instead into temporary expedients whilst new institutions had time to emerge. One historian remarks nostalgically that the period used to be seen as one of political repression and heroic popular agitation;[4] not so now as the less emotive distinction between government and governed replaces the starker delineation between oppressors and oppressed, which paid no attention to the problems of the governors, only to their sins. On this matter at least the Hammonds were wanting in sympathy, which they reserved entirely for those at the receiving end of government.

The most obvious novel aspects of industrial society were its greatly increased size and the fact that its members lived in areas of far greater concentration than previously. Whereas in the mid-eighteenth century less than one fifth of the population lived in towns of 5,000 or more, the proportion was three fifths by the mid-nineteenth century. This concentration and the growth rates that made it possible and necessary could not have taken place without enormous strain on the people involved and on the machinery by which they were governed. The ever-growing towns had a mainly young population, and in the deteriorating human environment which characterised most urban areas in the first half of the nineteenth century a high crime rate resulted. This, it has been argued, was not so much a consequence of poverty as such but of poverty of social institutions, the absence of adequate housing, education, and amenities such as public parks.[5] It would be difficult to establish statistically the growing crime rate which contemporaries believed in, since there are no records of the number of offences committed before 1857, but the slowness of response in terms of the provision of social institutions explains the high crime rate that preceded the identifiable decline in the second half of the century. The low priority accorded social provision in an economic system where the profit motive dominated has been offered as an explanation of why crime was high and the machinery of order strained during the first stages of industrialisation. And 'pure' crime was at the same time supplemented by growing social 'protest'. There had always been anti-papists and bread-rioters to occasion the periodic calling out of the military; the former were still present in the late eighteenth and early nineteenth centuries, augmented by the Church/King mobs who turned against Protestant Dissenters in the 1790s; the latter acquired a new bitterness in the closing years of the eighteenth century as they attempted to enforce what has been described as 'the older moral economy' of popular price-fixing in opposition to 'the economy of the free market' which was the new orthodoxy.[6] These customary recipients of policing action were to be supplemented after the turn of the century by all those groups whose industrial and political experience prompted them to forms of action which seemed to men of property to threaten the very fabric of society. If working men needed the mill to keep them from 'poaching, profligacy, and plunder', as some contemporaries doubtless believed, their industrial lives inside or outside mills might be prompting them towards other illegal courses, such as the Lancashire drillings of 1819 of which Samuel Bamford is said to have given 'idyllic and over-innocent descriptions'.[7] Whether more conventional crimes should be described as social protest in the same way that machine-breaking, for instance, can be so described is a matter of some contention: they certainly arose in part from the inadequacies of the social system and helped to highlight the outdated nature of the machinery of law and order. One particular anachronism that illustrates appropriately the predicament that existed is the fact that the new industrial areas which caused so much concern contained very few incorporated boroughs, that such rapidly-growing industrial towns as Manchester, Birmingham, and Bradford had no charters of incorporation at the time of the Municipal Corporations' Act, and until they had they remained under the control of manorial lords or county magistrates who happened to live near enough to be of assistance. The consequences for law and order of this kind of carry-over from a pre-industrial age are evident in every crisis that arose in these years, and the debate concerns consequences as well as causes.

When Luddism became a national problem in 1812, the country's peace-keeping machinery, was, it has been suggested, almost identical to that of 1588, an earlier year of domestic crisis, dependent on the public spirit of a few men and the capacity of its ordinary members for self-help.[8] Yet eight disorderly months and five Acts of Parliament later, local machinery for maintaining order remained very casual and incomplete; local government had broken down and could scarcely have been more taxed if the machine-breakers had started the revolution which some people expected them to do. Nor did the situation change much as successive crises ensued, for Middleton, in Lancashire, which had its mill attacked by Luddites in April 1812, was still equally vulnerable in August 1839, when renewed disturbances found the town without a magistrate within miles.[9] It could be said that in general the old incorporated towns made a fairly good job of policing themselves in comparison with the rural areas, though the Reform Bill riots of 1831 afflicted these towns in particular, causing doubts to be had about even their well-being, and it is easy enough to find examples, such as Leicester, of grossly inadequate policing arrangements prior to 1835.[10] On the whole, it was, however, the unincorporated towns and the industrial villages where disorder was most rife, and here the county magistrates held sway. The towns of Manchester, Stockport, Bolton, Huddersfield and Halifax were all Northern trouble centres in 1812 and at other times, and all these depended on the county magistracy. Where local administration was in the hands of the gentry and parsons it could not cope with anything other than routine life; this was the experience from the Northwest to Southeast, for the indolence and lack of will amongst the magistrates of Kent had been held in large measure responsible for the ineffective action taken against the Swing Rioters in 1830.[11] In contrast to the county areas, the boroughs were more compact, easier to police, and supervised by magistrates and permanent officials who could draw upon a substantial middle class to assist in watches or as special constables. In consequence they preserved higher standards of order, and even when the new boroughs of Manchester, Birmingham and Bolton were having to contend with political opposition to their establishment they soon acquired efficient professional police forces in spite of those who resented and resisted their new jurisdiction.

Beyond the boroughs the county magistrate, answerable to the Lord Lieutenant, was the man on whom the system depended. It was for him to be in attendance at any scene of trouble and take whatever steps were necessary, even if that meant calling out the militia or even the regular army. But this dependence on the magistrates was becoming ever-more precarious as the years passed. In 1812 they were about 5,000 in number and this was far too few; their socially exclusive basis meant that manufacturers, for instance, were kept out of their ranks in Lancashire until the century was well advanced, and their distribution left many populous areas without access to whatever protection they could offer.[12] Although their powers were very great, the actual exercise of them depended entirely on the personal initiative and zeal of the man concerned. This system depended on the personal character, will, and judgment of the individual man and called for the exercise of a discretion which few were capable of using satisfactorily. Home Secretaries grew to regard the over-zealous magistrates as the most menacing kind. Such a man was Colonel Ralph Fletcher of Bolton, whose zeal for entrapping Luddites led him to employ spies who instigated acts of incendiarism and fabricated evidence of illegal oath-taking.[13] Many had no time for civil liberties, were ready to interfere with little justification in peaceful meetings, and prepared to summon military assistance on the least provocation, as when a group of Manchester magistrates called out 1000 militia men in 1812 in what army and government leaders alike regarded as an improper and quite unnecessary manner.[14] Such men preferred the army to any costly police system that might threaten their authority, and they always appeared readier to recommend harsher penal laws than an effective policing system. They were, however, very much in the minority and easily outnumbered by their indifferent, apathetic colleagues who were causing the system to collapse by their inactivity. It would be quite impossible to list all the complaints that army officers had to make about their civilian masters on this score, but few who had to deal with them escaped unfortunate experiences of their lapses, through inefficiency, pure inertia, or even cowardice, and even the Queen was moved in 1842 to complain of their lax conduct in many places.[15] Government action in all crises had to come when magisterial action either failed to materialise or was inadequate. The magistrates were a poor set, Russell reported to General Napier, in 1839, on whom no reliance could be placed, and there were many who testified to the accuracy of this view.[16] The partiality of their conduct was notorious and even the Constabulary Commissioners seem to have accepted that it would be unreasonable to expect a magistrate who was a manufacturer to afford protection to the threatened machinery of one of his competitors.[17] Partiality took many different forms. In Yorkshire the county magistrates annoyed the Poor Law commissioners by their sympathy with those who took part in anti-Poor Law demonstrations, and in the 1840s Wellington accused the Lancashire magistrates of disaffection; he thought that their support for the Anti-Corn Law League was leading them deliberately to neglect their duty of suppressing riots so that the evils of the Corn Laws might be the more effectively demonstrated to the world.[18] The essential point was, of course, that magistrates were inherently unsuited to the role they were required to play in preserving law and order and that the role contained within itself an irresolvable conflict. As the Constabulary Commissioners very clearly explained in 1839, the executive function of the magistrate was basically incompatible with his judicial one, yet the executive function was permitted to remain for a further 50 years.[19]

The supreme test which the magistrates of old England faced in the administration of new England was Peterloo, in August 1819, an event traditionally cited as the classic illustration of oppressive governments, local and central, intent on stifling growing demands for reform. The story of Peterloo has been repeatedly told, yet in spite of much detailed examination of the events of that day and the preceding ones, several unresolved doubts remain about the actual facts of the situation; whether the decision to disperse the meeting by force was premeditated by the magistrates and, if not, at precisely what point such a decision was taken; whether the Yeomanry entered the crowd to disperse it or simply to make arrests and how they behaved, with a determination to cut their way through or otherwise; and how, in response, the crowd behaved, threatening with sticks or simply raising a few walking sticks aloft, throwing stones or not throwing stones, striking the first blows against a peaceful Yeomanry or receiving first the sabre-cuts of the cavalry. If doubts remain about the facts it is hardly possible to pronounce decisively on the motivation of the presiding magistrates, whether, for instance, they were fired with class hatred and class panic as one modern authority claims or whether, as the Hammonds maintained, they displayed a levity which revolted every onlooker.[20] What can be said is that any suggestion of Government conspiracy with the Lancashire and Cheshire magistrates must be abandoned. An extravagant hypothesis of government collusion before the event and suppression of documents afterwards is belied both by the advice previously given by the Home Office suggesting caution and non-interference and by the central government's traditional reliance on the discretion and initiative of local authorities, reiterated only a few days before the meeting on the 16th.[21] Naturally, the government felt obliged to give public backing after the event to the magistracy, whatever Sidmouth's feelings about the wisdom of their conduct. To have done otherwise would have indicated and further precipitated a mutual loss of confidence between the government and the magistracy; perhaps it might have done so with less haste and less apparent commitment to the correctness in detail of what was done.

If the government is exonerated the magistrates are less easily cleared of responsibility. On their behalf it can be claimed that they acted in the belief, not without some justification, that many radicals were intending revolutionaries, and that the recent history of drillings and disorderly meetings had filled them with apprehension, and that, with no pre-conceived plan of action, they acted as they saw best in circumstances of much difficulty. But whatever extenuation is offered of their conduct it must still be acknowledged that empirically they were wrong. They did panic, they exercised an ill judgment, they took wrong decisions, and these decisions were ineptly carried out. This is not necessarily to accept the extreme radical case against them, which must now be modified by the consideration that these men were the wrong people to have to exercise such power and take such decisions and that they had a totally inappropriate machinery at their command for implementing them. Perhaps the Peterloo magistrates like the people of Middleton were the victims of the administrative anachronisms that still prevailed; they have certainly been given a much gentler and sympathetic treatment of late than historians were once accustomed to supposing they deserved and 'massacre' has become a dirty word.[22]

If the local governors of England were too inefficient and indifferent ever to be consistently oppressive, the same cannot be so readily said of the over-worked and under-rated office of Home Secretary and the men who filled this post in the first half of the nineteenth century, and it is on the central government that the case must stand or fall, for supposing society to have been oppressively governed. But if it is not possible to argue that they were indifferent about their duties they were certainly quite hostile to any idea that these duties should involve them in acquiring increased responsibilities. Their constant mission was to try to persuade the magistrates to do their duty and they acted themselves most unwillingly and as a last resort by despatching police, spies, or soldiers as the occasion demanded. 'Amiable apathy' is one description that has been applied to the attitude of the central government at this time over its peace-keeping role, and this apparent apathy often caused it to be both late and inefficient in reacting to the crises that arose, even in the post-1815 years when government is commonly believed to have been at its most repressive.[23] Peel was still telling the magistrates of the south-east in 1830 as his predecessors had informed them in the North 18 years earlier that the protection of private property was their responsibility not his, and advising them to enrol special constables and not look to the central government for salvation; it was evidently not simply the geographical remoteness of most of the disturbed areas that prompted government attitudes.[24] By the time of Chartism the government was not even prepared to offer the expedients of law-strengthening or suspension that it had contributed in former times, and looked rather to the strengthening of locally controlled police as the proper means of tackling the problem. When the government intervened to ensure that police-forces were started under the control of the Metropolitan Commissioners, as at Birmingham and Manchester, this was far from being part of a grand scheme for centralisation and the denial of local liberties, but simply a temporary device to deal with a local political deadlock.[25]

Complementing this desire for non-involvement was a fairly consistent pursuit of a policy of restraint urged upon local officials for most of the period. Occasionally a Home Secretary might show an unwonted zeal for action against trouble-makers as did Melbourne against the Swing rioters in 1831 and Graham in 1842, when he urged the suppression of all large public meetings whatever their character.[26] But these were exceptional. The loudest demands for military action in 1812 came from 'owners of machinery, frightened manufacturers, nervous magistrates, Lord Lieutenants, and honest alarmists', and the reputation of the Liverpool government for alarmist attitudes and policies seems almost unmerited when official moderation is contrasted with the sensational and extremist tone of the majority of the Home Office correspondents whom the government had to pacify.[27] Melbourne's harshness where Swing-rioters and trade unionists were concerned must be set against his refusal to be panicked by Nottingham magistrates after the Reform Riots of October 1831 into believing that a conspiracy for armed insurrection was afoot in that town.[28] Lord John Russell remained very tolerant towards the often abusive and destructive behaviour of the anti-Poor Law demonstrators of the '30s, and in the early stages of Chartism he refused to put down meetings or to sanction secret service expenditure under this head. In December 1837, the Home Secretary was advised not to prosecute the *Northern Star* unless it could be shown that evil practical consequences followed directly from its preaching, and the usual government message to magistrates was to caution restraint when there was 'no reason to interfere'.[29] Peel too, as Prime Minister, instructed Graham in 1842 that when public order was threatened, as it clearly was in that year, the amount of severity used should be just enough to restore order and no more, and it has been argued that the government's policy shows no evidence of any plan to crush the popular movement, only a readiness to act as and when peace was threatened.[30] In the year of revolution, 1848, the government was unwilling, despite its show of special constabulary force, to take seriously the suggestion that the Chartists would resort to arms and this confidence was justified by events.

What is perhaps more surprising is that by this time popular protest was actually inspiring signs of an official response that something was wrong with the organisation of society and that it behoved the government to do something about it. Repression unmitigated by reform had characterised the response to popular outbursts in Luddite and the immediately post-1815 years. In 1837 Russell reacted to protest against the New Poor Law by urging delay in the implementation of the act, concession rather than repression. What are political and what humanitarian determinants of conduct is always difficult to distinguish, but even a recognition that a humanitarian line might be political marked a change in attitude. A more outstanding example of this kind of response came from Sir James Graham in 1842; 'I am by no means prepared to use military force to compel reductions of wages or to uphold a grinding system of truck'. He showed a conscious awareness of the feelings and complaints of the workmen, and argued that for the future government should look to the removal of food taxes, the fostering of education, and enquire into the fraudulent practices of employers upon their workmen.[31] This was no great all-time awakening of social conscience in government circles, but it represented, in the context of the law and order issue, a sophisticated and constructive appreciation of why popular discontent produced popular disturbance.

Amongst the supposed instruments of oppression the army holds pride of place. The traditional association of standing armies with despotism, whether based on the experience of Hohenzollern Prussia or Stuart and Cromwellian England, ensured an ingrained hostility from upholders of Parliamentary government. But the military arm became even more vulnerable to criticism when required to fulfil the policing role that the modern police force had not yet emerged to undertake. Nor has the passing of time entirely cancelled out this hostility, for there is nothing more successful in establishing a good reputation than a winning cause; the ultimate triumph of the police ideal and the almost universal veneration felt for the modern force have ensured that a heavy bias would afflict the reporting, especially by police historians, of that period when the British army was 'the police force of industrial England'.

How members of the regular army came to assume this role, for which they were not, of course, trained or paid, is a matter of some dispute. J. L. and Barbara Hammond, classic exponents of the liberal tradition, describe how Pitt's decision to establish barracks over England in 1792 was not a military measure but purely a police one. They quote his statement that a new spirit had appeared in some of the manufacturing towns which made it necessary that troops should be kept in large numbers in close proximity to those potential trouble spots. They believe that the army was deliberately selected by Pitt to be the means by which the early popular protests stimulated by the French and Industrial Revolutions were to be put down, and if this were so Pitt assuredly condemned the army to a bad press for the future.[32] E. P. Thompson has confirmed this general interpretation of action taken by the authorities 'to build barracks and take precautions against the "revolutionary crowd"' and has made the unsupported claim that Pitt's decision to erect barracks near the industrial towns was one of his most unpopular repressive measures.[33] Not surprisingly Pitt's action has been otherwise interpreted, though his executive action to implement his policies in advance of Parliamentary approval and the subsequent explanations and rationalisations with which he justified it make any clear assignment of motives more than usually difficult on this occasion. Pitt clearly accepted the vital role which the army had come to play in maintaining law and order and his Secretary of State, Dundas, argued that the civil power was unable to act without the military. This was an accurate appraisal of the law and order machinery in 1792; the army was being used in a police function and so it made sense to provide for its better discipline, loyalty, protection, and comfort within specifically-planned barracks than to continue the *ad hoc* expedient of random billeting on unwilling innkeepers amongst a possibly hostile population. There was undoubtedly social panic arising from the French Revolution and a growing awareness of the problems posed by the fast-growing manufacturing areas; neither of these is surprising and both called for a more efficient policing machinery than was currently available. In the absence of an efficient constabulary the army offered a possible solution and the military barracks became police stations, providing an administrative solution to a pressing problem rather than a means to a pre-planned tyranny. The Parliamentary case against barrack-building was couched in highly traditional terms of Whig opposition to standing armies and a separate military caste and the need for strict financial control by Parliament over the operation; there was no clear appraisal of any radically new role and policy assigned by Pitt to the army.[34]

Nor did the fear of the peculiar dangers that the manufacturing districts posed produce a policy of concentrated barrack-building in these areas, which would have been required to substantiate the Hammond view of a counter-revolutionary coup. Instead, it has been argued that of the 159 barracks built for the 17,000 cavalry and 138,000 infantry of 1815, only about a dozen were situated in or near the main industrial areas of the North and Midlands. Most of the smaller towns and manufacturing areas had no barracks, and the temporary barracks of the larger towns of Lancashire, the most likely centre of domestic tumult, were so poor as to constitute a health hazard to the soldiers stationed there, which was a highly inefficient means of subjecting the domestic population to military despotism. As late as the Chartist period General Napier found the Northern area desperately bereft of barrack accommodation and he was able to command the provision of comfortable, adequate barracks by the local population as the price for which he was prepared to allow his troops to remain in particular areas to protect the locals from the dangers that seemed to threaten them.[35] If a policy of barrack-building throughout the manufacturing areas was ever intended by Pitt in the 1790s it was clearly never implemented to the extent that would allow the army to maintain an effective permanent policing presence.

It might be supposed from the popular view of early nineteenth-century governments that successive Home Secretaries could barely wait to dispatch the army to suppress popular disturbances. In fact the situation was the exact opposite of this. For governments Whig or Tory the army was always the last resort, the ultimate means of defence when all else had been tried and found wanting. Pressure to employ the army almost invariably came from the provinces, whilst the government almost invariably strove desperately to refrain from taking this step. In the view of Lord Liverpool, as with his successors, responsibility for law and order lay with 'the gentlemen of the parish' and 'the property of the country must be taught to protect itself'.[36] It proved a difficult lesson to put across. General Maitland, in charge of operations against the Luddites in 1812, found men of property singularly unwilling to act on their own; instead they clamoured for troops and would gladly have abdicated all their responsibility. There were not enough troops in the entire British army, wrote Maitland, to meet the demands that he received from Yorkshire alone.[37] By the summer of 1812 he had become in spite of himself virtually the dictator of Northern England, because he commanded the only effective police force in existence, an army of more than 12,000 men, and because he had to act as leader rather than servant of the local officials whose own efforts were so inadequate to meet the requirements of the situation. And from this time on, the army could never escape the obligation to be at the ready to bale out the local officials whenever a crisis threatened. In 1819 Sir John Byng, the Northern Commander-in-Chief, complained that the manufacturers in and around Manchester were again refusing to bestir themselves and were all arguing that it was the government's duty to protect them and their property.[38] When the crisis came, as it did at Peterloo on 19th August, it was again to be the regular army which would be required to restore order after the Manchester and Salford Yeomanry Cavalry had preceded the 15th Hussars and left a trail of destruction which, in one view, allowed the Whigs to resurrect the bogey of military rule, and gave the reform cause its most celebrated martyrs.[39] Soldiers had again been required to perform a duty which they were simply not equipped for, a duty which they neither sought nor enjoyed. And the same situation prevailed through the Chartist period. It was government policy to withhold the supply of regular troops and to discourage their use until the very last moment and to withdraw them as soon as possible. Again typical of the local officials who preferred to hand over their responsibilities to the army were those Staffordshire magistrates who had to be coerced by the Home Secretary, Sir James Graham, who threatened to withdraw troops completely if the magistrates did not take steps to improve their county police force.[40] Since the Act of 1839 county magistrates had been encouraged to set up constabulary forces in their areas, but the massive apathy in implementing this Act had arisen, it has been suggested, from a universal belief that such forces would be inadequate unless supplemented and supported by a permanent military force.[41] What the government saw as a short-term expedient to the law-and-order problem, was seen by those responsible for maintaining law and order, the magistracy, as a permanent and indispensable aid. This conflict of views was typified by a request by Skipton magistrates in 1848 for the support of an armed force, to which the Home Office gave the standard reply that reliance should be placed on a well-organised police force.[42]

It is not then possible to argue that the government rushed to employ the army domestically whenever opportunity presented itself. Nor can it be argued that the army itself revelled in the role in which it was being employed. Soldiers had enough experience of suppressing riots in the eighteenth century to know that their presence was as likely to inflame as to pacify an angry crowd, and it could hardly have gratified the men in arms that their public appearances coincided with distress and often death among the domestic population rather than with victory against the foreign foe. Policing unruly crowds was an exasperating business as indeed was the hunting down of machine-breakers, a task set the army in 1812, and hard though army leaders insisted on the transitory nature of their role the difficulties over disengagement were severe. Even the Duke of Newcastle, Lord Lieutenant of Nottinghamshire and not the most perceptive of observers, saw that military power could not in the long run succeed in preserving law and order unless the local police were efficient, and the need to enlarge and strengthen the regular police became a constant theme of the generals, from Maitland onwards, who played leading roles in campaigning for police reform, especially in the North; the police would serve, in the metaphor of Napier, as a buffer between the army and the people.[43] The clash between Sir James Graham and the Staffordshire magistrates in 1842 had arisen because army leaders were wishing to withdraw from the area, and this had long been the picture. Throughout the North and Midlands during the Luddite period, for example, frightened magistrates had dreaded the day, as much as military leaders had eagerly awaited it, when the army would withdraw from their area and hand over to local defence associations and the special constables. Despite the general's advocacy of the new police, relations between the army and such forces as were established by the early 1840s were not necessarily good and in places considerable animosity existed. This is not surprising. Soldiers were still being required to spend their time doing policemen's work, for which they were getting paid far less than policemen's wages. For their part the police regretted the heavy drinking and boisterous, uninhibited behaviour which the soldiery traditionally practised, hardly suitable conduct for those expected to enforce law and order with all possible dignity. The soldiers would doubtless have agreed with this view but sought to change their role rather than their behaviour.

Any assessment of the army's sucess in performing the thankless task wished upon it from elsewhere must take particular note of the fact that many of its principle critics were propagandists on behalf of the new police and were somewhat unfairly belabouring the army with criticisms with which its leaders would have agreed. Its limitations as a police force were all too evident and clearly listed by the Constabulary Commissioners in 1839 as they argued their case for setting up a rural police; military action was often too drastic a solution for many of the situations confronting magistrates, in which case they were inclined to do nothing, which was too little, or call out the army, which was too much, for it was only against armed mobs that the army could be justifiably and effectively used in a preventive capacity.[44] Such arguments were legitimate and relevant material for debate in presenting the case for a police force, but they cannot be used to tarnish the army's reputation in the reluctant performance of a task for which it was unsuited. Nor have police historians been any more concerned than the 1839 Commissioners to give the army its due. The supposedly disastrous consequences of the army's employment have been lovingly listed with little regard for its successes and no mention of the fact that this 'broken reed' is almost universally regarded by modern scholars, as it was by contemporary magistrates, as the only effective force in the country for a half a century.[45]

In measuring the achievement of the army it is important to note the difficulties under which it operated. The size of the force available at any one time, whilst usually adequate to its commander's needs if all other arms of the law were functioning properly, was never sufficient to meet the demands on it in the absence of such efficient functioning. Secretary of State Richard Ryder admitted that the 3,000 soldiers sent to the East Midlands to contend with the early outbreaks of Luddism in the autumn of 1811 constituted a greater force than had ever previously been employed for such internal use, though a force four times this size was to be in action in the North and Midlands by the summer of 1812; even then General Maitland was refusing most of the requests he received for military assistance.[46] When trouble broke out in the South-east in 1830 in the form of the labourers' risings, these agricultural areas had only small and scattered forces available and could never be given more than a skeleton force because of government apprehension concerning events in France and Belgium and possible disturbance in the industrial areas of the North and Midlands.[47] The 7,500 soldiers stationed in the Northern District in 1820 had fallen to 5,300 by 1839, and although this number was raised to 10,500 by the end of that troubled year, the Tory government of 1841 reduced the military establishment by 6,000 on economy grounds during the brief lull that preceded the even more troubled year of 1842, the year of the 'Plug Plot'.[48]

Another problem faced by the army when serving amongst the domestic population was the likelihood that attempts would be made to seduce from their obedience soldiers who were themselves from the same social groups as those people against whom they might be required to act. The celebrated Campbell case of 1924, when members of the British army were urged not to shoot strikers, had many precedents in the nineteenth century, including the attempts made by Richard Oastler to incite soldiers to disobedience.[49] It was always an article of faith amongst would-be revolutionaries, part of the mythology of revolution, that the army was ready to join the insurgents when the latter had demonstrated their willingness to rise. The Pentrich rebels were informed, falsely, that Nottingham was in the hands of sympathetic soldiers during their march of 9 June 1817, and it was news that the London crowds had been joined by the soldiers on the Lords' rejection of the Reform Bill in October 1831, which helped to encourage Reform Bill riots in the provinces.[50] Certainly there were some occasions when individuals refused to obey orders; a private at Rawfolds Mill, on 11 April 1812, declined to fire on the attackers and was subsequently courtmartialled, whilst an officer involved in suppressing the Bristol Reform Bill Riots of 1831 was similarly disposed and later shot himself whilst awaiting court-martial. But these were isolated examples. Whatever the fears expressed by the alarmists, and occasionally by men of sounder judgment, the soldiers did what was required of them, though it remained army policy to isolate their living quarters and to encourage them to mingle socially for the sake of acquiring information rather than refreshment.

The biggest difficulty the army had to face on police duty was, however, its relationship with the civil authorities. Theoretically the army became a police force to be employed by the civil authorities according to normal civil procedures, and civil authorities were not superseded. When they were, as in the case of General Hawker's entry into the town of Southwell in February 1812, without a warrant from the resident magistrate, the Revd John T. Becher, offence was taken, though not intended.[51] The army could not win in this kind of contest, for they were just as likely to be criticised for observing protocol and refusing to act without the necessary warrant. Cases were cited where they had done nothing even within earshot of stocking frames being broken, and West Houghton Mill might well have been saved in April 1812, had not the local commander-in-chief, tiring of abortive exercises and fruitless missions, refused to move until properly summoned by the appropriate local official.[52] In practice, however, the civil authorities were usually only too ready to leave everything to the army and were not inclined to stand upon their dignity. Their need of the army and the central role in co-ordinating action taken by the commander-in-chief in any area ensured that the army was not too hamstrung in its actions by the sensitivities of local officials. The complaints were much more commonly to be heard on the army's side that the civilian authorities were not co-operating in the job to be done and were defective in their adherence to duty. When General Maitland went North to Lancashire in 1812 his endless trials and tribulations were a principle theme of his correspondence to the Home Secretary as he reported on the apathy, inactivity, confusion, and jealousy that prevailed amongst the local magistracy.[53] And an almost identical picture was painted by General Napier 30 years later, when he complained of magistrates who disappeared from the scene of action, leaving everything to the army, and on one occasion of magistrates who went off to shoot grouse at the height of the troubles of 1839. Poor Napier even found the Home Secretary Russell 'very ignorant of what is going on' in 1839.[54]

Faced with these difficulties the army had to act to the best of its abilities to do a job for which it was not trained, equipped, and intended. During the first half of the nineteenth century the ultimate horror to men of property and men in government was that of revolution, and it was to the army that people looked to ensure that armed insurrection was never allowed to succeed. In fact the actual insurrectionary attempts made were few and pathetic and easily suppressed, and it would be straining logic to argue that the army was the principal reason why the threat of revolution was averted. Nonetheless the threat of revolution was turned aside, the army was always available to deal with troubles as they arose, and its members constituted a loyal and obedient force which offered no encouraging signs to potential revolutionaries. Had the threat materialised only the army would have offered effective resistance, if the experiences of Luddism and Chartism are any guide. From the records of the army in suppressing riot and disturbance cases could doubtless be found when operations were not completed as speedily or as tidily as some might have wished. But the most striking overall impression left by army operations is how much better they were than any other kind, until the professional police, created for the precise task, were able to take over responsibility. And in a period when alarmists, reactionaries, and provocateurs so often determined the state of public opinion, the generals concerned with handling domestic disturbances stand out as the most intelligent, enlighted, humane, and liberal body of men to be found in places of authority, far removed from the pamphleteer's image of what a military man must inescapably be like. In the entire history of Luddism two men stood out from the rest for their good sense, level-headed conduct, and humanity; one was Fitzwilliam, the Lord Lieutenant of the West Riding, subsequently dismissed from office after protesting over Peterloo; the other was General Maitland, whose job it was to put down Luddism. His reports from Lancashire in particular indicate a sound judgment and ability to assess a situation and predict its development such as the local magistracy found quite beyond them. He quickly saw how exaggerated were the fears of the magistrates derived from unreliable spies' reports, and accurately estimated the small extent of political menace in the situation. Further, his conduct displayed a humanity lacking amongst local manufacturers, of whom he was critical for their neglect of the distresses of their workmen and for their willingness to try to exploit military support in establishing profitable settlements with their workers. Again, in 1819, when the Manchester magistracy were panicking at the prospect of trouble from parliamentary reformers and were in fact panicked into their disastrous handling of the meeting at St Peters Fields, it was Sir John Byng, the military commander-in-chief, who represented the still small voice of calm and who feared no disturbance, until the magistrates took their disastrous decisions.[55]

But even more outstanding was Sir Charles Napier, who showed all the prudence, good sense and humanity of his predecessors and more kindness. Politically radical, his personal opposition to the New Poor Law and his support for the Chartist programme permitted him to accomplish his task with a restraint and compassion quite remarkable. Conscious that the Yeomanry Cavalry were perhaps 'over-zealous for cutting and slashing', he sought to avoid confrontations with the Chartists, restraining them by tactful private approaches, and restraining the magistrates too from provocative interruptions of peaceful meetings. His moderation ensured that neither the central government nor the officials of local government were tempted to extremes. His perception and judgment are well illustrated by his shrewd comment that each magistrate thought his own village to be the focus of Chartism whereas it was merely the focus of his own fears, and his confidence in his judgment was based on the knowledge that he operated a better system of intelligence than the civil authorities ever achieved. Information acquired by his officers from the locals was, he believed, 'less influenced by any party, personal, or political bias' than that given to the Home Office by provincial magistrates, and there is no reason to question this view. And besides attending to the strict letter of his obligations Napier had time to notice such matters as the poor-relief schemes being operated in Nottingham in the winter of 1839–40, for which he was full of praise. In this period it was not uncommon for important army officers to mediate in local trade disputes, at times at the instigation of the Home Office, and army officers continued to deplore the tendency of some employers to try to use the army as a weapon on their own behalf in trade disputes with their workmen.[56]

In view of this kind of record it is hardly possible to subscribe to the Whig view that a standing army used internally necessarily involved threats to constitutional and individual liberties, especially when it is remembered that the magistrates and manufacturers so ready to make use of the security that the army offered them were in many cases the very people so fond of enunciating their Whig principles. The British

Army became, *faute de mieux*, the police force of Industrial England, and whilst it remained so it did a far better job than any other body of people or institution was able to perform at the time.

No aspect of the problem of maintaining law and order has aroused the passions of liberal historians more than the use of spies, and the government under which they are known to have been most extensively employed, that of Lord Liverpool in the years 1812-1820, has been uniformly condemned as the most illiberal and repressive, the 'worst', government of the whole century. But spies, like an army acting as a police force, need to be explained as well as denounced, and again the explanation of their existence is to be found in the poverty of social institutions and inadequacy of administrative machinery needed to face the problems that society was experiencing in the early part of the nineteenth century. It is pointless to blame the army for the absence of a professional police force and it is similarly pointless to blame the spies who operated in its absence. When the police emerged the police-substitutes became redundant, but until they did there was a gap to be filled. Spies existed because people in authority needed to have information which the squire and parson were not so able to supply for the new industrial areas and which could be obtained at this time only by the employment of paid secret agents. On a particular occasion, such as the spring of 1817, it was necessary to know exactly what was happening in the North and Midlands; historians have not found it possible to be sure and so it is not surprising, it has been argued, that Sidmouth should have sent Oliver the Spy, on what turned out to be something less than a mission of mercy, for there were no police officers to collect and organise reliable information.[57] What there were, of course, were hundreds of magistrates throughout the country, many of whom were themselves employers of spies, who based their reports to the Home Secretary on the reports that they received from their secret agents. Occasionally it proved necessary for the government to have a more direct contact, to spy on the spies, and hence the opportunity for such as Oliver. But it was the locally employed spies who were the most numerous; they might be shearmen from the West Country who were trying to penetrate the secrets of the Yorkshire croppers in 1812, stocking-knitters who were attempting to secure for the town clerk of Nottingham enough evidence for him to bring a prosecution under the Combination Acts, or militia privates employed in Lancashire by their Commanding Officers, Colonel Fletcher and Captain Chippendale, who doubled up as magistrates, to sniff out sedition or even to fan the flames a little. When no other efficient methods existed for the detection of crime and conspiracy, some such methods as the employment of spies was, it has been frequently argued, inescapable and therefore justified.[58] The spies and informers were an integral and essential part of the system of internal government, always assured of employment when trouble was brewing. They were the detective department of government, who forewarned of trouble to come, and helped in securing arrests and convictions, for without their assistance the authorities were dependent on criminal confessions to gain their convictions. They were then quite indispensable and the government recognised this by its willingness to allow them to become an expensive item of administration and by its readiness to foot the bill of those men employed by magistrates through the provinces.

Against their indispensable role in government must be balanced the obvious dangers and disadvantages of this particular mode of operation. The nature of the calling was not such as to attract society's most upright and reliable members, and the evidence produced by spies could be very unreliable and difficult to assess. The more astute employer, like the more astute historian, would weigh the nature of the evidence against the reliability of its source, and form his conclusions accordingly, but the less astute employer might too readily accept the reports of his spies at their face value. As spies were invariably paid by results so were they inclined to exaggerate the horror of their discoveries in order to justify higher payment and prolonged employment, and sometimes they presented reports that contained a large element of romance. The Lancashire spies of 1812, though numerous and well-paid, produced nothing of value on the important occurrences of machine-breaking, which were taking place, and reams on the threatened revolution which never materialised. Spies were also tempted on many occasions, either through their own temerity or at the instigation of their employers, to indulge in some provocative activity that would lead others deeper into trouble and produce clearer evidence of greater crimes. It is very clear, for instance, that Colonel Ralph Fletcher of Bolton actively encouraged Stones and son to plot the destruction of West Houghton Mill so that the other conspirators could be taken. Often the initiative of the individual spy would determine the exact role that he was to play; this was true in the case of Oliver, though it will probably never be known exactly what that role was; for generations of historians, including the

Hammonds, who devoted a whole chapter to his adventures, Oliver has been the arch-villain, instigator of the Pentrich Rebellion, who enticed innocent men to their deaths, though there is now a much greater readiness to see him essentially as an informer on the schemes which he did not initiate.[59] The exact borderline between informing and provocation is often a very difficult one to define, but classic cases were to occur during the Chartist period of spies who were to instigate some hair-raising atrocities in their search for the violent and rebellious. It was a spy, Daniel Lee, who led the turnout mob against the mills of Hyde, on 14 August, 1848, and another, Thomas Powell, employed by the Metropolitan police in that year, who, amongst other things, devised plans for the assassination of his employers.[60]

But what was perhaps the worst aspect of the use of spies was the fact that they were so badly and so casually organised and that the spies were such bad ones. It was Oliver's great redeeming feature that he supplied accurate intelligence to his employers in London and to the magistrates whom he visited in the provinces, for he correctly diagnosed that the plot he was investigating was not something to be feared and he permitted all the necessary arrangements to be made for its supervision without any undue panic. This was in some ways a model espionage operation; rarely did anything so useful emerge from such an undertaking. Yet in other ways it was a ludicrously inefficient operation that scarcely deserved to succeed, for Oliver had casually presented himself, been casually employed for his important mission, was allowed to go on his rounds without warning to the authorities within whose jurisdiction he would operate, and several times came near to disaster, at the hands of the forces of law as well as at the hands of the conspirators. Such a hazardous enterprise has been advanced as evidence against any notion that such a thing as a spy 'system' prevailed at this time; it has even been suggested that if spies were a necessary part of the government machine it would have been far better to institute some system in their employment rather than trust to the casual, unorganised means of operation of this amateurish network.[61]

It is well known that Pentrich discredited the use of spies and that Robert Peel abolished them because, it used to be thought, they were un-British, but that was not the end of spies. Individuals still presented themselves for service in times of trouble and still found employment. With the advent of the new police it was now possible to keep a closer watch on their activities and they were in any case now treated with much more scepticism by those who employed them. The range of employers remained fairly large. If the central government no longer featured, the Metropolitan police was as ready to utilise spies as were the rural magistrates, and this is not really surprising. The police needed on occasions to act secretly and the informer was still a source of valuable information as he is even today. The extent to which they were employed varied very much from place to place, but by the 1840s the central government was certainly helping to put on the brake. Sir James Graham has been described as 'almost puritannical' in his scruples concerning the employment of spies and his expenditure under this head was very slight. Whilst methods and means of detection were still in a very elementary state it was natural that governments should choose to pick up their information from whatever sources were available and use was certainly made of the old practice of searching mail during the Chartist period. The post-master, like the factory inspector, was a useful contact with public opinion and a likely informant on matters pertaining to public order; newspaper reporters too, who attended Chartist meetings, found their reports being used for the collection of evidence, a practice with which they expressed some discontent.[62]

On the whole it could be said that much of the heat has now gone out of the spy question. An issue that once inflamed passions and caused moral attitudes to be struck is now widely seen as just one aspect of the complex adjustment of the machinery of government that was necessary at this time. Neither the employed nor their employers are as likely to be condemned as evil men as was once the case: they are seen on the one hand as enterprising opportunists who exploited a temporary social need, on the other as almost well-intentioned men who, lacking the appropriate means to carry out their good intentions, turned instead to somewhat dubious expedients as men are inclined to do in such circumstances. But the spies were really no-one's fault. They just happened at this time.

The answer to the law-and-order question was, of course, the police force, and it is difficult, though important, to avoid the arrogance that hindsight brings to an investigation of why it took nineteenth-century society so long to come up with what seems the obviously right answer. The police are so much part of the British way of life that anyone who stood in the way of their establishment must now seem almost to have offered wilful resistance to the fulfilment of national destiny. Yet it was to preserve what many regarded as the British way of life that effective resistance was offered for so long. The arguments later to be extended to embrace the whole country were mobilised during the late eighteenth and early nineteenth centuries during repeated attempts to deal with what was generally recognised as a serious law-and-order problem in the capital city. They dwelt on the preservation of personal liberty, and the privileges and blessings of a free society which set Britain apart from her less fortunate neighbours. Adam Smith had emphasised the state's responsibility to preserve the rights of the individual and argued that a system designed to interfere with individual liberty was not likely to promote the greatest happiness of the majority and would be an abrogation of the state's responsibility. But as with all arguments on liberty and freedom, absolutes are rarely involved, and free men can always be found ready to threaten their fellows unless government is prepared to exercise some controlling influence. Jeremy Bentham and Edwin Chadwick were later to reconcile the apparently contradictory notions of liberty and policing, and freedom under the law, defended by the police, became philosophically acceptable to the Utilitarians. That did not mean the conversion of all, for *The Times* could still inveigh in the 1840s against an 'instrument capable of being used for purposes of arbitrary aggression upon the liberties of the people', though by this time it was probably no longer believed, as it had been earlier, that the police might be used to install the Duke of Wellington upon the throne, a perpetuation of the kind of tradition associated earlier with standing armies.[63]

Philosophical arguments rarely become the basis of popular belief and action unless they can find more mundane support, and the case against the police was well supplemented by the financial considerations involved. From the outset likely cost was always advanced as a principle reason for rejecting a professional police, and the reluctant payer of police rates became the antecedent of all those who in future generations would advance financial arguments for withholding services and amenities required by a community. And so ratepayers were repeatedly spared the burden through many decades when police-reformers were urging the need for action. When legislation did finally reach the statute-book from 1829 onwards, financial parsimony afflicted the implementation of proposals at all stages as it usually did where nineteenth century government was concerned, and in the middle years of the century residents in the rural areas of counties were continuing to object to making financial provision for policing the more industrial areas where lived the unruly elements in society.[64]

From the nature of the opposition to the idea of a professional police force it is difficult to advance any clear view of how the issue relates to the controversy concerning oppressive governments, popular rights, and an emerging working class. The Whigs and Radicals who opposed standing armies also opposed for much the same reasons the police who were the only means of replacing them, the Tory squires had an enormous vested interest in the perpetuation of the old system which they themselves controlled, and the new power in the land, the 'popular demagogues' and trade union militants, were also believed to share this attitude. Political extremists were said to be worried in the 1830s that the new police would bring an end to mob rule and terrorism, and the very fact that they were opposed to the police was evidence to its advocates that such a force was desirable.[65] It was doubtless hoped by the reformers that all men of good sense were in favour of law-and-order – and this included 'the great body of workmen' misled by their riotous leaders – and therefore of the police, but this was far from being so. The opposite was nearer the case, that most people were opposed to the idea, apart from a minority of reformers who managed to carry the day.

In view of this, it is the arrival of the police, rather than its absence, that requires an explanation, for the modern force was by no means predestined to emerge, and when it did so it was by fits and starts, the timing of the stages determined by expediency and accident rather than by design; so much so that the police cannot possibly be seen either as a naturally-evolving blessing on the one hand or, on the other, as an oppressive imposition that successive governments were determined to lay upon the people of England to keep them in check. The police force was set up out of necessity as people in authority came gradually to see the effect on society of the virtual absence of machinery for the enforcement of law and order. Robert Peel understood this and wished to combat crime, which could only be done by more efficient means of prevention and detection, at the same time supporting his case for reforming the penal law by ensuring that the law was enforced and therefore not in disrepute. He was an exponent of efficiency in matters of routine rather than an innovator attempting to deal with the newer problems of industrial troubles and large scale mob violence.

The next stage, the formation of a Borough Police as part of the Municipal Corporations Act of 1835, appears in no sense a logical consequence of the Metropolitan Act of 1829. The Whigs indicated no particular interest in the success of Peel's scheme, no particular concern for hounding the criminals who might have been driven from London, and no particular worry about the crime rate. Certainly the Reform Bill riots of 1831 had shown that the old corporate towns such as Nottingham, Derby and Bristol, were having their troubles as well as the new industrial centres, but the policing clauses of the 1835 act seem to have arisen principally out of a wish to rationalise and tidy up the confused situation of watchmen and constables, Improvement Commissioners and town magistrates, modernise police provision, and bring it under the control of popularly-elected councils. The Municipal Corporations Act provided the occasion and opportunity for further police reform, but it was not coming as part of any grand design, or conspiracy.[66] Nor did the next instalment, the Rural Police Act of 1839. Though a Royal Commission had toiled away producing unanswerable reasons why county police forces were necessary, it was only the Chartist disorders of 1839, and the threat of worse to follow, that finally stirred the government into action. And the action when it came was a typical piece of nineteenth-century legislation, determined more by expediency than by principle, which made a small step forward by conciliating and appeasing vested interests which prevented the issue being treated purely in terms of what was thought necessary. Unwilling to take on the Tory county magistrates and the newly enfranchised borough corporations, Melbourne's government found it politically impossible to accept the recommendation to set up a national force under central control, and settled instead for the much weaker permissive proposals which invited county magistrates to agree to the creation of county forces in their own areas for which the Home Secretary would lay down regulations. And again in 1856, in the County and Borough Police Act of that year, central supervision was combined with local management in a political compromise based on what was possible and politic rather than what the Home Office had thought desirable.[67]

It is an interesting comment on the nature of British society that the locally controlled and centrally supervised police system which evolved in the nineteenth century was contrary to the wishes of the outstanding Home Secretaries who were interested in police-reform, Peel, Graham, Simon and Palmerston, all of whom favoured a centrally controlled national force. For some this would be an indication of national perversity, for others the secret of English liberty. At all events, it is indicative of the total absence of any successfully accomplished design to impose a tyrannous police from above.

Where the motivation behind the establishment of a police force does appear in a form that could be seen as explicitly oppressive is in that part of the 1839 Report where the Constabulary Commissioners came very close to arguing that a rural police would be a good thing because it would keep down trade unionism and political fanaticism. They in fact reported that a police force would offer protection to capital and labour alike, though their arguments implied that the workmen were as much in need of protection from enthusiasts within their own ranks as were the manufacturers from the workmen's leaders.[68] It is perhaps significant that Lancashire with its industrial unrest was quick to set up a police force, though it must also be noted that the West Riding of Yorkshire was slow to do so. There is no indication, however, that governments were consciously and deliberately pursuing anti-labour policies in establishing police forces, and the latter were not to acquire any reputation for such attitudes in the years following their foundation. It is also necessary to exercise caution over the 1839 Report, for the commissioners probably overstated their case against trade-unionism knowingly in their desire to present as comprehensive an argument as possible for the adoption of their proposals.

Whatever the motivation of those who advocated and those who passed the proposals for the establishment of the new police, the new forces that emerged can hardly be regarded as the highly organised and responsive agents of the tyrannous governments that created them. The marked lack of enthusiasm evident in the passing of legislation was still to be seen in its implementation, and expediency and the pressures of the moment continued to dictate. The Metropolitan Police had a hard time from the governments of the 1830s who exhorted local corporations to seek help from them but refused the necessary financial help to allow for this to be properly given and who were prepared to tolerate, even encourage, public criticism of the police in order to divert it away from the government.[69] Outside London growth has been described as 'gradual, patchy and unspectacular'.[70] Boroughs were in many cases slow to respond to their obligations under the 1835 Act, and 20 years later it was discovered that 13 corporations had totally avoided their responsibilities. For the rest, though the big towns were generally efficient, many of the medium-sized towns and most of the smaller ones left a great deal to be desired. The London ratio of one policeman to 500 population was not carried to the provinces, where only half that proportion of police was the average; in the borough of Stockport in the 1830s the ratio was eight times worse than that in London. Inadequate staffing arose in particular from financial stringency and watch committee parsimony, and in general from lack of appreciation of realistic needs. Halifax, for instance, was preparing to adopt a force of 25 in spite of recent experience that it took 50 men to surround a building where there was trouble, whilst in Manchester local politics continued to bedevil the situation as the centrally-inspired police contended with the old police commissioners and manorial authorities that still fought a rearguard action over the Municipal Corporation Act and offered every possible obstruction. It has been claimed that there was no significant improvement of the borough police forces throughout the Chartist period and that there was even a fall in the percentage of well-policed boroughs.[71]

Nor did the counties set a better example. Chartism stirred them up to allow the Act of 1839 to make a slight impact, but the impulse was soon lost; only a minority of counties acquired forces in the early 1840s and the 1853 Select Committee found that half of the counties had declined to adopt the Act.[72] There was no confidence that the police could effectively take over from the army in bad times, and in good times the traditional machinery was thought to be sufficient. And so such response as there was to the Act occurred in times of political disturbance, and after successive disturbances there were lapses into former apathy and indifference. In spite of the advice of the 1839 Constabulary Commissioners magistrates continued to exercise their conflicting and incompatible responsibilities for law-enforcement and justice until 1888, and their retained vested interests, together with a general determination to avoid expenditure, ensured that police reform would continue through its experimental stage in the middle decades of the century. A comprehensive, rationally organised and effective system of police did not appear in these years; but any such new institution of government would have been unique in this period.

If the threats to law and order came primarily from the working classes, it would have been surprising if the new police had not been regarded in part as an instrument of class oppression. In fact, it was Peel's intention from the outset that his Metropolitan Police should recruit men 'who had not the rank, habits or station of gentlemen'; it was not to be a body apart from the people, nor was it to reproduce the caste system of either the army or the navy.[73] Yet by operating against the most violent elements in social and political protest it probably served to strengthen the hand of the more moderate leadership; in 1832 it probably assisted Francis Place to establish his hegemony over the radical reformers during the crisis of May, and its contribution nationally to the long-term evolution and success of moderates as leaders of popular movements could well have been important, if impossible to quantify.[74] The Metropolitan Commissioners operated with a degree of impartiality not always previously characteristic of policing enterprises, and their wish to avoid repressive policies earned them criticism from property-owners during the Chartist period for their failure to put down working-class meetings. They defended their policy of non-interference where no breaches of the peace were involved. And when intervention did prove necessary it could now be correctly timed, as at Clerkenwell on 31 August 1848, when a riot was prevented.[75] It was not simply that the police were usually good-humoured and restrained in their handling of disorderly crowds, despite their own ill-treatment in their early years, but also that a technique of crowd-control was now being learned. Unlike the unfortunate men who exercised responsibility at Peterloo, the police were beginning to understand the behaviour of human beings in the mass.[76] Again it could be argued that the change from anarchy to order, from failure to success, was not so much a question of virtue triumphing over vice but experience and professional expertise being brought to bear on the solving of problems. And if the working classes could hardly be expected immediately to view the new police as their natural protectors, there were at least signs that a measure of accord was being established. In July 1840, for instance, the Birmingham Chartists sought police help at their reception for the release of Lovett from prison, indicating their growing confidence in the police and the new prestige with which they were now invested, confirmed by their skill and the impartiality of their conduct. In Manchester too the police won working-class friends by refusing to align with the manufacturing interests of the Anti-Corn Law League, and in June 1841, actually saved the Chartists from the even more alarming Irish in the troubles of that month.[77]

The traditional case against the oppressive governors of industrialising England, if not in a state of collapse, is at least to a small extent undermined. A last aspect of it that warrants discussion is the suggestion of the Hammonds that the law itself, far from being 'the true embodiment of everything that's excellent', was partial in its application to the different social classes; that it was impossible for working men to have their rights justly upheld, as for example over the notorious non-enforcement of successive Truck Acts; that the traditional rights supposedly attaching to Englishmen were meaningless for the working classes; and that some laws, for example those against seditious publications, were used only against the working classes.[78] It would be impossible to quantify any accurate response to these accusations, but such evidence and opinion as exists on them tends to support the general trend of the Hammonds' argument and to establish the partiality of the law as a prime working-class grievance of the period. Certain laws such as the Vagrancy Laws, Poor Laws, and Game Laws were designed to apply to the poor rather than the rich, and they would operate exclusively upon certain sections of society. The poor, it has recently been argued, offered excuses for their 'unseemly behaviour' in terms of the customs and excise laws which tempted people to ill-treat the enforcement officials, the law prohibiting the sale of game which, according to McCulloch, encouraged murder and robbery, the despotic behaviour of magistrates, and the oppressive and ineffectual Combination Laws.[79] These last were supposed to apply equally to both employers and employed, though it was admitted before their repeal that the only convictions that had occurred under them had been of workmen. The reasons for this are largely a matter for inference; in 1839 the Constabulary Commissioners reported that they had not 'adduced full evidence as to the illegal proceedings of masters, only because we have found it more difficult to obtain for public use than evidence of the proceedings of workmen'.[80] But when Gravener Henson, attempting to exploit the rash behaviour of hosiers who advertised their combination in the local press, instituted proceedings against them under the Acts in 1811, he found the magistrates totally unwilling to co-operate, offering the technical objection that they had no proof of the parish in which the combination had occurred.[81] The 1828 Select Committee on Criminal Commitment heard complaints that offences passed over when committed by the sons of the wealthy led to prosecution when committed by the children of the poor; it was a commonly held view. A proffered explanation of this was the reluctance to prosecute children of a respectable background because of the contaminating effects of prison, which did nothing to assuage the working-class sense of grievance.[82] Quite apart from being better placed economically to avoid the petty crime of lower classes, the rich also enjoyed the social privilege that allowed them, for instance, to take for granted the right of physical assault upon their subordinates and to escape detection in the vices they chose to practise. It can hardly be doubted that the balance was unfavourable to the poor where the impartiality of the law was in question and this fact alone would militate against any rash supposition that the traditionalist views of the Hammonds have been thoroughly discredited.

3 *The New Towns*

'Life in such a town brought no alleviation of the tyranny of the industrial system'

—*The Town Labourer*, p. 56.

Between the middle of the eighteenth and the middle of the nineteenth centuries the British people ceased to be mainly country dwellers and became mainly town dwellers. In 1750 less than one-fifth of the population lived in towns with a population of more than 5,000; in 1850 more than three-fifths lived in towns of this size. In 1750 only London and Edinburgh had a population of more than 50,000; in 1801 there were eight such towns and by 1851 there were 29, so that by this date one-third of the population was to be found in such cities. For individual towns the growth-rate was spectacular; Manchester grew from 17,000 to 180,000 in the years 1760–1830, having increased itself nearly six times over in the course of 60 years. Across the Pennines Bradford was growing even more dramatically, always increasing itself by 50% in each decade of the period 1811–51.[1] During the same 40-year period the number of mills in Bradford rose from one to 67, for it was industrialisation that was the cause of this rapid and unprecedented growth.[2] This new industrial world was to be seen in its most obvious form, it has been suggested, in and around Manchester; the cotton towns were the first to be dominated by factories, which other places acquired, if at all, mainly during the second half of the century, and it was the cotton towns that illustrated best the so-called 'system of life constructed on a wholly new principle', life as experienced in an industrial town.[3]

Yet to say that Manchester represented this new world in its most obvious form is far from saying that Manchester was necessarily typical of developments elsewhere; in many ways it was unique as a pace-setter. Even before the coming of railways it was changing over from manufacture to commerce, and the young Coningsby was advised to visit Stalybridge or Bolton if he really wanted 'to see life'.[4] The investigator has been given many warnings against the dangers of facile or 'thumping generalisations' over the new industrial towns; he should expect to be able to observe how towns differed from each other as well as what they had in common.[5] The typical industrial town will probably turn out to be a myth in view of the great variety of industrial experience undergone by different places. Ancient towns like Nottingham and Leicester were important economic centres long before they underwent their great growth periods through the expansion of the domestic hosiery trade in the late eighteenth and early nineteenth century, an expansion which did not involve conversion to factory production. Manchester, Leeds, and Birmingham, probably the three most important industrial towns in the nineteenth century, were previously places of minor consequence; and their economic and social development was to produce political pictures of fascinating contrasts rather than similarities.[6] Other towns, Middlesbrough, St Helens or Crewe, for example, were literally new towns, but again their history would be determined by their specific economic structure, whether, for instance, they were single-industry towns and therefore highly vulnerable to depression or centres of mixed economy which enabled them to withstand crises more successfully. A study of St Helens, for instance, suggests that experience there should relieve the gloomy generalisations inspired by less fortunate centres. This town enjoyed the advantages of comparatively late development, it was not so overcrowded and insanitary as many other places, it had a higher proportion of well-paid workers and lacked the 'horde of domestic weavers' that characterised many Lancashire towns, and its workpeople enjoyed a wide variety of leisure activities. The origins of the labour force might determine quite markedly the nature of a particular town.[7] The country folk are thought to have helped set the St Helens' pattern, whilst the peculiar predicament of Manchester was rarely explained without reference to the fact that one-fifth of its population in 1840 was Irish.[8]

A lack of uniformity is in fact what would be expected in the absence of any central government planning and direction in the process of industrialisation, for, like industrialisation, urbanisation was unplanned. This was not an unmixed blessing. In de Tocqueville's eyes everything in the outward appearance of the cities he visited testified to the power of individuals and nothing to the controlling and directing power of society; government was noticeably lacking and 'at every turn liberty shows its capricious, creative form'.[9] In Lewis Mumford's words, the industrial town revealed an 'uncouth disorder'. The location and operation of its constituent parts were determined by private enterprise in search of private profit, but the 'pre-ordained harmony of the economic order' that this would supposedly accomplish 'turned out to be a superstition'; instead the town became a mere 'fortuitous concourse of atoms', discredited as an institution for promoting the good life.[10] The state had no interest in what today might be called 'social investment', the provision of administrative and welfare services such as local government, sanitation, and education, which, if not strictly necessary to aid economic growth at first, were soon desperately needed in consequence of it. Towns grew unchecked by public control and without those public services which might have cut down the costs in social, if not in economic, terms of conversion to an urban, industrial economy. And when the central government did begin to interest itself in this kind of area, it met the usual nineteenth-century arguments against interference and centralisation. Sir John Simon claimed in 1868 that one-quarter of the country's mortality resulted from the ineffective application of nuisance laws; and the need to register contagious diseases was later to be resisted as an infringement of personal liberty.[11] At a local level some services, such as gas and water-supply, could only be brought within the reach of the poor by a fully planned and efficient public enterprise, but this was delayed and resisted by the sanctity of the notion of competition.[12]

But perhaps more important as a deterrent than a need to preserve private enterprise was the need to preserve profitability, though these are essentially aspects of the same issue. In a flourish of rhetoric the Hammonds asked what the new industrial towns were to be like, their schools, their houses, their places for leisure and pleasure, their facilities for co-operation and fellowship, the whole fate that they offered to the masses of people within their boundaries. For an answer to their questions they said that capital must be consulted, and capital always gave the same reply, that all these aspects must be left to the mercy and direction of the spirit of property.[13] And so piped water and gas-lit streets, possible from the start of the nineteenth century, were denied to the town-dwellers until much later; the town grew at the pleasure of the profit-seeker, and no Act of Parliament encompassed town-planning before the twentieth century.[14] In less rhetorical language, economic individualism and common civic purpose were difficult to reconcile, and a high rate of industrial investment might mean a total indifference to the social costs of industrialisation.[15] Or, in the words of another modern authority, cities, like houses, were constructed on the cheap, and catering for public services was minimal; by excluding from calculations all needs which arose from matters of social provision it was possible to achieve phenomenal economic growth rates, at least until a point was reached where the cheapest course was proving to be uneconomic because it undermined efficiency.[16] For instance, the failure to invest in education would ultimately have proved disastrous because the industrial system eventually required large numbers of educated men to operate it. Similarly, there was a limit to how far employers and governments could afford to neglect social amenities and welfare if they were to retain an economically productive work force; this would be all the better for being healthy and happy, and so health and happiness were eventually seen to be worth pursuing on grounds that made sense in economic terms. In general, it could be said that modern opinions have largely vindicated the Hammonds' view that the rapid economic growth of the late eighteenth and early nineteenth century took place at some 'social cost', that developments in the social sphere did not keep pace with those in the economic, and that this occurred because industrialisation and urbanisation were carried out without central direction and financed on a free enterprise basis.[17]

Opinions on the quality of social environment offered by the new industrial towns are dictated, it has been suggested, by prejudice rather than by science.[18] The allegedly offensive nature of the new urban environment has yet to be quantified, and until this statistical assessment has taken place it would be premature to speak of scientific investigation, yet contemporary literary evidence is sufficiently strong to have permitted a fair measure of agreement on this issue. The 'general assault on the senses' can be broken down into its obvious divisions: the smell of towns arose from a combination of industrial activities, such as brewing, tanning, dyeing, and the manufacture of gas, the effluence of animals and human beings, uncleaned, defectively drained streets and unwashed people.[19] Particularly memorable are Engels' 'revolting blackish-green puddles of slime from the depths of which bubbles of miasmic gases constantly rise and create unbearable stench'.[20] The dirt of the streets and the houses was reinforced by the dirt of the chimneys, and this whole 'toxic refuse of urban life' was not tackled effectively until the 1870s.[21] Mumford lists the various poisonous gases that pervaded the atmosphere and refers to the 200 cancer-producing chemicals that they helped to disseminate, creating the 'acrid evil-smelling environment' that still awaits unprejudiced assessment.[22] The 'dense acidic smoke from the alkali works' of St Helens 'was soon to blacken the countryside and kill the trees and hedgerows', an illustration of the immediate visual impact of the towns, what the eye could see or what the eye could not see because of smoke.[23] In the manufacturing town, wrote Robert Owen, people were enveloped in smoke; it was the smoke-nuisance, according to Cooke Taylor, that was driving everyone from the centre of Manchester who could afford to buy a house elsewhere, and it was the prospect of the 'smoky nuisance' that caused the respectable inhabitants of Tyrrel Street, Bradford, to threaten legal action against John James, in 1793, when he proposed to build a factory at the bottom of Manchester Road.[24] Their victory was only a transitory one and the extent of the continuing problem is evidenced by the fact that only in recent years, since the establishment of smokeless zones, has it been possible to see across the city from one hillside to that opposite. The trading of Sheffield left no industrial debris behind but created a particularly severe smoke nuisance.[25] But it was the cotton towns that were the most smoke-filled of all and their steam-engines that were responsible; in 1838 Manchester and Salford possessed about three times the steam-power of Birmingham and doubtless a proportionally greater problem as a result.[26] And if the smells and sights of the industrial towns are more readily imagined than the sounds, there can be little doubt that town-dwellers lived in an 'atmosphere vibrating with clamour', from the machinery of factories, the hammers in the forges, the new railways, or the horse-driven transport of the cobbled streets.[27] When the 1808 visitor from Rotherham to Manchester could report that 'the town is abominably filthy, the steam engine is pestiferous, the dyehouses noisome and offensive, and the water of the river as black as ink or the Stygian Lake', the man's apparent credentials entitle him to a respectful hearing.[28] That a deteriorating urban environment was one of the most disastrous and continuing consequences of industrialisation seems a proposition of sufficiently obvious veracity and one so generally upheld as to remove it from the realms of prejudice. Controversy might appropriately be confined to recent more extravagant speculation that this was the 'most degraded urban environment the world had yet seen' and to the bitterly ironic comment that the transformation of rivers into open sewers, massive pollution had it occurred a century and a half later, was 'a characteristic feat of the new economy'.[29]

The overwhelming dominance of the profit motive in determining the nature of the nineteenth-century towns ensured a neglect not only of those aspects of life which were not immediately necessary for the realisation of profit; it also entered their treatment where they were essential support subsidiaries of the industrialisation process, as in the case of housing, which was not simply a social amenity to be enjoyed when there was spare money available for its development but a necessary accompaniment to the building up of a large and concentrated labour force in the towns. Again the Hammonds, in memorable language, see nineteenth-century urban housing as 'the avarice of the jerry-builder catering for the avarice of the capitalist', quoting Nassau Senior, who said that towns were erected with the utmost disregard for everything except the immediate advantage of the speculating builder.[30] Once again the language has changed, but the message remains much the same, for a recent survey of working-class housing in this period confesses that it brings little of comfort to the optimistic historian of the standard of living issue;[31] nothing that has been learned since the Hammonds has made the condition of working-class housing in this period seem any better and it would still be easy enough to subscribe to the views of H. G. Wells on the 'massacre, degeneration, and disablement' that arose from the way people were housed during the nineteenth century.[32]

The problem of housing arose in part from the phenomenal growth in the population and from its redistribution, which placed a huge strain on the urban areas. It arose in part too from technical problems, 'structural bottlenecks' as they have been called, on the supply side of the building industry; firms remained typically small, employing only a dozen or so men, no new techniques were introduced and building remained a high-cost craft industry; and urban land remained at a premium in competition with the prior claims of industry and railways.[33] This last was more than a technical problem; it was a political problem of determining social priorities, and housing for workers clearly came very low, a 'residual affair' in terms of land available and the money and imagination that were invested in developing sites.[34] In Nassau Senior's words, working-class housing was erected by small speculators whose sole concern was immediate profit; in consequence Cooke Taylor found that the population of Manchester quickly outstripped the accommodation available and that the houses of workers below the status of factory operative were the most wretched that could be conceived.[35]

are some of the general factors influencing housing provision, ndividual places there were specific factors that produced a ristic kind of working-class dwelling associated with these places. In Leeds in the period 1797–1850 almost all working-class houses built were of the back-to-back variety; these were tiny houses, highly defective in their water supply, sanitation, drainage, and ventilation. In the town centre this high-density housing can be explained in terms of the need to get the maximum number of rentable or saleable houses into each acre of expensive land. Further from the centre the existing narrow fields became narrow plots and imposed their pattern upon further back-to-back developments. The Commissioners on Large Towns were told in 1844 that this was a cheap mode of building and that to outlaw it would be to deprive poor people of accommodation. Parliamentary legislation left the back-to-backs untouched, and, although other large northern boroughs had by-laws banning this type of construction in the middle years of the century, Leeds continued to build them until 1937, 28 years after they had been proscribed nationally.[36] In Liverpool the notorious working-class residence was the cellar-dwelling, occupied by 24,000 in 1841; this was a square area, of ten or twelve feet, some 4-5 feet below ground level. There was no check on this kind of development prior to 1842; some cellars were used as daytime schools, housing 40–60 'consumptive, disease-ridden children'; double cellars might house up to 30 Irish for the night. Not surprisingly the cellar-dweller was the worst sufferer from epidemic diseases. As the cellar declined in importance the court system, cul-de-sacs of high density back-to-backs, became the standard working-class house; one-third of the working classes were so housed by 1835. The courts were undrained and unpaved, standing in fluid refuse of every kind, and had defective water supplies. The justification for this type of development was the high return on capital invested. Manchester too had its cellars, occupied by 20,000 people in 1834; here would live the Irish immigrant accompanied by 'his disgusting domestic companion, the pig'.[37] In Glasgow the tenement was the characteristic working-class dwelling. In Birmingham the problem of slum tenements was avoided and cellar dwellings were uncommon, but the town had over 2,000 courts in the 1830s.[38] Nottingham too was characterised by courts and 'rookeries'; here the old town was surrounded by large private estates and common lands, compelling housing development to take place within the restricted area of the old town. Members of the Corporation, which opposed enclosure of the commons, were in some cases slum-property owners who benefited from the artificially inflated land prices in the town centre.[39] Similarly in Coventry the town was unable to expand geographically and built inwards upon itself, courts and yards again supplying the answer.[40] In Leicester in the year 1789 even the lower orders were said to have had their neat gardens; over the next 60 years these gradually disappeared under the almost universal pressure for land.[41] In many large towns the artisan élite used their higher earnings to move into superior dwellings; the Nottingham lace-workers, for instance, forsook the courts in the town centre for the new 'garden communities' such as New Basford and Hyson Green beyond the 'green belt'.[42] But these were only the minority. The vast majority of the working classes were condemned to the sort of conditions that Robert Baker described in Leeds; houses built without reference to health, decency, and morality, conveniently sited for their work and built in the smallest space in streets unpaved, unsewered, and uncleansed.[43] When Engels wrote of the 'scandalous and demoralising system of housing the workers' in the 1840s, he was not measuring against mid-twentieth-century standards but displaying the capacity of contemporaries to be shocked by what they saw.[44] And no amount of modern emphasis on the new materials of stone and slate that the working classes were now enjoying and favourable comparisons with rural dwellings can obscure the insanitary nature of working-class dwellings which gave nineteenth-century England its public health problem.

The existence of a causal connection between living conditions in the industrial towns and the ill-health of their people was widely observed. When Mr Balwhidder left his rural parish to visit Glasgow in 1791 he was struck by the long, white faces, the 'cast of unhealthy melancholy', of the weavers he saw in the Trongate, and this condition he attributed to their overcrowded conditions and the absence of 'wholesome country air', a mild analysis compared with Robert Southey's a few years later; he identified the dwellings of the poor as 'hotbeds of infection' bequeathing to the labourers 'a plague of their own'.[45] Cooke Taylor found Manchester's mortality rate of 1 : 30 indicative of the great misery and suffering attributable to purely physical causes, but it was Dr Robert Taylor, whose Leeds cholera map of 1833 so clearly related the incidence of the disease to the undrained, unsewered, and unpaved areas, who first offered something more than an intelligent inference from the facts before him.[46]

Chadwick used the work of Taylor and other medical men to produce his sensational revelations of 1842 that life expectancy was dramatically less for all town dwellers than for country dwellers and that within towns the labourers and mechanics who lived in the least sanitary, worst-housed areas had less than half the life expectancy of the gentry and professional classes. The poor of Manchester had also less than half the life expectancy of the poor of rural Rutland. In the words of one modern authority Chadwick set out to establish 'the correlation between insanitation, defective drainage, inadequate water-supply, and over-crowded housing with disease, high mortality rates, and low expectation of life'.[47] It is difficult to resist the conclusion that he succeeded. E. P. Thompson shows an unwonted caution in regarding as literary rather than statistical evidence the reports on which Chadwick, whose views 'needed to be fed on a diet of statistics', based his findings.[48] He effectively demonstrated that the urban environment was a killer. His own crankish ideas of how disease was contracted are now of little importance; but there is no difficulty in seeing how the pollution of the air and water supply were responsible for diseases of the respiratory and intestinal systems, for periodic epidemics, the new cholera and typhoid specifically. The boom towns of the Industrial Revolution had the worst conditions, and prosperity, as Chadwick argued, was no safeguard against epidemic disease, even if the endemic typhus and tuberculosis, the latter almost entirely confined to the towns in the nineteenth century, were diseases of poverty and undernourishment.[49] The high urban death rates did not fall until some 30 years after Chadwick's sanitary report, and infant mortality rates remained constant until the end of the century. Indeed it has been suggested that only constant new immigration from the country-side enabled town life to survive at all since the towns were killing off their people faster than they were able to renew themselves.[50] Those who survived the urban experience were a race of defectives, for as early as 1830, it has been argued, the average industrial worker was assumed to be of stunted growth and unfit for heavy manual labour.[51] There is no measuring the psychological strains imposed upon him by his new life, though Mrs Gaskell noted of townspeople that 'Their nerves are quickened by the haste and bustle and speed of everything around them, to say nothing of the confinement in these pent-up houses, which of itself is enough to induce depression and worry of spirits'.[52]

It is very difficult to know where the worst conditions were to be found since any particular town currently being inspected would invariably convey the impression of being the worst of its kind. Gaskell might have believed Manchester in 1832 to be in a lamentable condition where everything relating to the 'health, decency, or comforts' of its people was concerned, and there were plenty others to testify to the evils of that place, yet other towns too staked their claims to paramountcy.[53] The old market town of Leicester, for instance, remained one of only four municipal towns without improvement commissioners prior to 1835, and was said to be unequalled for filth and unhealthiness because of the absence of proper drains.[54] Nearby Nottingham presented a fearsome spectacle to the town commissioners of 1844, who found its slum areas second only to those of Bombay inside the British Empire, and its entire working-class districts one vast nuisance.[55] In Yorkshire Dr Baker contributed his graphic account of the offensive nuisances of Leeds, whilst nearby Bradford appeared to one visiting commissioner 'the dirtiest, filthiest, worst regulated town in the kingdom'.[56] The horror stories could be culled from almost any of the towns; a league table would be of little value. Nor did the revealing of these horrors necessarily lead to their prompt removal. The Hammonds were able to argue that in 1867 the death rate was higher in many towns than it had been in 1842, and it must be acknowledged that not until the last quarter of the century did health conditions begin to improve in the poor parts of the cities.[57]

In this sort of context to look for social amenity and the facilities that distinguished between life and existence seems almost a fatuous exercise. The towns had after all brought together people who were in search of profit of one sort or another rather than attempting to create a social community. It is not surprising then that Southey found it impossible to visualise 'a place more destitute of all interesting objects than Manchester', and it is in their reflections on this subject that the Hammonds strike their most mournful note as they contemplate the new Manchester of rundown and squalid buildings, of 200,000 people without a single park to enjoy, and melancholy streets without gardens or orchards.[58] They have an almost infinite regard for what the city could represent; in man's highest moments he has rivalled the beauty of nature with the beauty of cities, but in the nineteenth century this can be nothing but ironic comment, for nineteenth-century towns they see as the barracks of an industry not the refuge of a civilisation, as they ought to be. With the lofty ideal of the ancient world before them they lament the decline of 'the art of living', 'degraded to its rudest forms'.[59] Chadwick had regretted the absence of open spaces for recreation which would have been conducive to better health; in 1842 Preston was the only town in Lancashire with a public park, and not until the last quarter of the century was this problem seriously tackled, Sheffield, for instance, making its first public park provision in the 1870s.[60]

But the Hammonds' town labourers were not to be pitied simply because they were denied access to museums and participation in guilds and pageants, for the Hammonds were not so unrealistic as to suppose that all labourers were so inclined. They were to be pitied because their sports had been converted into crimes and their holidays into fast days, as they put it, because it was thought that the less amusement a working man had the better he would be, since working men were not capable of profiting by leisure. They were intended for work alone and their towns were so constructed.[61] The spirit of the age, Coningsby was told, the spirit of utility, was against popular customs such as maypole dancing; 'the best thing we can do for the labouring classes', said Lord Everingham, 'is to provide them with work'.[62] These ideas, according to Cobbett, derived from 'the Scotch feelosofers, who seem all to have been by nature formed for negro-drivers, have an insuperable objection to all those establishments and customs which occasion holidays. They call them a great hindrance, a great bar to industry, a great draw-back from "national wealth".'[63] Traditional habits and customs did not fit the patterns of industrial life and so they had to go as a new work discipline was erected. They might be condemned as 'pastimes of village buffoonery and rudeness' and their elimination, like the attempted assault on drinking habits, was part of the process of assimilating the work-force to a new society and a new way of life.[64] In some places, as at St Helens where 'pigeon-flying, prize-fighting, and foot-racing' continued unabated, pre-industrial practices survived; in others the working classes had to wait until late in the century before a new urban working-class culture filled the void, replacing the 'healthy, rational sports and amusements' that Robert Owen would have preferred for his work people.[65] In 1842 Cooke Taylor commented that Manchester had become essentially a place of business where pleasure was unknown as a pursuit and amusements scarcely ranked for consideration.[66] These were to be found only in the inns, beer houses, and gin vaults, of which the town was said to have almost 1,000, where temporary escape from the realities of life could be purchased; the other form of escape was the 'even grimmer Protestant chapels' which constituted the only other facility for social intercourse that the town offered, for the inhabitants' need to congregate was as neglected by the town as his need for personal comfort.[67] Opportunities for social contact outside work were few anyway as wrestling, cock-fighting, and bull-baiting, the sports that had been declared crimes, were dying after 1840, leaving behind a 'stony desert' of a society which workmen would have to make tolerable by their own efforts and by the development of new pastimes and entertainments later in the century.[68] Meanwhile, they must experience 'deteriorating town-life' which brought 'social losses not embodied in any index', hoping to avoid the depressions that would throw them to the mercy of the soup kitchens of the distress committees, which could make only the most superficial impact on the problems experienced by town workers during times of slump.[69] From the middle of the century a park or a library might become accessible if some public-spirited individual had campaigned successfully or bequeathed sufficiently, but most towns had to wait until the last two decades of the century before they began to enjoy a share in this kind of cultural amenity.

Not surprisingly this physical environment is believed to have had important consequences for social relationships. The worse the working-class areas of towns became, the less acceptable they were to other social groups for residential areas and the more confirmed they became as areas of exclusively working-class residence. Though there has been recent warning that relatively little is known of precisely where men lived in relation to their jobs, there has been a general readiness to accept Cooke Taylor's view of the physical demarcation of living areas between the poor and the rich, with the latter increasingly moving away from places where they would be conscious of the existence of the poor.[70] Engels commented on the clear distinction between the two areas, suggesting a planned exclusion of working-class people from the main streets of Manchester so as not to offend middle-class eyes or nerves.[71] Working-class ghettos became increasingly isolated and unvisited by other social groups, except for law enforcement; the middle classes left the town centres, aided by the growth of suburban railways and the horse omnibus, and there remained only the shopkeepers, the innkeepers, and the police to attend to working-class needs or to deal with working-class crime.[72] Physical separation of this kind would certainly exacerbate the social gulf and the lack of sympathy and understanding between the social classes which had an obvious economic base in the desire of the employer to buy his labour as cheaply as possible. In the industrial North, it has been said, a new kind of society was coming into being, 'torn by conflicts of attitudes and interests', where actual social disintegration accompanied the physical separation of the different classes.[73]

Again Manchester is the archetypal town, for there was no place, according to a local clergyman, where the gulf between rich and poor was so great.[74] As the growth of industry greatly increased the power that the few were able to exercise over the many, economic divisions reproduced themselves socially, and the social classes went their separate ways. In some old towns like Coventry and Nottingham it had been traditionally possible to resolve local trade problems by the common action of the parties concerned; this became an increasingly obsolescent approach to issues as distinct and separate interests emerged and profit became a more important consideration than 'the good of the trade'.[75] In Manchester Prentice saw two classes ranged in bitter hostility against each other, and as early as 1819 a local newspaper had remarked that there was 'no sympathy between upper and lower classes of society, no mutual confidence, no band of attachment'.[76]

A retrospective identification of a class-conflict situation in the towns is a less hazardous experience for the historian than an attempt to identify the first stirrings of class consciousness there. The wealthy cotton manufacturers of Manchester were, it has been suggested, perhaps the first group of men to think of themselves as a class, and there would be wide support for the view that the towns as a whole helped to foster class consciousness amongst the working classes too.[77] This would probably be tempered with a cautious enjoinder to avoid sweeping generalisation and remember the way in which the structure of the local economy helped determine class patterns. As a result of a detailed investigation of Oldham, for instance, it has been suggested that within the town's three principal employments three-quarters of the cotton workers were employed by 60 firms, four-fifths of the engineers by three firms, and that almost all the coal-miners worked either for one combine or subsidiaries of the cotton firms. This, it is alleged, amounted to 12,000 workers, without prospect of social mobility, selling their labour to 70 capitalist families. Here was a working-class, unstratified and not divided against itself, living in the immediate presence of its employers and therefore acutely conscious of the exploitative relationship, experiencing a high degree of class consciousness which paved the way to some notable political triumphs at the very start of the nineteenth century. By contrast South Shields experienced social mobility, and active identification of employees in a common purpose with their employers through investment in their enterprises, together with their physical absence from the town, helped to keep back any latent class consciousness. Similarly in Northampton, which equalled Oldham for its poverty and low life-expectancy, no class consciousness developed because there was no resident employing class to pull the workers together and they fragmented into their occupational groups instead of coming together as a class.[78] The best publicised case of the town which avoided stark class confrontation in its social structure is Birmingham, where small workshops and small employers helped to ensure a situation of class co-operation which carried over into politics.[79] A similar situation prevailed at Sheffield. Here there was no large gulf between merchants and manufacturers on the one hand and workmen on the other such as occurred in a textile or mining context. There were few very wealthy employers, social transition was still relatively easy in the middle of the century, and the absence of clear economic hostility encouraged class co-operation in politics and inhibited both working-class consciousness and the emergence of an independent political labour movement.[80] In St Helens during the first half of the nineteenth-century four fairly distinct working-class groups of miners, Irish, glass-makers, and domestic workers looked to themselves rather than to each other, and not until the second half of the century did they tend to merge into one recognisable body.[81] In general it has been argued that the structure of the employing group and the occupational make-up of the labour force determined the extent to which a sense of class was experienced. These were highly variable and so there is no uniform pattern of working-class consciousness to be observed throughout the nineteenth-century towns, certainly not before 1850. And particularly is this to be emphasised in the light of recent comments about the local sentiment and traditions that remained inside relatively isolated colonies within towns, or mill-communities in which the first loyalty was to the mill rather than to a class grouping.[82]

Whether the new towns displayed signs of class-consciousness or not, the latent menace of immense numbers of working-class people contained within the narrow confines of their own quarters was one more reason why early nineteenth-century towns were looked upon with a mixture of horror and fear. Those who extolled the virtues of towns in the eighteenth century lost their voices when confronted with the problems brought by the urban growths of the early nineteenth and recovered them only when those problems were in some measure nearer to control in the second half of the nineteenth century.[83] One explanation of their silence is the suggestion that the new social evils made the city an emblem of guilt, and so most Victorian writers repressed their knowledge of the city in the same way that they repressed their knowledge of sex.[84] The guilt might have been compounded amongst the sensitive and artistic, such as Ruskin, by the latter's conviction that the manufacturing cities manufactured everything except men.[85] And even with the partial recovery of the town's reputation later in the century it still remained and remains to some extent the sinful and depraved alternative to the rural environment of which man dreams and for which he substitutes his plot of garden. At some point before William Morris's dreamland was described, 'the town invaded the country, but the invaders . . . yielded to the influence of their surroundings and became country people'.[86] Towns were places of horror because they were places, according to one distinguished historian, where problems overwhelmed people, where filth, physical suffering, and moral disorder seemed to exist in excess of that which John Howard had encountered in his investigations of the country's prisons.[87] In consequence, the towns conjured up black images of despair, dissolution, and corruption. In towns the rural, food-rioting crowd became an uncontrollable fury which governmental machinery was not structured to contain, part of the problem of those masses who would eventually, it was feared, scatter their employers, patrons, and governors to the four winds. Even the classical economists who might have felt almost a parental pride in the new towns (for Cobbett noted how the jolterheads congratulated one another on the growth of Manchester and similar places) are said to have had misgivings over the restlessness of their people, a turbulent and inflammable populace.[88] These people constituted a danger to religion because they were irreligious, a danger to traditional politics unless it could somehow assimilate their wishes to those of the political establishment, which for long seemed so improbable though it was in fact achieved, and were a danger to bodily safety because of their occasional resort to violence and their imagined readiness to rise in rebellion.

As events turned out they were too indifferent to religion to threaten its survival and so highly susceptible to political accommodation that the physical threat had gone out of politics by the middle of the century. And as the worst fears proved unfounded, so the worst conditions that were responsible for them have themselves seemed somewhat more understandable, and even excusable, than once looked likely. Although the Hammonds were good enough Whigs to know that evil conditions resulted from the actions of evil men, they were fair enough judges to admit that difficult problems were made more difficult by a sequence of events over which British industrialists could exercise but little control. They believed that industrial expansion would have produced fewer social problems had it proceeded at a slower pace, and they blamed its actual pace upon the fact that the French wars accelerated the rate of industrial expansion and had the customary catalystic effect that wars do have on so many branches of national life and development. And the war against Revolutionary and later Napoleonic France was fought in an atmosphere of anti-Jacobin panic and bitterness which helped to exacerbate tensions that were growing fast enough as a result of industrial development. Thus they believed that the coincidence of the French and Industrial Revolutions was a catastrophe for the whole of society, but for the working classes in particular.[89]

Another nuisance and uncontrollable element in the situation was the unprecedented population growth which accompanied, in part prompted, industrial change. Not only was population expanding rapidly in general; it was expanding very rapidly in particular places and in these places it was virtually impossible for basic public services such as water-supply, sanitation, and street-cleaning to keep pace with growth; towns were places where people were overwhelmed by problems. And the experience from which solutions to these problems might be found was not present in rural England to supply the necessary remedies. Sanitary science was, as Clapham suggests, 'as new and raw as its name'.[90] Chadwick made only a minor impact in the short term on the problems he identified, the Public Health Act of 1848 permitted rather than required the establishment of Local Health Boards, and the *Economist* opposed even this on the grounds that 'Suffering and evil are nature's admonitions; they cannot be got rid of'.[91] Some towns, like Sheffield, were worse in their housing and sanitation in the 'sixties and 'seventies than they had been in 1842, and the dreadful housing conditions of Leeds remained too in spite of the 'remarkable legislative achievement' of the Leeds Improvement Act of 1842 which gave the Corporation wide powers in this area.[92] Concepts of 'capital investment in social overheads' which urbanisation necessitated are familiar enough today but were unknown at the time for which their absence is so regretted.[93] Nor could governments have moved much quicker, even had they possessed the inclination to do so, for there was no administrative machinery in being to handle the whole range of social issues that were becoming matters of national concern. Apologists for the early nineteenth-century find cause for admiration that so much was done so quickly. And on the question of the uncontrolled growth of towns comes the timely comment that modern experience of planning new towns from scratch can produce only sympathy for those people confronted by the problems of nineteenth-century urbanisation when knowledge was that much less adequate than it is today.[94] The nineteenth-century town should not be judged according to ideal, and therefore false, criteria, the hypothetical alternative; it should be judged inside the context of contemporary knowledge and experience, and this should ensure for it a more understanding approach, which it is perfectly possible to reconcile with E. P. Thompson's view that conditions were produced by a combination of ignorance and avarice and become no better for being explained.[95]

But it is not necessary to adopt a totally defensive position where the new towns are concerned, for an accurate balance sheet will need to show entries on the credit as well as on the debit side, and the towns of the early nineteenth-century gave hope for the future as well as almost unmitigated gloom for the present. At first sight it is difficult to see why their inhabitants should have had any reason for supposing that things would ever get any better, since it was common doctrine that they would get worse. Malthus was telling them that population increases would consume any gains that might result from economic growth. Gaskell, another prophet of doom, came very near to predicting that increasing mechanisation would eventually create total unemployment, whilst the social critics of the 1840s saw catastrophe rather than adaptation as the outcome of the problems they were describing.[96] Yet there were others who saw life in the towns holding out new opportunities for the development of man, not least of these being Engels, who was scornful of country dwellers, 'comfortable in their silent vegetation' and looked to towns as a liberating influence which would free men to think and demand a position worthy of themselves.[97] In similar language R. Guest described how, from being only a few degrees above their cattle, men would become political citizens.[98] According to Engels, urban life would assist the development of powerful groups, developing social attitudes, becoming aware of their class position, and exploiting the distress and disorder of their lives to become conscious of their destiny. The *Edinburgh Review* had the same message in 1824, a message of hope or fear according to the viewpoint; only after men had been condensed into masses, collected into cities, and provided with the strength that concentration gives could they sense their own consequence and begin to act in a collective capacity. This was to be the foundation of future collective action through trade unionism and eventually through Labour politics.

'It is the cities', runs a splendid declaration of faith, in *Alton Locke*, 'where the light dawns first, where man meets man, and spirit quickens spirit, and intercourse breeds knowledge, and knowledge sympathy, and sympathy enthusiasm, combination, power irresistible.'[100] Even the countryman Cobbett sensed the romance, the power and the possibilities:

'They call it black Sheffield, and black enough it is; but from this one town and its environs go nine-tenths of the knives that are used in the whole world,' and the men who made the knives were amongst those who helped persuade him that 'there is no hope of any change for the better but from the working people'.[101] Whether that change would be sought in reaction against experienced evil or because large numbers of concentrated people made comparisons, envisaged possibilities for themselves, and developed rising expectations, is a matter of argument, but whatever its derivation the process of social and political emancipation would be assisted by the urban environment.[102] Towns would eventually develop a wide range of organisations with specialised interests in which aspiring men could participate, newspapers through which opinions could be explored, and municipal government which would provide opportunities for political action and involvement away from the traditionally restricting hand of the aristocracy.[103] Towns would also compel governments at a national level to extend the scope of their authority in order to tackle the problems that the urban centres posed, to impose social controls on those aspects of society which the towns demonstrated as defective. In a sense it is a somewhat circular argument to suggest that public concern became directed to social abuses previously accepted without question, for towns produced a need to solve problems which urbanisation itself partly caused and certainly intensified. This is like the argument that towns gave the working classes a base from which to organise and a need to organise. Towns were at once the cause of, the occasion, and the opportunity for action. On what the working classes themselves achieved in terms of their own cultural development the questions have as yet been posed rather than answered.[104]

4 *The New Machines*

'The struggle is not so much against machinery as against the power behind the machinery, the power of capital.'

— *The Town Labourer*, p. 28.

New machines, like new towns, were vital to the process of carrying forward industrialisation. New machines, like new towns, created social problems, but because industrialisation was an act of free enterprise the social aspects of its implementation were always subordinate to the economic aspects, whether in town-building or the mechanisation of industry. If towns provided the context of industrialised life, machines provided, or denied, the livelihood itself and so became the focal point of much of the debate on industrialisation. For both manufacturers and workmen they became symbols, to the one of progress, to the other, in many cases, of despair.

The Hammonds saw clearly that the issue was not about machinery as such but about the power that lay behind the machinery, the power of capital; this they believed to be universal, though it might be locally manifested in the displacement of some particular form of hand-labour by some particular form of new machinery. They believed that the social problems arising from industrialisation came about because this new power was not subordinated to the 'common will', and they believed that it would menace the freedom and happiness of men until some kind of social control were imposed upon it.[1]

This attitude is another illustration of the theme of the hypothetical alternative that runs through their work, the historian's lament, as a social critic, that affairs were organised as they were and his conviction that there was a better way that could have been adopted. In *The Skilled Labourer* is voiced the speculation that if only the introduction of machinery had occurred under workers' control, it would have been used to increase their leisure and their happiness.[2] Instead it bound them ever more tightly to the capitalist, whose concern was not a better life for his workers but a greater profit for himself. The missed opportunity is a favourite theme, illustrated again by Oastler's biographer, Cecil Driver, when he describes the 'social tragedy' which arose from 'the indisputable fact' that the paternalist role of the state was being abandoned at precisely the moment when it was most needed, 'when expanding technology most obviously menaced the welfare of those least able to protect themselves' and divided society into a minority of wealthy exploiters and a mass of exploited.[3] Once again the criteria of judgment are human and not economic. Increased productive power is not regretted, only the absence of the appropriate social philosophy and political machinery that might have ensured a better purpose for it to serve. 'By what social alchemy', asks E. P. Thompson, 'did inventions for saving labour become engines of immiseration?'[4] Other systems would have produced other results, and the alternative political or moral philosophy will always have its believers.

This is not to suggest that historians are simply obscuring the past by introducing a totally irrelevant ideological content into their work, for their disagreements are modern reflections of the very real contemporary debate that accompanied the technological revolution. And that contemporary debate at least is a proper field of enquiry. The Hammonds' support for a 'common will' was a repetition of the arguments of Oastler and Robert Owen and their rejection of individualism. Oastler lamented the passing of a way of life and condemned the greed which prompted employers to replace men by machines. He would doubtless have preferred to end the technological revolution and return to a pre-industrial society, but faced with the fact of industrialisation he asked that society should be responsible for those whom the new machines made redundant and that it should adopt only such machines as would ensure good wages to their operators.[5] William Cobbett, an even greater romantic, was concerned about the social effects of machinery and discriminated against that which took industry away from the home and converted his self-sufficient peasant producers into impoverished labourers. Mechanical invention, when carried beyond a certain point, was 'productive of great calamity', and such he believed to have been the case within the West Country woollen trade by 1825.[6]

Robert Owen, by contrast, accepted the Industrial Revolution and the technological changes involved and regretted only that under capitalist control they had brought exploitation and pauperism. They were vital to future welfare but needed to be placed under social rather than private control.[7] Similarly, John Doherty, the cotton spinners' leader, argued that if life were to be enriched by the new industry, machinery must be made subordinate to the interests of the men who used it, though how this was to be done was not an easy question to answer. Gaskell thought in terms of parliamentary regulation: he argued that the steam engine should be legislated for rather than the children who served it and suggested that temporary benefits might accrue from taxing new machinery; masters and men had a common interest in avoiding a 'life of servitude to an iron-master' and should therefore coalesce to keep it under control, though he admitted that 'to endeavour to arrest its progress would be madness'.[8] The notion of taxing new machinery was not an unusual one; the masters and men of Rossendale, for instance, requested a tax on steam-looms in 1822 to try to hinder their introduction, but this kind of legislative interference was anathema to prevailing economic orthodoxy.[9] So too was the alternative or complementary notion that the wages of those who were threatened by machinery might be guaranteed by law, a nonsense to those who argued that the whole purpose of technological innovation was to increase production and reduce its costs. And so the complaints and demands of those who advocated an alternative philosophy to laissez-faire economics might be listened to but would never prompt government action. Central control of mechanisation was simply not a possibility within the value system of those men with power; whether it was desirable is a matter of opinion.

In its absence the machine became a symbol, of evil and of good, of disaster and of progress, and a once neutral word now has connotations that make it as emotive as the word 'factory', with which it was and is still linked to suggest the horrors that industrialisation brought upon working people. 'Machines symbolised the encroachment of the factory system', and both were portents of evils.[10] The Industrial Revolution, 'with its wholesale adoption of power-driven machinery and the factory system', derived its horror from these twin blights.[11] Toynbee's workmen were 'fighting with machinery for a miserable existence', whilst the Hammonds' worsted and woollen weavers 'fought against this menace to their livelihood' in resisting the advent of power-looms.[12] Each invention, the workers said, seemed to bring their final enslavement a day nearer; appropriately, the labour-saving machine introduced to break up bales of cotton was called a 'devil', and steam-engines were 'those terrible machines for superseding the necessity of human labour'.[13] Machinery was the capitalists' 'slave that has supplanted the labour and ingenuity of man', 'the gigantic and untiring energies' which dehumanised the workers before casting them upon the industrial scrapheap, a master that never tired but drove its servants endlessly without respite or relaxation, dooming them to a life of total dependence on its generating power before dismissing them as no longer necessary to its increasingly sophisticated operative.[14] And before Mary Barton's father left to represent his fellow-workers at the Chartist Convention he was reminded that 'machines is th' ruin of poor folk', and 'them newfangled things (power-looms) mack a man's life like a lottery', and requested that he 'ask 'em to make th' masters break th' machines'.[15]

Amongst the manufacturers machinery was invested with a mystique, an almost magical quality which carried it beyond a mere tool of man and made it rather the salvation of mankind, the grand panacea for all social ills. In the argument of the *Leeds Mercury,* machinery would enable the rich to grow richer and the poor would grow richer with them, since both parties shared a common interest.[16] Or, in the equally rhapsodic language of the *Manchester Commercial Advertiser,* any invention for abridging human labour was infallibly followed by an increase in the wages of every description of artisan, a proposition which it would have found difficult to demonstrate but one which nonetheless represents the kind of faith that many shared in the good life that the mechanical revolution would make universally accessible.[17] When the young Coningsby travelled north, he declared that he had never seen anything he so admired as Manchester and its machines.

'"But after all", said Coningsby with animation, "it is the machinery without any interposition of manual power that overwhelms me. It haunts me in my dreams", continued Coningsby, "I see cities peopled with machines. Certainly Manchester is the most wonderful city of modern times".'[18]

And, not surprisingly, if machinery was capable of arousing such deep and varied emotions, those who in any way sought to impede its introduction would arouse similiar passions, and were in fact considered guilty of the greatest folly and infamy. The liberal orthodoxy which so strongly condemned the opponents of mechanisation in the eighteenth and nineteenth centuries has persisted into the twentieth century and been reinforced by the familiar Whig tradition of writing history in terms of successful causes and by the strange inability of some historians to understand the predicament of those who were threatened with redundancy. Understandably the governments of the day viewed machine-breaking as a simple law and order issue, but the historian has no excuse for such a limited vision. Workmen who were living through situations which the uninvolved could view in purely legalistic terms were not concerned to create a law and order problem for the government but to preserve a livelihood for themselves. Their actions were not 'blind vandalism', a 'blind display of hatred', or 'pointless', because they arose from a situation which men were experiencing and to which they were reacting; if the men who broke the power-looms in Lancashire in 1826 were poor, ignorant country weavers, they were nonetheless capable of understanding the undoubted causal connection between their plight and technological change, and they adopted their specific course of action as a result of this appreciation.[19] This kind of action has been almost universally condemned as unsophisticated, old-fashioned and primitive, and even where machine-breakers enlist sympathy for the plight they suffered they earn disapproval for the means they adopted to find a way out of that situation. Instead of breaking machines workmen should, it seems, have turned to trade union organisation and political representation, the approved and eventually the supposedly 'successful' way of tackling working-class grievances. They should, in other words, have anticipated the eventual outcome of nineteenth-century history and made their particular contributions to this outcome rather than attempting to stop its natural flow and employ techniques that would eventually be discredited. They should, in addition, have been prepared to take the highly philosophical, long-term view that short-term expedients were no substitute for long-term organisation that would allow future generations of working men to reap where they had sown, an act of collective altruism which defies credulity. It is a matter for argument how far the working classes have ultimately found salvation through politics and a political labour movement; it is a matter for observation that this was not an available option during the first half of the nineteenth century.

Equally general has been the condemnation of machine-breaking as an irrational tactic, doomed to inevitable failure, in view of the inevitable triumph of mechanisation, a force not to be resisted; and again hindsight has helped to produce this kind of verdict. Again the short-term goals must be considered alongside the long-term achievements, for unemployed and starving men cannot afford the luxury of long-term amibitions. In the short term the destruction of machinery might mean the preservation of a job; it could be a rational step in a particular situation. In the long run, in Keynes' phrase, the croppers and the handloom-weavers would all be dead anyway. And they could hardly be blamed for drawing the inference from free enterprise economics that their own immediate gain and profit were more to be sought after than the eventual realisation of some idealised role for working men as partners in an industrial democracy.

The problem of knowing what to think about machine-breaking is not then an easy one, though the very recognition of a problem represents a transformation in traditional attitudes. Marxist scholars have produced some of the most illuminating insights into machine-breaking, and none more important than the distinction first drawn by E. J. Hobsbawn between the anti-machine movement and 'collective bargaining by riot', a recognition of machine-breaking as a technique used by industrial workers to put pressure on their employers in the pre-trade union era.[20] Yet even these perceptive observations are not free from internal contradictions; machine-breakers appear alternately as primitive rebels and sophisticated upholders of working-class traditions, refugees from a pre-industrial society who insist on practising their outdated techniques when they should have been flexing their proletarian muscles, or forward-looking exponents of an alternative working-class morality to rival that of capitalism.[21] Whatever views might be expressed about machine-breaking as a form of behaviour, modern experience of automation has at least predisposed commentators to see the problems of technological change in terms of people and their problems, to balance social cost against economic profit. And this experience has undermined the former tendency to dismiss as fools and villains the earlier victims of technological redundancy who refused to collaborate in their own destruction. There is a readier sympathy available for the predicament of William Farren in *Shirley* whose head and heart were clearly pulling in opposite directions when he remarked, 'Invention may be all right, but I know it isn't right for poor folks to starve'.[22]

It was, of course, impossible for the Hammonds to be insensitive to such a dilemma, and they observed with some bitterness that men and women whose livelihood was being destroyed by some new invention could hardly be expected to enthuse over 'the public benefits of inventive genius'.[23] Yet, curiously, they refrained from passing judgment on the machine-breaking that occurred when threatened workers embarked on violent protest, despite their willingness to offer judgment on virtually every other topic that concerned them. Their approach was to describe machine-breaking when it occurred and to explain sympathetically the situation in which it arose. But they have neither praise nor condemnation for the methods employed; nor do they attempt to measure its achievements as a technique or dismiss it for its futility. Neither the legitimacy nor the efficacy of the method is evaluated, and though they invariably stress the context of popular support in which machine-breaking occurred they offer neither their own support nor their own disapproval of it. Perhaps it could be inferred from their work as a whole that violent working-class behaviour was something of an embarrassment to them. The rejection of any accusation that the working classes had revolutionaries in their midst, a readiness to accept that all conspiracies were the work of spies and provocateurs, and an obvious approval of trade unions and constitutional political organisation all suggest that the contribution of the machine-breakers was probably unwelcome to them. But they kept faith with the workers by observing an unwonted neutrality and silence on the subject.

The rights and wrongs of a situation are always a difficult matter; the facts of a situation sound easier to elucidate, though in practice it is usually attitudes that make history rather than history that makes attitudes. Yet attitudes do require to be validated or invalidated, and attitudes towards the new machines of the Industrial Revolution can be questioned by reference to the historical problems of what motivated the technological changes of the late eighteenth and nineteenth centuries, what inhibited these changes, and what were the consequences of the revolution they brought about.

The classic case of those who advocated more and more machinery put the inventions of the Industrial Revolution firmly in the context of other inventions through the ages, the wheel, the plough, the cart, by which man had triumphed over nature and improved his lot and 'progress' had been made.[24] In modern times progress would continue and bring with it prosperity through successful competition where mechanisation went ahead; where it failed to do so Britain would fall behind her rivals and the non-co-operating occupations would find themselves first depressed and then disbanded. The welfare of the people was dependent on technological advance to such an extent that Andrew Ure was able to persuade himself, in one of his moments of self-delusion, that 'the constant aim of scientific improvement is philanthropic'.[25] A harsher, but more realistic, judgment was that of

Beatrice Webb, who maintained that 'the accepted purpose of the pioneers of the new power-driven machine industry was the making of pecuniary profit', a purpose, she added, that they fulfilled 'beyond the dreams of avarice'.[26] Philanthropy is rarely offered as a prime motive of entrepreneurial enterprise, and a more common assumption has been that new machines were intended to control the working classes rather than to advance them. This has arisen from the ambiguity present at almost every stage of the argument for new machinery, which helped to ensure that machinery would be seen as much as a threat as a promise, for it featured alternately in the two roles as Engels so clearly recognised.[27] As often as it was being commended to workmen as a means of fostering their interests through increased production and prosperity, it was being held out as a threat of what they might have to suffer if they persisted in unacceptable behaviour of combinations and strikes. Whilst the *Manchester Commercial Advertiser* in 1812 was in one breath extolling the virtues of machinery for having raised cotton from nothing to the leading manufacture in the kingdom, it was in the next one listing the bad habits of the handloom-weaver, who took advantage of good times to demand higher wages so that he could do less work and devote more time and money to drink; from such dissipation and human folly the power-loom would save the employers, since it was capable of producing a given quantity of cloth of uniform quality at reduced prices and ensuring that raw materials would be honestly applied.[28] It would serve as a corrective to the handloom-weaver as well as a means to commercial expansion. The case was more fully developed by Ure: on the one hand he erupted in almost lyrical praise for the power-loom, which would enhance wages, eliminate muscular fatigue and be conducive to good health, protecting the workman's eyesight and his bodily frame, and preserving his mind for higher thoughts; on the other hand he ominously warned workmen how surely science would defeat every unjustifiable union which they might form; taking the example of the self-acting mule, he argued that this had been devised only 'under the high pressure of . . . despotic confederacies' and that larger mules would enable their owners to rid themselves of 'indifferent or restive spinners'.[29] Similarly, in 1839 the Constabulary Commissioners attempted to argue the case for having the manufacturers of Norwich protected by police by listing the virtues and advantages that well-defended machinery would bring to the town. They had earlier argued that the results of recent strikes in Norwich would be the introduction of the power-loom and that if the weavers suffered as a result it would be their own fault.[30]

In view of this kind of confused argument it is not surprising that the workmen did not know whether to believe those who threatened them with redundancy or those who tried to cajole them into a belief that it was for their own good that new machinery was being introduced. And where direct action was taken to resist new machinery, as in cloth-finishing in 1812, the action of the men only confirmed the desire of the employer to become less dependent on his workmen, made him more anxious to press on with mechanisation, and caused the men to complete their own vicious circle by promoting that very development which they were attempting to resist. Earl Fitzwilliam had in 1802 frankly urged the need to supersede the croppers by machinery so that 'their consequence would be lost, their Banks would waste, their combinations would fall to the ground, and we should hear no more of meetings of any sort of description'.[31] The Yorkshire Luddites destroyed shearing-frames in 1812, but with the invention of a cloth-cutting machine in 1820 the croppers, in the words of the Hammonds, 'Pass out of the pages of history'.[32] A similar mixture of motives helped to promote power-loom weaving, which would be performed by a more tractable labour force of women and children than that of the adult male weavers, and the self-acting mule, which freed employers from the control of the troublesome male-spinners. The irritant of strikes, according to Samuel Smiles, was responsible for the adoption 'of many of our most potent self-acting tools or machines'.[33]

In view of such evidence it would not be difficult to construct a theory of technological change in terms of employers' pursuit of anti-worker policies, yet a recent investigation of this kind of change has, whilst recognising the desire to limit the power of the skilled worker, concluded that that worker resistance to technological change was often enough of a deterrent to inhibit innovations and that retarded technology was frequently the price paid for good labour relations.[34] The power was not always, it seems, on the employers' side, though there were some vulnerable groups such as the weavers and the wool-combers who experienced decades of decline under the shadow of machinery which finally eliminated them.

The resistance of the workers to technological change is in fact one of the great themes of the Industrial Revolution and has been widely held responsible for many of the delays in its implementation. Certainly worker opposition is a factor that must be recognised, though it was based on the same mixture of rationalisation and honest belief that characterised employer attitudes in the opposite direction; the debate was never simple and paradoxes abound. The same machine that was advocated as a means of making work almost physical relaxation was seen by its enemies as the instigator of hours of unremitting toil. And if workers questioned the machine's ability to make hard work easy, they even more fundamentally questioned its ability to perform successfully many operations which hand-workers undertook. It is a persistent theme of the resistance to machinery that it was an inferior and inadequate substitute for the skilled labour that it was replacing. Resistance to gig-mills in cloth-finishing had long been dependent in part on the argument that mechanical rollers and wire combs would damage all but the coarsest cloth, which required the gentler human touch and the caresses of natural teazles to preserve it from harm. The Jenny-rioters of 1779 similarly argued when destroying machines of more than 24 spindles that the work was better done on small Jennies; whilst in stocking-knitting it was firmly believed that the 'function of the eye in co-ordinating movements of the body meant that human motive power could not be replaced'.[35] The survival of hand-weaving in finer cottons and silks when the coarser articles had all transferred to power-looms helped to confirm this view that the machine could not match hand-labour in the best work and that its use implied a fall in standards.[36]

But such an argument became increasingly a rationalisation to be expected in the struggle for survival. This was the central issue which dominated the argument. As Ure admitted, it was the aim of every improvement in machinery to supersede human labour or to diminish it by substituting the work of women and children for that of men or ordinary labourers for trained artisans.[37] This was menace enough to explain attitudes of hostility from men who believed that improvements in machinery would soon enable their employers to manage without them, for they had been told by as respectable an authority as the *Edinburgh Encyclopaedia* that all the workmen of England would be turned into the street if the manufacturers could employ steam engines in their place at a saving of 5%.[38] And if a further ingredient were necessary to confirm the hostility to machinery it was supplied by the association of the new machines with factory production. The Jenny rioters spared the domestically-operated machines and destroyed those which needed to be sited in factories; similarly part of the resentment of the Yorkshire Luddites arose from the fact that manufacturers were not only operating shearing-frames and gig-mills but also gathering them together in large numbers and housing them in factories, alongside other processes in cloth-production from which they had traditionally been kept separate.[39]

Yet it would not be accurate to claim that hostility towards new machinery was an inherent working-class characteristic uniformly displayed on all occasions or to suggest that the years 1750–1850 witnessed anything resembling a general confrontation between the innovators and their workmen. The Manchester manufacturers, it has been argued, saw themselves as heroic figures who fought to establish British industry in embattled towns against frightening and perpetual opposition.[40] In creating this myth about themselves, they created a myth about working-class attitudes. Against this myth it has been very plausibly argued that the workers were not concerned with technological progress in the abstract and that they resisted it only when it threatened their employment, their standard of living, or even such immeasurables as freedom and dignity which cannot be quantified and are therefore often dismissed. The mining industry and the printing trade have been cited as cases where technological change provoked no opposition at this time because it posed no threat, and the specific example of the hand-spinners of Nottingham and nearby Leicester contrasts clearly the difference between a threatened and a safe group.[41] When Joseph Brookhouse of Leicester attempted to adapt Arkwright's roller principle to worsted spinning in 1787 he provoked a serious riot in which the mayor of the town was killed and his machinery destroyed.[42] There was an established vested interest of domestic spinners who were threatened but who succeeded by this direct action in prolonging the putting-out system for a further 20 years. Nottingham by contrast welcomed the Lancashire spinning pioneers, Arkwright and Hargreaves, who had provoked the hostility of workmen in their own county, and they were encouraged to establish factory cotton spinning in the town without opposition, for it supplemented rather than threatened the established hosiery trade that existed there.[43] Furthermore, Nottingham was one of the towns that developed Brookhouse's process for spinning yarn, again because the yarn had previously had to be brought into the town from outside and there was no established interest that considered itself under threat. And this was the town that was to acquire such a notorious reputation for machine-breaking in 1811 under very different circumstances.

The war against machinery fought by the working classes during the Industrial Revolution was by no means so widespread as has sometimes been supposed and in the context of a century's history of technological change, 1750–1850, could even be described as a number of local contests at precise and limited moments in time. Mechanical spinning certainly provoked bitter localised opposition in Lancashire in the 1760s and 1770s, but not as has been seen in the North-East Midlands. The quick absorption of the displaced hand-spinners into weaving and the prosperity of the two trades until the end of the century helped the process of reconciliation, and there were no more Lancashire spinning riots after 1779. There was a further bout of disputes in spinning in the period 1820–45, when conflicts arose from the adoption of further new machinery, such as the self-acting mules, but these disputes were essentially concerned with negotiating the new conditions under which the machines were to be operated, wage-rates in particular, rather than with manifesting opposition to machines as such. It has also been suggested that many of the tensions of this period resulted from the changing employment patterns that new machinery involved, the break-up of the family as the traditional working unit being the principal factor: but these tensions found outlets in industrial and political action other than anti-machine movements.[44] Power-weaving too had its problems but had been practised for 40 years before there was anything resembling a widespread assault on power-looms in 1826, when distress was acute and there was a genuine threat of technological redundancy. Prior to that there had been only occasional gestures of protest against steam looms, as in the attack on Grimshaw's mill in Manchester in 1792; the events of 1812, so-called Lancashire Luddism, were almost certainly a reaction to the general distress of that period rather than a deliberate attempt to stop power-looms, which were a negligible factor in the workmen's plight.[45]

As an older industry wool had longer traditions and more conservative attitudes. The first attempt to introduce the jenny into the woollen trade, at Shepton Mallet in 1776, caused all the woollen workers to combine with the spinners in riots, which failed to keep out the innovation, whilst disturbances, including riots at Hunslet, Leeds, accompanied its introduction into Yorkshire from 1780.[46] Bradford weavers rioted and attacked Horsfall's mill in 1826, destroying the power-looms which the owner was attempting to introduce.[47] The woolcombers, for all their opposition to technological change, were as powerless as the weavers to resist its gradual take-over during the second quarter of the century. Perhaps the sternest fighters were the croppers. Gig mills had been outlawed in mid-Tudor times and successfully resisted until the end of the eighteenth century, when their introduction prompted riot by the West Country shearmen, soon to be followed by the West Riding croppers, who fought a bitter battle against gigs and frames in 1812, which merely added a few more years to their own survival as an occupational group.

In the Midlands textile trades, hosiery and lace, though experiencing much machine-breaking in pursuit of 'collective bargaining by riot', were relatively free from anti-machine demonstrations, though an incident is recorded in 1773 in which Leicester framework-knitters destroyed an exhibited stocking-frame which was reputed to be capable of making 12 pairs of stockings simultaneously.[48] The attitude of ribbon weavers to improved machinery, Dutch engine-looms capable of weaving several ribbons at once, and later steam-looms, seems not to have been one of outright opposition to improvements but to be concerned rather with supervising their introduction so that women were not able to supplant men in the trade nor power operators supplant hand workers.[49] Such a phased and controlled introduction, however selfishly inspired and at variance with the wishes of the innovators themselves, did represent a corporate effort to control the social consequences of technological change. That it was sufficiently successful to stop Coventry from being competitive with the rest of Europe and virtually to kill the local ribbon trade suggests some moral to be drawn about the compatibility of business and social ethics.

It would on the whole be more accurate to suggest that anti-machine attitudes arose and were longest sustained where mechanisation posed or seemed to pose a threat to established interest or when change coincided with a period of acute depression rather than to suggest that they were an inherent, in-born characteristic of workmen. It would also be more accurate to suggest that technological change represented an area where the workmen's organisations attempted to slow down and thereby alleviate the impact of change rather than wage outright war on new machinery.

And if it is necessary to qualify the traditional account of a monolithic working-class hostility, it is also necessary to identify elements beyond the working classes who were identified with anti-machine attitudes. When the Hammonds suggested that 1811–12 was 'an unfortunate time for the introduction of labour-saving machinery', in view of trade depression, unemployment and bad harvests, they were echoing the query raised, strangely enough, in the *Leeds Mercury*, which had questioned the propriety of introducing new machines in a period of unemployment.[50] If the *Mercury*, the champion of the Leeds manufacturers, was sufficiently sensitive to register this doubt, there can be little grounds for suspecting the frequently asserted claims that the Luddites operated against a background of considerable public sympathy and the survival into the nineteenth-century of older paternalist attitudes which had required protection for a man's skill and his labour against the encroachment of the machine.

But considerations of public morality were of less importance than considerations of private interest, and it was these which created over the issues of new machinery and factory production divisions of opinion amongst the employing classes and a substantial anti-machine element there too. Large jennies were not only too big for the home and allegedly unable to produce high quality yarn; they were also too costly for the small man to handle and were part of that general tendency of technological change to isolate from the innovators those of insufficient capital, insufficient daring or enthusiasm, who, for whatever reason, could or would not compete in the highly competitive world of mechanical mass-production. It need occasion no surprise that Arkwright was unpopular with his fellow manufacturers, however great his contribution to the cotton trade. Many manufacturers had reservations about machinery, because of its cost, its profitability, or perhaps because it undermined their concept of how society ought to operate, and they are to be found supporting the men in many of their campaigns to control it. In the woollen trade the workmen and independent clothiers joined forces to fight for their independence against the large clothiers and merchants in an effort to uphold the act of 1555 forbidding the congregating of machinery into one place and banning the use of gig-mills. William Cartwright, whose mill was attacked by Luddites in April 1812, had antagonised his fellow-employers by his enterprise as well as the local croppers, and his demise would have given satisfaction in more than one camp.[51] From Norwich there came reports that strikes and violence against certain employers had been instigated by their trade rivals because of the improved machinery that had threatened the business interests of those who were not involving themselves in the new methods.[52] Similarly, inside the hosiery trade the stockingers throughout the first half of the nineteenth century could always be sure of the support of many employers in their attempts to enforce traditional standards of production and to resist innovation. Luddism was hardly an internecine war amongst the employing classes, yet it would be folly to overlook this aspect of the anti-machinery case.[53]

And in addition to the commercial reasons why some employers found it appropriate to resist mechanisation, there were other reasons outside trade why men of property should have doubts about the desirability of replacing men by machines. One of these was the possible effect of this development on the poor rates, which featured as an argument in both eighteenth and nineteenth-century debates on the subject. As late as 1836 Gaskell was claiming that the effect of mechanisation had been to push up poor-rate expenditure to £8m. per annum.[54] The issue of machinery was then far from creating any clear class division between its advocates and its opponents, and was never less than a complex matter. Anyone doubting this might care to ponder the mixture of motives that prompted farmers to put out their threshing-machines to be broken by the Swing Rioters in South-Eastern England in 1830.[55]

The uniformity and persistence of worker-resistance to technological change were not so great as is often imagined, yet they have often been held to have been decisive in retarding mechanisation. Just as it was invariably the warning used against machine-breakers and other opponents that they would scare away capital investment and condemn themselves to industrial stagnation, so was it widely argued after the event, when the advice had been rejected, that these consequences had in fact materialised. Two of the foremost interpreters of this age, Halévy and Mantoux, have both accepted the view that the long-delayed establishment of the power-loom in cotton-weaving arose from the deterrent effect of the handloom-weavers' action when they declared their hostility by attacking Grimshaw's power-looms in Manchester in 1792 and confirmed it in the incidents of 1812.[56] Within the cotton area the rise and fall of individual towns have also been ascribed to the location of machine-breaking incidents. Ashton-under-Lyne and Stalybridge, for instance, are said to have owed their prosperity to the early destruction of power-looms at Stockport, Blackburn, and West Houghton, whilst Cooke Taylor in 1842 ascribed the absence of industries other than coal-mining from West Houghton to the fact that it had been the scene of Luddism in 1812. Similarly the decline of Norwich was ascribed in 1839 to the fact that manufacturers had been deterred from introducing steam-weaving by intimidation from the unions; the town's trade was allegedly being lost to Halifax, Leeds, and Bradford, where power-looms had gone ahead. It was, however, also admitted that combinations of masters had attempted to deter the innovators and that many manufacturers had shown a greater taste for politics than for pursuing the interests of their trade.[57] The most dramatic example of the disastrous consequences of machine-breaking to suggest itself to Andrew Ure was that concerning bobbin-net lace, which he described as the foster-child of Nottingham, Loughborough and the villages in between until it had been frightened away in 1816 by the attack on John Heathcoat's mill at Loughborough.[58] It then took flight to the remoter provinces of the South-West, 'away from lawless ruffians', emigrating to Tiverton, Barnstaple, Taunton and Chard. This account of the alleged effect of the 1816 attack was also told by Edward Baines, and later confirmed by William Felkin, a business associate of Heathcoat, who accused the Luddites of having robbed the area of many thousands of pounds in weekly wages by the loss of this great lace-innovator. Heathcoat's migration to Tiverton, apparently the classic example of how the prophecies were fulfilled, was later shown by the Hammonds to have been decided upon before the attack on his mill.[59] Nor were its consequences as disastrous as many supposed. In spite of Ure's comments, Loughborough continued to thrive and expand as a lace centre and Heathcoat's old premises were quickly taken over by a new manufacturer. Even Ure's own figures, an early and unsuccessful exercise in quantification, fail totally to substantiate his claim that the lace trade was lost to the East Midlands and was gained by the West Country. If anything, it became more concentrated there during the course of the nineteenth century.

It is well established that the croppers and shearmen successfully resisted gig-mills for 250 years, and it is in this kind of limited, local enterprise that a resistance movement had some hope of success, for these cloth-finishers were a tiny occupational group who were nonetheless in control of a vital operation in the cloth trade. As late as 1816 the shearmen of Wiltshire could claim a successful opposition to gigs and frames whilst the war lasted, though they admitted to losing ground afterwards, and a few years later their trade had gone.[60] The Coventry ribbon trade supplies a more unusual case of reversion to hand-weaving in some factories in 1861 after a successful strike to bring steam-powered production into line with hand work on list prices. Mechanisation was being prevented from showing its intended profit, but its successful resistance produced only a decline and disappearance of the industry, not a guaranteed future.[61] It could fairly be argued that this action proved counter-productive, and this was the lesson that some contemporaries sought to put across to the opponents of technological change. The greater the resistance, argued Gaskell, the greater would be the stimulus to change; the greater the turbulence of the workmen, the more the energy that would go into attempts to replace them. If the men had possessed wisdom, he continued, they would have seen that riot could serve no useful purpose and that they could not prevent the introduction of new hands or improvements in machinery.[62] Modern scholars would probably agree with E. J. Hobsbawm that machine-wrecking could not prevent the overall triumph of industrial capital but would look for individual cases where, in the short term at any rate, some influence could be exercised on the pace and timing of technological change.[63] They might too be less inclined to see this influence exercised entirely through the dramatic and overt tactics of machine-breaking and look instead to the less obvious but perhaps equally effective resistance of shop-floor organisation which made second-phase mechanisation a hazard to good labour relations.[64]

Naturally the Luddites and their fellow saboteurs have had all the publicity, and generations which were disposed to see their history as the deeds of human beings and the consequences that followed them inevitably looked to the machine-breakers for an explanation of why certain machines were slow to be adopted, why certain industries experienced technological obsolescence, or why Britain as a whole seemed to lose the impetus in the nineteenth century which had made her the pace-setter in the eighteenth. Today the inclination is to seek explanations elsewhere, not in terms of the futile and petty actions of mere human beings but in the economic factors which really determined the national fate, including its progress in technology.

In the case of the long-delayed steam loom, there were very basic technical problems to solve before the machine would work efficiently. Steam looms were far more difficult to make than they were to break; the early models which followed Cartwright's invention of 1784 were unreliable and a very dubious investment, and the engineers faced a long experimental period. The same is true for those who attempted to prepare suitably dressed yarn for the machine to use. The availability of plentiful cheap labour was also a disincentive to technological change. From the turn of the century the vast army of handloom-weavers was continuing to grow in spite of wages which were continuing to fall steadily towards starvation levels, and there can be little doubt that the steam-loom would have been perfected and introduced much earlier and much more widely but for the cheap alternative that existed. The challenge of the power-loom was met by the handweavers by the two-fold response of increasing output and lowering rates. In the decade 1819–29, as wages fell and the labour force at last began to decline, the handweavers managed to increase their output per loom by over 25% just by working harder, so remaining competitive and applying a brake to mechanisation.[65] It remained a matter for fine calculation until after 1815 whether the savings through the adoption of power-looms were sufficient to justify the expenses of setting up and maintaining the considerable establishment necessary for steam-weaving. And when the technical problems had been largely solved and the economic gamble minimised, there still remained the fact that steam looms were not necessarily suited to every kind of fabric. It has recently been argued, for instance, that Middleton, one of the scenes of Luddism in 1812, retained its handloom-weavers until the 1860s not so much because of the Luddites as because of the fact that the town specialised in silk and fine cottons; in the manufacture of muslins, nankins, and ginghams, all of them delicate fabrics, the power-loom was no substitute for the handloom, and so the two ran side-by-side until the 1860 Cobden Treaty made it impossible for local industry to compete with the cheaper imports from France.[66]

Amidst all these other factors that of machine-breaking seems to acquire a trivial status. It does not appear to have discouraged investment in power-looms or deterred their advance when conditions made them worthwhile, in the 1820s. By 1826, when they made their most determined stand, the machine-breakers were quite powerless to achieve the complete and simultaneous destruction which alone could have given them a major influence in determining weaving technology.

The example of the transition from handloom to power-weaving does in fact illustrate some of the main general principles that have been offered as an explanation of why British industry as a whole remained technologically backward in the first half of the nineteenth century in comparison with American industry.[67] Power-weaving was not alone in posing the problem of balancing the profit of labour-saving against the expense of power and machinery; spinning, too, offered labour-saving machinery which required higher capital costs per unit of output than the machinery to be replaced, and this inhibited, for instance, the employment of self-acting mules. The ability of the domestic industries to survive by increasing output at lower wages is also to be seen in nail and chain-making in the West Midlands and in tailoring and cabinet-making, whilst the domestic system in general offered advantages to the manufacturer in terms of low fixed capital costs and flexibility both of composition and volume of production which allowed it to resist the factory system under some circumstances and thereby inhibit the technological change that the factories helped to produce. Above all, mechanisation was a response to labour-shortage; it came in where labour was in short supply and remained absent where labour was plentiful. The vast numbers who flooded the weaving trade in the early decades of the nineteenth century were the biggest deterrent to power-loom weaving, the unlimited supply of framework-knitters in the East Midlands was an important reason why the hosiery trade was not power-based until the second half of the nineteenth century, and, in general, the generously supplied labour market that existed in Britain, for a variety of reasons, after 1815 denied industrialists the stimulus they required to press on with mechanisation. This, together with the failure of the market to expand sufficiently to force technological change, induced a certain apathy amongst employers and encouraged them to succumb too readily to worker-resistance, which, as a result, appeared more important in determining the ultimate outcome than it really was.

In 1812 the *Manchester Commercial Advertiser* had felt it a matter for speculation how far the extension of machinery might be ultimately beneficial or prejudicial to the interests of a community, a surprising want of conviction from such a source.[68] Criteria for such an assessment are so variable as to make judgment on an agreed basis quite impossible. The imaginary traveller of Cole and Postgate, returning to Britain in 1846, would have been 'astonished by the mechanical inventions but shocked at their results'.[69] The machine had, in the view of the Hammonds, come to dominate everything, subordinating the quality of civilisation to the system of production.[70] To recreate civilised living William Morris abolished factories and powered machinery and had his people collecting in 'bonded workshops to do hand-work', but this romantic response to industrialisation, though having its adherents at every stage of the development, has always been a minority strand.[71] To blame the machine and pardon the capitalist would be to confuse symptom with cause. E. P. Thompson stresses the weavers' sufferings before they were ever faced with the competition of machinery, and the Hammonds argued not against the technological revolution but against the power that directed it, a power which turned to the workers' disadvantage the alleviations that science made possible.[72] They illustrated this proposition by arguing that the more successfully science was applied to the hazards of coal-mining, the greater the new hazards to which the men could then be exposed.[73] They might also have cited Nassau Senior's comment that in industries where the amount of fixed capital in plant was proportionately high to the amount circulating in wages and material, longer hours would need to be worked so that expensive machinery did not stand idle.[74] Capitalists would use scientific discovery and invention for their own advantage, not for that of their workmen.

But political philosophies were less a matter of concern to the working classes than their immediate work prospects. Gaskell was hardly reassuring when he argued that trade would soon reach its maximum and that the fate of the handloom-weavers was the first sign of the great social crisis being precipitated by the substitution of machinery for human labour.[75] Sufferers were being identified in 1796 by Eden, who noted this reverse side of the coin in the Wiltshire village previously dependent on hand-spinning which paid the price of the prosperity enjoyed elsewhere through the introduction of powered-machines.[76] It was demonstrably so that some crafts declined and disappeared as others developed; as woolcombing machines improved, the wages of the hand-combers decreased, and in time the hand-combers were eliminated. It was a process of gain and loss, and nowhere was this more clearly demonstrated than in the case of the weavers, the 'large and deserving class of operatives' who became 'the largest case of technological unemployment' ever experienced in Britain, whose plight was so pitiful in the 1840s that commentators, and historians later, were prepared to speculate that their fate would have been better had the power-loom been invented in so perfect a state and in such favourable economic conditions that it could have superseded them in a sudden and complete takeover, eliminating all hopes of possible survival.[77] In making his calculation of the benefits of mechanisation, Gaskell estimated that against the good wages being enjoyed by machine-operators must be set the 'wretched penury' of an estimated one million people dependent on handloom-weaving, together with an equal number at least of other handworkers displaced by automatic machines.[78] His totals were not broken down and his estimates are highly questionable, but he was at least aware of the need to present the two sides of the balance sheet in measuring the consequences of technological change, a two-sided calculation that remains a necessary part of any more general exercise in assessing the consequences of industrialisation for those involved in it. Machines meant vast social upheavals, and their short- and long-term benefits were not achieved without heavy social cost.

5 *The Handworkers*

'For half a century after the introduction of steam power, domestic industry, as well as factory industry, was increasing, and the condition of the people engaged in it was growing worse.'

—*The Town Labourer, preface.*

It is a popular, misconceived caricature of the Industrial Revolution that at the same time as it rapidly converted a population of country folk into town-dwellers it was also turning a domestic labour force into factory workers. That this was not so has, of course, repeatedly been shown in all serious studies of the process of industrialisation, many of which have used the very survival of the hand trades to point contrasts between those who earned higher wages and enjoyed improved standards of living by going to work in factories and those who were left behind in the domestic trades to suffer degradation and declining standards.[1] There is, however, a danger in this kind of argument. If it is used in all its force to demonstrate the well-being of the factory worker, this can only be done by emphasising the fate of the domestic worker, and if it is agreed that industrial revolution involved domestic as well as factory workers the argument that publicises the delights of the factory worker cannot at the same time be employed to establish the claim that industrialisation was a good thing for the workers as a whole. This ignores the balancing exercise that needs to be done between the advantages achieved by mechanisation and the social cost of this achievement in terms of displacement and redundancy, between the benefits of industrialisation and the 'long agony of poverty, starvation, and degradation' experienced by large numbers of people who lived through this process of industrialisation, in some cases the victims of technological change, in some cases suffering because it never reached them and some of whose children and grandchildren were still there to shock the social investigators at the end of the nineteenth century.[2]

This is no new realisation; Gaskell's noting of the gains and losses of industrialisation has already been observed, and his point, although based on crude quantities, was a valid one, supported later by Kydd's testimony that 'the social and moral progress of the majority of English society is not by any means an undisputed question'.[3] It was not enough simply to follow the successes of those factory workers who were the standard bearers of industrial progress. There were still great numbers, as the Hammonds were to explain, who worked in their own home to a very late stage; and the issue which united them all, factory and domestic workers alike, was the struggle to maintain their standard of living against the growing power of capital.[4] Again, the Hammonds' quantities were somewhat crude, even non-existent at times, but they were anticipating what later historians were to make more explicit, the importance of the domestic workers in any overall view of the situation. They argued that far from disappearing, the domestic industries continued to grow for half a century after the introduction of steam power and they observed that this growth was accompanied by deteriorating conditions.[5] Few would quarrel with this view today. Rather would it be supplemented by observations that not only did the domestic industries continue to grow but they remained bigger employers of labour than the factories in the middle of the nineteenth century. Technological change and the factory system were by no means so all-embracing as was once commonly supposed; the factory operative was not the typical industrial worker in 1850, still heavily outnumbered by the millions of domestic outworkers who were surviving the technological revolution. The working class contained only a minority of archetypal members, the factory workers, and far more handworkers of various sorts who, in numerical terms, are far more demanding of attention. It is quite unacceptable to regard the outworkers as 'special groups' or 'a small section of the working population', unfortunate exceptions to the general pattern of prosperity, who can be relegated to a brief mention for the sake of completeness, but who cannot be allowed to detract from an otherwise impressive economic achievement.[6] The weavers were, after all, the largest single group of industrial workers in England in 1830 and sufficiently numerous to invalidate any generalisation that fails to take account of their progress.

What can now be seen very clearly is that industrialisation in its early and even in its middle stages involved a considerable expansion of the hand-trades, that the pressures which produced industrial expansion in the eighteenth century could for a long time be accommodated within the existing structure of many industries and that expansion did not necessarily imply structural change, even when some technological change was involved such as the introduction of the first spinning jennies. The need for greater production might be satisfied within existing trade structures, which simply expanded to take in great numbers of handloom-weavers, or framework-knitters, or nailmakers, 'the swollen armies of unskilled domestic outworkers', to produce the increased quantities in demand.[7] The nailers of the West Midlands, for instance, probably increased from around 10,000 to around 30,000 in the period 1770–1810, and they were domestic workers.[8] In cloth-making, which remained a good step behind cotton in its translation to factory production, weaving remained essentially home-based until the middle of the nineteenth century, though the spinning of both wool and worsted as a domestic industry was, according to the Hammonds, obsolete by 1830.[9] It was, however, the cotton handloom-weavers who experienced the most phenomenal growth, and decline, during the Industrial Revolution; in three generations, it has been said, economic change created and destroyed a new type of labour, that of the handloom-weaver, who constituted the very backbone of the Industrial Revolution.[10] After the jenny and the mule had guaranteed the supply of cotton yarn, the demand for weavers attracted enormous numbers from a variety of sources, the old fustian weavers, displaced spinners, agricultural labourers, Irish immigrants, the unplaced and displaced members of society, who could quickly make a good living from a trade requiring minimal skill.[11] It was the loom, not the factory, E. P. Thompson reminds us, that attracted the new cotton workers in their thousands, and ranks swelled to probably a quarter of a million by their peak in the mids–1820s.[12] In 1835 a Select Committee reported that they and their dependants numbered about 840,000, after farm labourers the largest single occupational group, and, like the labourers, an unskilled body, who mistakenly found their way into the Hammonds' *Skilled Labourer* a century later.[13] The apparently insatiable demand for weavers in the late eighteenth century encouraged their growth and permitted them to sample the prosperity which industrialisation could bring, but it was a short-lived prosperity, declining by the end of the century, though numbers in the trade continued to grow for two further decades. Similarly, industrialisation multiplied the stocking-knitters, giving them a brief prosperity in the late eighteenth century, and in the same way they continued to grow beyond the demands of trade and to their own detriment. Trades such as handloom-weaving and framework-knitting were crafts of little skill and therefore very vulnerable to flooding with unskilled labour from outside; they were also easily accessible to female and child labour, which made it difficult for fully employed men to earn a proper living. And the same ability of females to undercut male labour in hand-weaving made women a more attractive, because cheap and pliant, labour force for power-loom weaving with which the hand-weavers were to be supplanted, though handloom-weaving was already overstocked with labour before power-weaving became competitive. Through the first quarter of the nineteenth century industrial expansion was such that handloom-weavers could still find fair employment in good times to complement the output of the new steam looms and in bad times were willing to work so cheaply that they remained competitive, a willingness that doubtless prolonged their own agony.

The inability of the handloom-weavers to find alternative employment has sometimes been argued, and there were certainly practical difficulties in the way of going into factories since powered weaving tended to be concentrated in the South of the county, away from the main hand-weaving areas of the North-East, and was in any case a job that could be done by women. But it has alternatively been argued that the case of the weavers is not explicable on economic grounds, for their motivation and behaviour defied the operation of simple economic incentive.[14] In terms of the free operation of market forces, low pay and bad conditions should have driven the weavers into other employment, yet in spite of their squalor, their ill-health, and all the other disadvantages that they endured, they seem to have preferred these conditions to the discipline and regulation that factory life would bring. The man's status within the family production unit, the family employment, the independence and the self-imposed controls, all combined to produce a way of life that was thought preferable to that which a factory could give and to deflect the weaver from a choice that would be rational on economic grounds to one that was justifiable only on emotional and traditional ones. And this, according to the historian's inclination, might be dismissed as stubborn conservatism.

It was not, of course, unique to the weavers. The nailers of Worcestershire and the Black Country 'stuck by their trade' and continued to put their children to it when only the hope and never the reality of a decent living remained.[15] Andrew Ure believed that young women who were prepared to sacrifice their health and comfort in lace-embroidery at home were averse to the discipline and continuity of factory work, which implied a loss of caste or gentility, whilst the ribbon-weaving trade offered its humblest members the alternative aspiration of first-hand status, attainable in the traditional framework, as a more attractive yet economically less rational future than that of a factory weaver.[16] In hosiery only the blandishments of bobbin-net lace creamed off the more highly-skilled stockingers in South Nottinghamshire and North Leicestershire, but for the vast majority life as a domestic framework-knitter was predetermined both by the absence of any serious attempt to change the technology or organisation of the hosiery trade and by the absence of alternative employment in the principal centres of Nottingham and Leicester before the second half of the century.

And so for whatever reasons, economically intelligible ones or otherwise, reasons within and reasons beyond their personal control, hundreds of thousands of people remained within domestic hand trades whose interests would, arguably, have been better served had they been subjected to sharper, more decisive instruments of social change such as irresistibly efficient technology or wholesale introduction of factories. The relative morality of the 'prolonged agony' and its converse is a matter of mere academic concern and no relevance for the fate of those who did actually experience the fate of handloom-weavers or framework-knitters in the nineteenth century.

Under the impact of the demand for greater production the hand trades expanded, but as the demand continued to grow in such a way that it could only be met by structural changes within the industries and technological innovation the hand trades began to decline, at first in prosperity, eventually in numbers. The putting-out system involved a vast amount of time-wasting and other inefficiencies, and hand methods could not compete with the quicker, cheaper, and more efficient job that the increasingly sophisticated machines could accomplish. It is not necessary to investigate Ure's charge of the 'discontinuous industry of handicraft people' and other aspects of the case to see why it was thought better to locate industry centrally and to operate it by machines rather than to site it in people's homes and to apply traditional hand-power.[17] The handworkers would eventually have to go, at different speeds in different places, but they would all in time have to go. But the process of their going was a painful one, and the pain was so widespread because of the enormous build-up of the hand trades immediately prior to their collapse. Amongst the handloom-weavers it was the coarse weavers who went first and the fancy ones who were able to survive the longest, in some cases into the second half of the century, but the overall picture was one of decline from a quarter of a million in 1825 to less than one-tenth of that number by 1856. And whilst they declined they suffered and were subjected to repeated investigations. The Select Committee of 1835, appreciating that the increase of steam-weaving contributed to their plight, failed to explain their basic predicament which had preceded the widespread use of power-loom and chose to advance 'political' arguments about oppressive taxation, currency problems, and the export of yarn to rivals, as an explanation of the weavers' condition.[18] The Royal Commission Report of 1841 got nearer the heart of the dilemma by emphasising the relationship between supply and demand within the trade but made its own 'political' point in devoting 20 pages to a largely irrelevant section on 'releasing working men from the tyranny of combinations', which could hardly be said to have featured prominently in the weavers' story.[19] Under the very eyes of the investigators, the weavers were destroyed 'inexorably' or by 'slow strangulation' according to the view taken on the degree of deliberate exploitation that entered into their employment during their years of decline, for they were gradually eliminated by the simple device of starvation, kept in being to save manufacturers the expense and risk of mechanisation, served both these apparently contradictory functions simultaneously, or were simply the unfortunate victims of fateful circumstances which men failed both to control and to understand.[20]

The role of individuals in promoting this process of decline has indeed provided one of the more bitter aspects of the whole controversy in both contemporary and academic settings. E. P. Thompson, for instance, strongly implies that only a minority of selfish manufacturers frustrated the willingness of the humane majority to accept a fixed minimum wage for the handloom-weavers.[21] Similarly the hosiery workers had always distinguished between the good men and the bad ones, the 'respectable' and the 'unscrupulous' employers; the ones co-operated with the workmen to preserve list prices, the others undercut their rivals to the detriment of all, for it was, according to Gravener Henson, their leader, the 'want of good faith in a few' which 'destroyed the confidence of the rest'.[22] These men had their counterparts in the ribbon trade who took advantage in 1814 of the repeal of Elizabethan apprenticeship regulations to employ women in engine-looms and apprentices at half-pay, and who paid as little as possible at all times.[23] No doubt the unscrupulous, undercutting master was a feature of economic expansion, but the 'few bad masters and bad men' who had 'passed beyond the effective control of the majority' and were tending 'to bring the good majority down to their own level', could only have been a major influence on the situation if an industry's capacity for growth would otherwise have ensured high wages.[24] The sweated handworkers in weaving or knitting were going down with their trades, and not because of the malevolence of individual employers. Similarly, it is mistaken to suggest that power-looms and shearing-frames were introduced during the depression years of Napoleon's Continental System largely because wicked employers were deliberately seeking to depress the handloom-weavers and croppers beyond their present state.[25] The actions of the innovators make too much sense in the context of their flagging trades to require any explanation that depends on personal malice or social purpose of this kind, though the croppers had over the years given their employers little cause to love them. In the case of the woolcombers, who claimed 60,000 members in their various associations, the Bradford strike of 1825 does seem to have been a direct confrontation between employers and a rather superior group of skilled workmen which the former were determined to win. 20,000 were said to have been out of work for 22 weeks, after which their resistance was broken and they were coerced into unprotected outworker status by the destruction of their unions before suffering extinction at the end of the 1840s as improved combing machinery made them redundant.[26]

A noteworthy aspect of the incidence of decline amongst the handworkers is the differing patterns of town and country experience. The weavers of Coventry successsfully denied the country weavers the use of engine-looms and in consequence the country weavers remained the poor relations of those in the town. They worked on the single looms for low wages and without the protection of the 'list', which was much easier to administer in the town, and they were the most vulnerable to being laid off during recessions as it was undesirable to allow the fixed capital of the more highly mechanised town ever to remain idle.[27] In cotton-weaving too a 5%–10% differential has been noted between the town and country weavers right through to the end of the handloom period and a further 2/- – 3/- differential observed between those who worked their handlooms at home and those who worked them in factories.[28] Towns also offered the even greater advantage of opportunities to leave the trade altogether for alternative employment. On the debit side the urban domestic weavers were thought to be much worse housed, in their cellars and garrets, than their rural counterparts. In hosiery it was the towns such as Nottingham and Leicester where the most skilled and therefore best paid branches of the trades were concentrated, and the country villages which housed the unskilled branches, subjected to the worst exactions of the middlemen and again much less protected by list prices than the urban workers. This distribution might well have made some contribution to the law and order and other political patterns that emerged during the first half of the nineteenth century.[29] Whether it was a cause or consequence of urbanisation or, as in the case of population growth, both a cause and a consequence, is not easy to determine.

One very obvious result of the declining status of so many handworkers in the nineteenth century and of the many grievances that workpeople felt as a result of industrialisation was the growth of the myth of the 'golden age', the idealised society, described by Cobbett, amongst others, that was supposedly inhabited by contented domestic workers in the days before factories and industrial towns made their appearance. This myth is to be found in a very complete form in the writing of Gaskell, who ascribes to the domestic worker all the virtues of which man is capable and more besides, and who generalises and falsifies to the point of caricature.[30] Gaskell's domestic worker was a respectable member of society, a good husband and father, and a man of simple habits and few wants. He earned a sufficient wage by working when he needed to and spent his vacant hours in farming or in gardening. He was without question 'as a moral and social being infinitely superior to the manufacturer of a later date', and with all this excess of virtue he lived to a good age, on the strength of his healthful occupations, wholesome food, and clean living, for he never needed to join a trade union in his rural innocence. The development of the pure 'cash nexus' relationship between employer and workman which was a characteristic of the Industrial Revolution has led even historians to fond descriptions of the more complex social relationships between master and man, the alliance of mutual obligation that characterised pre-industrial society. By contrast many timely warnings have been given of the danger of romanticising this situation in a search for times which never were, and a scepticism bred of the experience of nineteenth century domestic trades is usually directed against any sentimental approach to this question. What must still, however, be said is that within the major hand trades that were disappearing or about to disappear in the early nineteenth century, there was a fairly consistent memory amongst workmen of a golden age which they had enjoyed during the later eighteenth century which was something more than nostalgic yearning. Most weavers encountered by the Handloom-weaving Commissioners recollected the 'good old times' 'when their labours were four-fold remunerated, compared with their present rates of earnings' and the Commissioners, who were by no stretch of the imagination romantics, recorded this as fair memory.[31]

Like most myths this one was rooted in reality, and if wages had never been as consistently high as some accounts suggest this was because the weaver settled for a moderately low standard of living which could be obtained by that 'rhythm of work and leisure' which sometimes kept him from his work on weekdays.[32] The spinner, newly established in his factory, regarded the decade 1780–90 as his golden age for he had enjoyed increased earnings then without the structural changes in his way of life which removed him from the home and placed him in a factory;[33] domestic spinning was remembered for this rather than for the tedious work, the long hours, and the employment of young children that it had involved. The stockinger, whose standards began to tumble shortly after the weaver's, at the start of the nineteenth century, could also look back to pre-war days when even plain cotton workers were earning 10–12/- per week, most skilled branches up to 30/-, and the stockinger had his pig or cow and grew his own vegetables.[34] The animals and the gardens feature prominently in all the memories, and the handworker remained at heart a countryman. This was Cobbett's reason for extolling the virtues of cottage industry, that it provided supplementary work for the rest of the family and kept the menfolk on the land. And it was to the land that the woolcombers of the towns would return at hay-time and harvest. Of course this industrial yet rural existence became idealised more and more as time passed. The Hammonds acknowledged that the weavers' golden age was neither so golden nor so long-lasting as they fondly imagined, and they conceded too that factory workers were guilty of painting an over-indulgent picture of the happiness they had enjoyed when working at home.[35] But it was the myth rather than the reality in which these men believed and it was that myth that made their existing condition the more intolerable.

The plight of the domestic workers in the nineteenth century remains one of the least controversial and contested aspects of the nineteenth century standard of living debate, if only, as suggested earlier, because the evils of domestic employment have enabled factory work to be presented in a more favourable light, with the result, as one historian put it, that compared with framework-knitters, for instance, factory hands and their children seem to have had a more tolerable existence than was really the case because it was in the old domestic industries where the worst conditions were encountered.[36] Ure had employed this technique of argument, describing the 'abject conditions of the so-called independent handicraft workers', enquiring into the lives of the stockingers, the weavers, the woolcombers, the lace workers and others who worked their 12–16 hours per day for bare subsistence, so that he could present the existence of the factory worker as one of comfort and affluence by comparison.[37] The technique has been perpetuated in those accounts which dwell on these and smaller groups, the nail-makers, glove-makers, button-makers, and straw-plaiters, whose womenfolk and children worked all day long in insanitary cottages for nominal payment which gave them less than they needed for survival, powerless to resist such payments and the other petty exactions of the middlemen who supplied them.[38]

It is, of course, more than a technique of argument. The factory commissioners in 1833 themselves made the same point that the weavers, knitters, lace-runners, and others in domestic manufacturing trades began work at an earlier age, worked longer hours, and for less wage than did the factory children, that the motives for state intervention on their behalf might be stronger than in the case of the factory children, but that regulation could not be considered because it could not be carried out without 'such an extent and expense of police and such a vexatious scrutiny of private dwellings and occupations as could not be borne'.[39] It was desirable but it was inexpedient. And so those trades that met the demands upon them by undercutting and exploitation of their labour forces rather than by technological change were allowed to develop into the sweated trades that remained, in many cases, until the end of the century.

Some happily were rescued or disappeared completely long before then, though not before their members had experienced the most acute distress for many decades. The framework-knitters, belonging to an industry that was structurally obsolete, technologically stagnant, and unable to produce a cheap pair of plain stockings, could advance many witnesses to support the Leicester man who testified in the 1840s that he was working 20 more hours than when he first began in 1799, for a much lower standard of living.[40] Felkin estimated that in the 40 years after Luddism the stockingers averaged no more than 6/- per week. They worked harder, for longer hours, apprenticing their children earlier, surviving on a diet described in 1845 as 'low and precarious', unable to shake off the occupational diseases of the respiratory and digestive organs, and experiencing a marked deterioration in all those aspects of life normally accepted as criteria of judgment.[41] It took powered machinery, factories, and alternative employment to rescue these men in the second half of the century. Their fellow workers in the ribbon trade did at least have the option of factory work open to them from the 1830s, but many declined to take it and the fate of the country weavers in particular was disastrous. Their wages in the 1830s fell to less than 5/- on average, and Richard Oastler estimated in 1834 that the single hand weaver was down to 2 – 3/9d and in a totally hopeless state.[42] Not surprisingly the country weavers were feeble in health and physique; living on a diet of bread, potatoes and a little tea, eked out by occasional scraps of bacon and some milk, they suffered great demoralisation until their trade was effectively killed off by the Cobden Treaty of 1860 and Coventry gave up the unequal struggle against French competition.[43]

After their defeat in the strike of 1826 the Yorkshire woolcombers sank into a pitiful state; in the words of one of them 'we are sunken debilitated, depressed, emasculated'.[44] The Spitalfields silk workers lost their protection in 1824 and here again, in the Hammonds' words, 'labour continued to find its own level of starvation'.[45] By 1812 West Midlands nail-makers were said to be working up to 18 hours per day, which contributed 'a degree of slavery to the mere business of earning a livelihood which is startling to think of', and after 1830 'truck, oppression, and misery of every kind throve in South Staffordshire'.[46] But of all the depressed hand trades none was so large and so clearly seen to be slipping into disaster as that of the handloom-weavers in the cotton industry. From about 1798 their wages began to fall and in the years 1805–33 fell from 23/- to 6/3d per week.[47] Recent suggestions that their years of decline were not a period of unrelieved gloom and that extreme poverty was periodic rather than permanent brighten the picture very little.[48] Clapham's view of their 'infinite misery', the contemporary accounts of sufferings 'scarcely to be credited or conceived', and E. P. Thompson's horrifying reconstruction of their experiences leave scope for disagreement only on the precise degree of their suffering.[49]

The response of the domestic workers to their growing plight was varied. There was certainly a tendency to idealise the past and an attempt made to move industry back to the patterns that seemed in retrospect so satisfactory. But ribbon weavers such as Gutteridge or stocking-knitters in their thousands whose aspiration was to become owners of their own looms or frames were finding themselves left behind by the capitalistic development of their trades.[50] The independent workman was a character from the past and if he attempted to survive as an individual machine-owner in the nineteenth century he found himself the first without work as employers in times of recession worked through their own machines in factories or on hire in vast numbers in their workers' houses. Over-production often seemed to be the explanation of trade depression to the numerous competing hands of the declining trades, and frequently they thought in terms of solving their problems by producing less. Gravener Henson, for instance, could advance many reasons for supposing that his framework-knitters would be better off, financially and in health and happiness, if they spent less time at the frame and diverted part of their labours to subsistence gardening.[51] This kind of aspiration, to satisfy so many cravings, reached its highest form of expression in the cottage factories of Coventry, to unite the factory and domestic systems, reacting against industry as a full-time occupation by planning a partial return to the land as a supplement to industrial earnings and an avoidance of the thorough commitment to factory life. In practice the cottage factories were able neither to compete with factories on the production side nor to build up the necessary food reserves that a total economy required to protect it against possible dearth.[52] A similar range of aspirations was met by the early co-operative movement, when it was still concerned with community-building and not yet with shop-keeping, which appealed powerfully to the handloom-weavers, in part perhaps because Robert Owen was attempting to reconcile the mechanisation of industry with domestic employment, in part perhaps because Owen promised a return to the rural existence, with family and community life determining the pattern to the exclusion of the income and status issues which were dominating the real world.[53] William Cobbett made a similar kind of appeal to them in seeking somehow to undo the whole process of industrialisation and return to the unspoilt countryside in which power had supposedly been accompanied by social obligation. Similarly the land scheme of Feargus O'Connor, the anti-industrialisation limb of the next stage of the Parliamentary Reform movement, Chartism, was to provide a rural Utopia of peasant proprietors where the ills of industrial society did not extend; it is not necessary to invent a term like 'dedifferentiation of roles' to understand why schemes of this kind had such a powerful appeal to the depressed and the displaced.[54]

If this was the escapist approach to problems, and therefore one unlikely to provide a general solution, a more practical approach was to seek to exercise some kind of control or regulation of developments as they occurred to prevent them from getting out of hand. If trades like handloom-weaving were becoming overcrowded the solution was obviously to attempt to stop unapprenticed workers entering the occupation; in the context of the late eighteenth and early nineteenth centuries with its climate of opinion on a free labour market such a solution was never within reach. If falling wages were the problem, the answer for many was to attempt to regulate wages. From 1799 the handloom-weavers attempted to secure legislation for a legal minimum wage, just as the ribbon weavers met in 1828 to ask the government to regulate their wages by law. The framework-knitters on this question were a step nearer reality than their comrades in their appraisal of the situation in 1812, when one of their leaders wrote his now classic statement that 'it is well known that governments will not interfere with the regulation of the quantum of wages which shall be paid for a certain quantum of labour' since the influence exercised on polite society by the writings of Dr Adam Smith.[55] In spite of this appreciation the framework-knitters persisted in the belief that many other aspects of their trade were susceptible to Parliamentary regulation and continued to have faith, ill-founded as it turned out, in Parliament's willingness to interfere in industry for their protection. Parliament in fact dismantled the one piece of protective machinery that existed when they withdrew in 1824 the wage regulation previously enjoyed by the Spitalfields silk-weavers.[56]

The alternative to Parliamentary regulation of wages was attempted control through trade union organisation, but this means too could be rebutted by reference to prevailing contemporary economic doctrine; the carpet-weavers of Kidderminster, for instance, who tried to preserve their list prices were told in 1828 that any agreement to fix wages was both a conspiracy against the consumer and the community as a whole and an infringement of an individual's right to sell his labour at whatever price he could command.[57] The ideal of strength through solidarity was on occasions realised, but with fatal consequences, as when the outdoor ribbon weavers persuaded the factory weavers to act in concert with them against employers who were reducing list prices by mechanised production; their success in the great strike of 1858 removed all incentive to further mechanisation and left Coventry highly vulnerable to the foreign competition that swept it aside within a few years.[58] The scattered handloom-weavers found combination very difficult, more because they possessed a commodity which was barely saleable than because of their dispersed employment. A massive strike in June 1808 brought a supposed rise of 20% which in fact lasted no more than a month, and other efforts in 1812, in Scotland, and 1816 and 1818 in England, brought no more joy.[59] On the whole the weavers were believed to be well-behaved workmen who rarely combined, in contrast to their unruly cousins, the spinners, who were always ready to express their discontent.[60] The contrast was, however, less a matter of their nature than of the relative importance of their roles in industry. It was barely possible for trade unions in this area, or in that of hosiery, to learn the techniques of striking on a rising market, since the market was never rising as far as they were concerned. The framework-knitters do seem to have detected this possibility in 1814 and 1824, virtually the only bright years in half a century of gloom, but for most of the time their trade unions were born of despair, the last resort of underemployed and unemployed men in the depths of depression, who vainly attempted to halt price slumps by some sort of collective action which might include striking or the even more direct form of collective bargaining by riot, Luddism, which belonged to the years 1811–16. The handloom-weavers too, to a very slight extent in 1812 and more actively in 1826, supplemented their efforts by machine-breaking, but these outbreaks were exceptional and apparently quite abortive in terms of their aims.

What now seems to some, with hindsight, the most sophisticated weapon of self-defence that these groups could all have used was that of political action. Many were not unfamiliar with political techniques as their constant attempts to petition Parliament for legislative protection indicate, but such behaviour was only a continuation of the age-old tradition of petitioning for the safeguarding of threatened rights rather than any modern awareness of the political power that working men might possess if they organised themselves for political action and attempted to gain control of the machinery of the state. It has been customary to regard the handloom-weavers as foremost participants in the political protest movements of the early part of the nineteenth century such as the Blanketeers' March, the Peterloo demonstration, and later Chartism, though it has never been clear how far the reform of Parliament was being sought so that power might be obtained to alleviate grievance and how far it was simply a grand panacea which would provide instant solutions along whatever lines appealed to particular groups, even if that implied a complete reversal of the Industrial Revolution and a return to pre-industrial society. A growing sense of political consciousness is something that the historians have been delighted to find amongst the weavers. The growth of a reform interest in 1816 was very satisfying to the Hammonds in revealing that 'the best minds' amongst the weavers were now prepared to follow the right course, and Cole and Postgate, another pair of good Whigs, described how the political reformers became aware of the hopelessness of resistance to machinery and saw the real enemy not in machinery but in the power that controlled it.[61] Whether the weavers as a whole shared this clarity of vision is another matter, and the Hammonds admitted that they were as a body non-political.[62] But if a detected inclination towards Parliamentary Reform gives pleasure in some circles, a supposed inclination towards physical violence gives pleasure elsewhere. The cool handling of the weavers in 1841 allegedly transformed them into 'confirmed physical force men', and it is standard interpretation of Chartism that the weavers were its most loyal supporters and those most attracted to desperate measures.[63] Yet many of these assumptions have probably been made on insufficient evidence and a recent enquiry has suggested that the weavers' enthusiasm for politics was lukewarm and short-lived, that the Chartist weavers were not obviously more loyal to the cause or more violent than men from other groups, and that the whole assumed connection between social depression and radical politics is worthy of closer scrutiny.[64] What is perhaps most interesting is a total rejection of the Whig tradition and the heretical suggestions that the resort to politics was a substitution of the improbable for the practical, a last resort and an act of despair, which reverses nicely the 'first things first' arguments of the nineteenth century parliamentary reformers and their supporters amongst the historians.[65]

However opinions might differ on what was the most sensible course open to the weavers, it is certainly not easy to reconcile the view that the weavers were on the one hand the political activists of working-class campaigning in the first half of the century and on the other that they were a well-behaved, quiescent group who bore their troubles with fortitude and resignation and showed 'patience unexampled'.[66] The framework-knitters, notorious for their industrial violence at particular times, showed few signs of political awareness until the years following the Great Reform Bill and persisted in regarding the industrial struggle as quite independent of any struggle for political power in which they might have been involved. Politics was even a proscribed subject in some organisations, and it was not until Chartism that industrial and political campaigning came together when the stockingers of Leicestershire and Nottingham supported this movement in great numbers in the hope that the Charter might perhaps bring their salvation when all else had failed. But for the domestic workers, some of whom might have been attracted to physical force Chartism, as for the working classes as a whole, political solutions had very much a minority appeal, at least until the end of the century, and when they sought to organise it was to trade unionism that they turned and not to politics.

From the middle of the century the problems of the principal groups of domestic workers were in one way or another solved. The Utopian solutions had all failed and the quest to produce a miraculous handloom that would compete effectively with the powerloom was seen to have been a vain one. The Handloom Weavers Commissioners of 1841 concluded that it was up to the weavers themselves to adjust supply according to the demand for labour and advocated activity and intelligence in the search for other employment.[67] Thus were the grievances of the weavers 'handled' and 'channelled'.[68] Their skills as weavers were modest and so the alternative occupation would have to be unskilled or would involve a learning of new skills. 'Mobility of labour', a concept beloved of economists and practised by middle-class professionals, becomes a working-class reality only in times of utmost extremity. Such times arrived between 1820 and 1850 when, according to Clapham, the weavers' resistance was broken and their children left the crowded cottages and cellars for the mills and other occupations.[69] A modern, rosier view is that by the mid-'Thirties the great bulk of the weavers had found 'more promising occupations', many in cotton factories and in the textile trades. The healthy young men among them might have become labourers or coal-miners; indeed, they had open to them the 'whole range of occupations appropriate to a rapidly developing industrial society', vistas apparently unlimited.[70]

Popular tradition is said to have recorded that many ribbon-weavers emigrated to the United States and to the Dominions; others probably moved to Lancashire from where they might have moved yet again in the Cotton Famine of the '60s.[71] Such mobility, like that of the emigrant Irish, was the product of only the harshest necessity. In political terms the disappearance of the hand-loom-weavers as a class, and the absorption of the stockingers in a factory industry, their own or new ones which were coming to the East Midlands towns, removed the main groups to whom political revolution might have seemed a not unjustifiable gamble and thereby contributed to the decades of political stability, even inertia, that followed the collapse of Chartism.[72] Apart from lowering the political temperature in this manner, the decline and disappearance of the domestic industries and the growing concentration of industries in factories had, it is argued, another implication for industrial peace, which is not altogether the obvious outcome of this development. Whereas it is frequently argued that organisation and solidarity were difficult to achieve among domestic workers in scattered, fragmented industries, and that conversely the factory system permits such consolidation to take place, it has also been argued that the factory gave to the indispensable and specialist workman, in the immediate presence of so many dependants, a growing sense of his own importance in relation to his fellow-workers. This it has been suggested helped to make the 'labour aristocracy' more self-conscious and more prominent as a sub-division of the working-class movement, which left it more vulnerable to the blandishments of employers and the traditional political parties, less ready to act in a united manner industrially, and disinclined to seek political independence.[73]

To claim that the problems of the major groups of domestic workers were solved from the middle of the century is not, of course, to say that the problems of all domestic workers were dealt with by this time. There were an estimated 30–50,000 workers in the nail trade in 1830, many of them women and children, who were required to produce 1,000 nails per day in the heat and smoke of a forge, whose homes were like pig-sties, and whose life was mean and savage; many of these survived into the 1880s in the Birmingham area as an anachronistic domestic trade on the fringes of the world's most sophisticated light-engineering centre. In 1843 London dressmakers and milliners were shown to be working 18–20 hours per day for several months of the year and in many cases for all-night sessions on top of their day-time ones, hours which were unequalled in any of the much-crticised manufacturing industries of the North. These workers in houses, garrets and small shops, of the tailoring and dressmaking trades, were to achieve notoriety as the sweated trades of London in the social investigations of the 1890s, when a further round of enquiries revealed that those of the first half of the century, whilst exposing many abuses concerning many large groups of workpeople, had left submerged minorities still to find their champions.[74]

A postscript to an examination of the nineteenth century problem of the handworkers, of whom the weavers were the most numerous and the most publicised, will almost inevitably pose the question of whether that problem need have been so great and whether the governments of the day might have done more to mitigate distress. Schemes for wage-regulation, the most commonly advocated alleviation, have been described as 'quite outlandish' for the time and, in the Hammonds' words 'contrary to the spirit of the nineteenth century', but, as E. P. Thompson argues, conditions do not become any more defensible for being the consequence of 'natural economic forces' at play.[75] The decision to allow the natural economic forces to play freely on this question, like decisions to proscribe trade unions, or prevent certain forms of political activity, was a political decision, taken by individuals and groups in their own interest and, arguably, contrary to the interests of others. After all, an alternative approach was available in the proposals before the 1835 Parliamentary Committee for a legal minimum wage to be administered by local Boards of Trade and for the regulation of machinery by taxation. To reject this alternative in favour of non-interference involved a conscious and deliberate political decision, however much that decision might have been seen as subscribing to natural economic laws and common-sense procedures. 'Handling and channelling', synonyms for doing nothing, were not a pre-ordained response. Whether the alternative response was workable and would have achieved anything must, of course, remain purely a matter for speculation. Some will continue to believe that the weavers might well have been spared their worst sufferings; others will believe that schemes for their salvation were administratively unworkable and took insufficient account of the market situation. Again the view might be that society did its best with the limited experience and machinery at its disposal; or alternatively that things would have been much better had another course been followed. They could hardly, in the view of some, have been much worse.

6 *The Factory Workers*

> 'Stunted, diseased, deformed, degraded, each with the tale of his wronged life, they pass across the stage, a living picture of man's cruelty to man, a pitiless indictment of those rulers who in their days of unabated power had abandoned the weak to the rapacity of the strong.'
>
> —*The Town Labourer*, p. 171.

If the large but, by the mid-nineteenth century, dwindling number of hand-workers is likely to be overlooked in a general assessment of the process of industrialisation, the same is hardly true of the small but fast growing number of factory workers. These people, especially those employed in the textile mills of Lancashire and Yorkshire, have always been the main focus of attention, and their factories the best known symbol of the new industrial society. Yet familiarity has not bred accord. Historians are no more in agreement on the subject of factories than were contemporaries, and if such a thing as historical truth is still being sought it will assuredly not be found in this area of study, where emotions run high and contending versions of the truth proliferate.

This is not the place to investigate in any detail that rural companion of the factory debate, the argument on the social consequences of the enclosure movement, yet the one lends both substance and tone to the other. It was the cataclysmic consequence of enclosure, according to the Hammonds, that it broke down the life and economy of the old village, dispossessing large numbers of small agriculturists, who were driven into the towns, becoming thereby the reluctant fodder of the all-consuming factory.[1] And the sense of grievance felt by the new work-force, according to Christopher Hill, was as much a result of the recently perpetrated land swindle as a consequence of their being forced into factories.[2] It is tempting in retrospect to rationalise the whole enclosure process as a deliberately calculated dispossession of the peasantry for the creation of a labour force without which industrialisation could not go ahead. After all, there were contemporary philosophers of the European enlightenment who were recommending precisely that course to their princely patrons. But whatever arguments persist about the degree of rural misery caused by enclosure, it is more likely to be seen now rather as a consequence of the need to feed an ever-growing population than as a deliberate fulfilment of one of the essential pre-conditions of industrialisation, the creation of a mobile labour force. And if the mobile labour force did appear it came not so much from the artificial conditions of dispossession as from a natural increase in population, for if greater numbers of people were needed to produce greater food supplies, the demand for rural labour was growing far less quickly than the population which supplied it.[3] Agrarian change, 'symbolised by enclosure', can no longer be viewed as 'the chief recruiting agent of the industrial proletarian army', and Engels' 'tale of the sturdy independent yeomen driven off their land' has become merely an illustration of how history used to be taught.[4] It is not then necessary to believe in the coercive role of enclosure in driving men into towns and factories; it is not even necessary to believe what Engels was prepared to concede and unlikely disciples happy to adopt, that is the attractive power of higher wages which brought the crowds flocking from the countryside into the factories, genuine though these higher wages were.[5] The real attraction, or the real coercion, was that the town and the factory offered employment and therefore survival, which the countryside did not, an incentive reinforced by the new Poor Law of 1834, which drove or encouraged paupers from the South East into the factories of the North as the alternative to the workhouse.

Yet in spite of the fact that the factory held out a life-line to the otherwise unemployed and prospects of higher wages to the unskilled from a great variety of trades, the financial inducements were insufficient to counteract the widespread antipathy of domestic workers in whose industries factory production was beginning to operate. The failure of many workers to follow the obvious route of highest economic advantage was indeed an irrational thing if we assume that men are motivated by financial considerations alone; but rarely is this so. In 1806 a House of Commons Committee reported that amongst the domestic woollen workers 'the apprehension entertained of factories was not only vicious in principle but practically erroneous'; factories would have the opposite results from those they feared and so their attitude was misguided.[6] Financial recompense was, however, evidently considered insufficient to still the emotions that were felt on the subject of factories; handloom-weavers, faced with the alternatives of factory work or starvation, might well choose starvation. The opposition, it has been argued, was in part the result of traditional thinking of two centuries standing that wage labourers were thought to have forfeited their birthright as freeborn Englishmen; the freeborn would not go voluntarily into factories and for a long time considered it a disgrace to surrender their children's birthright by allowing them to take such a step.[7] More practically they hated the factories from what has been described as the 'reluctance of an immemorial social order to accommodate an institution so alien in its assumptions about the way in which people should spend their lives'; the nature of the new institution condemned the worker to a fate reserved previously for the pauper.[8] The turning of many poorhouses into workhouses of enforced labour, and the apparent modelling of the new buildings on workhouses and prisons confirmed the association of the new factories with these institutions of unfree labour and assisted their reputation as 'centres of exploitation, monstrous prisons in which children were confined'.[9] In one view the factories were 'barrack-like buildings'; for the Hammonds it was the image of the pyramid that came to mind, a symbol of man's enslavement rather than his power.[10]

And so the domestic textile workers shunned the factories. The Jenny rioters of 1779 in Lancashire preserved the small jennies which could be operated in the homes and broke only those which would need to be housed in factories. The framework-knitters of Arnold near Nottingham helped to make life miserable for the philanthropic Davison and Hawksley in the 1790s who established a large spinning mill in the village which failed to prosper amidst labour troubles and popular discontent.[11] The West Riding woollen workers confirmed their longstanding opposition to the factory system before the 1806 House of Commons Committee of enquiry, and the ribbon weavers of Coventry attacked and burnt down the first steam loom factory erected in 1831.[12] The ribbon trade is a most instructive illustration. The popular prejudice against factories was so strong that the factory worker was regarded as the lowest form of life. The journeymen who worked for the first hands might find themselves forced into the factories in bad times, but once good times returned they would quit the factories and aspire again to becoming independent first hands themselves. And when it became clear that steam power must triumph and that their resentment of the factory system surpassed their ability to compete with it, they produced the ingenious compromise of the cottage factory, that curiosity which combined domestic work with steam power by the careful arrangement of cottage blocks to accommodate the necessary powered machinery. Cottage factories were still operating in Coventry's last days as a ribbon-weaving centre.[13]

The staffing of the early mills was then a difficult problem, and not simply because they were often built in remote country areas where there was water-power but an insufficient local population on which to draw. It is notorious that the early labour force was made up of migrants and casuals. It is not necessary to romanticise the Englishman's traditional self-respect to explain his absence and the presence instead of Irish and Welsh labourers, pauper-children, and women, who occupied the Lancashire and Derbyshire spinning mills in the late eighteenth century.[14] The Scots too, according to one contemporary, were accustomed to their personal freedom and comforts and so declined to enter the mill.[15] As a result their mills in Glasgow and Paisley were worked by Irish labour and by dispossessed cottars and the roving and dissolute elements from inside their own ranks, some of whom roved as far afield as Lancashire to the mills there.[16] The hostility of the domestic textile workers in particular towards factories meant that where the mills were drawing on a native population, it was agriculture, domestic service, and the unskilled elements of other trades, together with the parish paupers, that supplied the work force. The early factory workers were described as 'transient, marginal and deviant', an unreliable labour force of 'restless and migratory spirit', whose tendencies would have to be curbed and behaviour stabilised before they could properly serve their purpose.[17] Undoubtedly the higher wages eventually eroded this hostility and resistance in many cases, though the handloom-weavers held out to the bitter end and power-loom weaving was largely performed by women who could be had cheaply because of the competing presence of an army of depressed, hand-working men. The framework-knitters in hosiery were never required to take a personal decision on factories before the second half of the century, since their employers were content to retain the industry's domestic structure which continued to pose its own problems for men who had virtually no chance to leave their homes.

On the question of the timing of eventual working-class reconciliation to the factory system there is room for argument, but on the general and prolonged hostility there can be no doubt. This is reserved for the ever-flowering but rarely fruitful controversy concerning the judgment to be passed on factory conditions. Agreement is still far from being reached on whether the factories were the evils that their opponents alleged and how we should view the conditions that prevailed inside them. The most testing problems of methodology, moral judgment, hindsight, and partiality exacerbate the historian's predicament.

No aspect of factory conditions has aroused stronger emotions than the employment of small children. For the Hammonds the employment of masses of children was the foundation of modern industry and had become the most important feature of English life.[18] They were aware that child labour was nothing new, but would doubtless have agreed with a later view that in the years 1780–1840 there was a drastic increase in the intensity of the exploitation of child-labour, which became the *sine qua non* of industrial life.[19] The factory system, they wrote, began with serf labour, that of the pauper apprentices from the large towns, and the prosperity of English manufacturers was erected on a basis of 'helpless misery', during which time the rulers of the land abandoned the weak to the rapacity of the strong. The Hammonds delivered a massive indictment on early industrial society for its cruelty towards and exploitation of children, almost echoing in tone one of the first historians of the factory movement who alleged that 'Tens of thousands of the little children . . . have been destroyed because of the owners' lust for gold', a destruction arising from overwork and physical cruelty.[20] Overwork, illustrated once by philanthropic factory-owner John Fielden's assertion that a child would cover 20 miles in a normal day's work, was challenged by the protagonists on behalf of the factory system. Fielden's claim, cited by the Hammonds, has been treated with some scepticism, though very recently it has been suggested that boys in the throwing department of a silk mill were required to keep up almost continuous activity for 12 hours during which time they would run a distance of 20 miles.[21] By contrast, Andrew Ure believed work to be light, the factories as comfortable and easy as any occupation open to the working man, and the work such that the child remained inactive for nine hours out of the 12 which he nominally worked;[22] Cooke Taylor, another defender, suggested one hour in three, but both would have agreed with the overwhelming majority of employers who argued that the work was light, and rejected the views of reformers such as Oastler or Parson Bull that excessive physical fatigue resulted.[23] The reformers' views were represented by Sadler's Select Committee Report of 1832, which produced, according to one authority, 'a dreary picture';[24] certainly critics have worked hard to undermine the truthfulness of his acount and validity of his conclusions ever since. The Hammonds used the report as their prime source and others have confirmed its status as 'a classic social document', the charges of which have never been successfully refuted.[25] The subsequent reports of the Factory Commissioners are less open to the accusation of special pleading, have been suggested as a better guide to the situation as it really was, and put forward 'authoritative conclusions' that even the coolest sceptics have been willing to accept.[26] The commissioners found that children worked the same hours as adults, that a 12-hour working day had become the norm in Yorkshire and Lancashire, but that in the clothing districts a refusal to work overtime meant dismissal. They found occasions of 14-year-olds working from 6 am until 12 pm, of children made to work continuously for 16 hours, of some cheated of their meal hours, and others, working as pieceners for slubbers in woollen cloth factories, who troubled their employers by falling asleep at their work. They found only rare instances of children at work in factories at five years old; children of six were not uncommon.[27] Whether or not these findings suggested that children were wrongly treated must, of course, remain a matter of opinion according to what is thought to constitute right and wrong treatment. Speaking for the more sensitive, Tawney asked why the 'average decent Englishman' should feel it disgraceful to buy and sell human beings without at the same time finding the exploitation of child labour equally disgraceful.[28] But Tawney was a sensitive man.

An objective definition of cruelty is also beyond reach. After the horror stories of the 10 Hour movement and those related to Sadler's Committee the Factory Commissioners provided welcome relief for the harassed masters in a report that has enabled historians to say that by 1833 cruelty was not being systematically practised inside factories. Perhaps the children at the Catrine cotton mills had been 'very much beat at first before they could be taught their business', but gentler norms prevailed by 1833.[29] Even Gaskell, no friend to the factory system, rejected in 1836 the notion that cruelty was extensively practised, whilst Andrew Ure confidently asserted that factory owners set their faces against every species of oppression; far from being injured, ill-treated, or overworked, factory children resembled 'lively elves' at play.[30] In more recent times has followed further insistence that there was no systematic cruelty, that abuses were things of the past (which at least admits their one-time existence) and exaggerated, and, most reassuring of all, that 'the majority were not markedly ill-treated or permanently harmed'.[31] The historian's capacity for moral outrage normally encompasses the fate of minorities too. Again, the commissioners have provided grounds for this more favourable view. Their evidence from Leeds, Manchester, and the Western District showed them that within the past few years a great improvement had taken place in the treatment of children. Now they were able to report that the worst cases of cruelty occurred in the small and obscure mills, and that Scotland and the Eastern district of England were the worst areas, which they illustrated by citing cases of what appeared even to them as sadistic behaviour in Scotland, the North-East of England, and Lancashire, where they had found a greatly if recently improved situation.[32] Again, personal taste alone will determine how satisfactory this situation was.

Bad health should be more amenable to clear definition than cruel behaviour, but here too the picture is clouded. There were discrepancies in what the medical experts had to say about the health hazards of factory labour because medical science was at a primitive stage and no one was able to state with precision what the actual consequences of factory employment were for young children. As usual, the masters generally took the optimistic view and told Sir Robert Peel's Committee in 1816 that their children were in excellent health. According to Cooke Taylor the proprietor had an obvious and immediate interest in the health of his employees which ensured their well-being, though what was obvious to Cooke Taylor was not necessarily so to all manufacturers.[33] Again, Andrew Ure could offer assurance that accidents to children were rare and that factory children were not prone to disease.[34] Others were less confident and might have agreed with the Leeds surgeon, C. Turner Thackray, who argued, moderately enough, that the term of physical growth ought not to be a term of physical exertion;[35] good health, according to Kydd, was not consistent with constant confinement and excessive labour.[36] Modern authorities have appeared to take a more favourable view than this: perhaps the deformities of factory children were the consequences of their being tightly wrapped as babies rather than severely rapped as workers, or perhaps factory work merely exacerbated the problems of what were poor specimens anyway; scholars are as yet falling short of Southey's comment, deliberately ironic in his case, that to be sure many of the factory children would die of consumption as they grew up but consumption was, after all, the disease of the English.[37] It is still believed that the working mothers of very young children were a contribution to high infant mortality, but the factory is generally held less lethal than its opponents could once argue and the limited state of contemporary knowledge is emphasised.[38]

On this matter the factory commissioners, so frequently praised for their moderation and impartiality, expressed the view that the effects of factory labour on children were both immediate and remote; the immediate effects fatigue, sleepiness, and pain, the remote effects the deterioration of the physical constitution, deformity, and disease. From all the manufacturing towns they had received evidence that 'grievous and incurable maladies do result in young persons from labour commenced in the factory at the age at which it is at present not uncommon to begin it, and continued for the number of hours during which it is not unusual to protract it'. Their conclusions were that in a great number of cases these resulted in permanent deterioration of the physical constitution and the production of disease often irremediable. And because children suffered these injuries at an age when they were not free to choose otherwise, an argument which Professor Hutt says can be ignored because it is platitudinous, the commissioners believed that the case had been made for legislative interference.[39] Contemporary medical authorities were, not surprisingly, unable to fix a limit to the physical endurance of the child, a fact which strengthened the belief of the employers and some later historians that contemporary practice did not reach that limit. The commissioners, in their ignorance but with a fairness that has been much admired, believed current practice unacceptable.

In addition to the purely physical features of factories and their alleged effects on people who worked in them there was another area of influence where the factories are believed to have had damaging consequences, what could be termed the 'spiritual' and social sides of people's lives. Contemporary critics of the factory system were quick to develop the contrast between the domestically employed family, living and working together, with the benefits that this was believed to bestow on all members, and factory employment which removed the child from the pastoral and instructional role of the parents and the woman from the proper exercise of domestic duties; the results of the change, in terms of education and morality, were believed to be very serious. The disappearance of the family as the industrial unit and the disturbed patterns of family and community life which the factory system introduced have continued to seem important. Contemporary and later accounts of the pre-Industrial Revolution family at work at home have undoubtedly idealised and romanticised this old order, exaggerating its attractive and wholesome features and ignoring many of the evils involved, yet at least one modern scholar has found this aspect of the case against factories the one which contemporaries found the most difficult to rebuff; it has been argued with some force that the social and political impact of industrialisation should be seen essentially in terms of its impact on the family and the responses that this involved.[40] For industrial labour was now being removed from the familiar, meaningful context of family life into a strange, harsh context, where, in Cobbett's words, the masses of slaves were called together by a bell and kept at their work by a driver, and they had to learn the formalised impersonal rules of factory discipline.[41] On the question of the moral standards of the new factory population, the factory commissioners found the evidence conflicting but did not believe that factory people were any better or worse than working people outside factories, and the factory workers have received good character references from those who have stressed the sort of thing that provoked contemporary moral outrage, drink and tobacco, which the Evangelicals found so offensive, and Parson Bull's quirkish objection to ready-made clothes.[42] The proper remedy to this kind of problem, according to the commissioners, was a 'more general and careful education of young people', and it was one of their main complaints against factory employment that it denied children the means of obtaining adequate education.[43] This argument in fact begged the question of whether adequate education would have been obtained had factories not intervened and raises the wider problem of deciding just what proportion of blame can be apportioned to the factories for the evils that coincided in time with the beginnings of the factory system.

The lot of the factory children continues to promote debate and the particular side taken invariably corresponds with the overall judgment of the industrialisation process and its social consequences. In the contemporary debate the pessimists certainly made the memorable contributions, the operatives who attacked the right of avarice 'to grind to the dust the helpless child', Shelley who saw children turned into 'lifeless and bloodless machines', Southey who thought that if Dante had peopled one of his hells with children the factories would have supplied him with new images of torment, or Cobbett who simply found child labour unnatural.[44] But all these people were opponents of the whole Industrial Revolution as such and not just its social accompaniments, and were perhaps determined to exploit any cause to its maximum. There never was an age more fond of sickly sentiment, writes one scholar, by which he is presumably implying that the factory children were used to foster spurious emotions rather than being themselves a cause of deep, committed feeling.[45] It evidently requires an impossible imaginative leap to envisage that motives other than self-interest can determine human response.

Yet the whole debate on industrialisation did tend to focus on factories and the factories did provide ammunition for a battle that was much larger than the factory issue as such. They provided, according to R. M. Hartwell, a scapegoat for all the ills of industrial England.[46] What has in fact happened, however, with some historians, is that having examined the charges made against the factories and found them unsubstantiated, a matter of contemporary propaganda sustained only by continuing ideological commitment, they have then sought to make assurance doubly sure by listing a whole string of arguments showing that there were extenuating circumstances which explain or qualify those fictitious evils that supposedly came only from the pens of propagandists.

One common and acceptable proposition is that the evils associated with factories were rarely new; there were bad cases at the end of the eighteenth century, but bad conditions were not originated by the factory masters; child labour, for instance, had been praised by Defoe as a means by which families would find survival and was widely established inside and outside industry long before the Industrial Revolution, which did, however, concentrate, multiply, and publicise the phenomenon. If affairs were bad, a point not necessarily conceded, they were all the time getting better; the pauper apprentices were a passing phase, the small mills that had been the scene of early cruelties quickly disappeared, and hours were all the time getting shorter. If factory conditions were bad, those outside were equally bad, if not worse; : women and children worked long hours whether in factories or elsewhere, and the really grim conditions were to be found in the domestic industries; Peel and Bright both argued in 1844 that there were worse conditions outside the factory industries than inside them, but it is a moot point whether this made factories more tolerable to those who occupied them.[47] The Commissioners on the Employment of Children had already reported in 1843 on the children of the poorer classes who were not under the protection of the Factory Acts and found their condition such as to require the government's immediate attention.[48]

And if the workers had their problems, so too did the masters. The task of creating a disciplined labour force out of the unpromising material confronting the early employers was formidable, and Ure rated Arkwright's success in this sphere one of his prime achievements; this preoccupation with discipline, it has been argued, arose in part from a long history of dissatisfaction with worker-discipline under the putting-out system and in part from the already observed 'transient, marginal, and deviant character of many early adult labourers'.[49] Where the masters were slow to ameliorate conditions, this resulted from 'the apathy of ignorance' rather than 'cupidity' on their part.[50]

And if the workers and their children had a bad time, it was partly their own fault; they were themselves, as parents who sent their children into the factories, or over-lookers, responsible for most of the cruelty that was practised, especially the notorious slubber in the woollen mill after his famed bouts of drinking. Indeed the general standards of the times were low, which helps to explain why they were low in factories; it was a brutal age and so punishments of offending children were brutal, even according with the best educational theory of the day: some factory owners acquired very bad reputations, but investigations show that the cases were no worse than practiced elsewhere. If behaviour standards were low amongst the factory workers, they were low amongst workers generally, and if their domestic standards were low so too were those of the working class as a whole. In fact, a more leisured existence for the working classes would have served no purpose since they had no facilities for enjoying leisure outside the public houses; so runs one modern variation of the contemporary theme that factories kept children off the streets where they would have been idling their time away and acquiring vicious habits.[51] And if factories were as evil as some have suggested employees should have been more consistently concerned to reform them;[52] though a somewhat incompatible argument is also used that if employees were concerned to improve conditions they should not have supported legislative interference which was positively harmful to their interests.[53]

To attempt to summarise this welter of rationalisation and special pleading is virtually impossible, though a recent view suggests that it can be assumed that all the mitigating claims about healthy children, benevolent masters, and exaggerated accusations were little more than special pleading motivated by self-interest.[54] The conflicting verdicts roughly represent strongly held positions on each side. On the one hand is the view that for the majority the factory meant higher wages, better food, clothing, and an improved standard of living; with all its faults it was the direct route to all these ameliorations. On the other hand is the view that the man who entered the factory lost his independence, his freedom, and the right to variety, abandoning the right to choose when, how long, and how hard he worked; for all the ameliorations that higher wages might lead to, man paid a high price in terms of his sense of dignity and personal freedom.

In the context of this kind of debate the Hammonds stand up very well. Though clearly committed to the view that the factories were one of the most evil aspects of a civilisation which they found wanting in many important aspects, they were able to anticipate much of the case that would be argued against their viewpoint. They admitted that scarcely an evil associated with the factory system was entirely a new evil of its kind, they knew that life before the factories was far from paradise, and they knew that conditions were evil in industries not organised on a factory basis, this last a reason for questioning the value of the industrialisation experience rather than a cause for complacency on factories. The novelty and the horror for them was the systematisation and the discipline now involved as 'infant man soon became in the new industrial system what he never was in the old, the basis of a complicated economy'.[55] The Industrial Revolution did not create quarrels of class or wrongs and discontents; it introduced few new evils but gave the old ones a far greater range and importance.[56]

One aspect of the controversy that can be developed further is the respective roles of the worker and the employer in determining conditions, and these can be examined in the context of factory legislation. The reasons why Factory Acts were sought and introduced follow readily enough if the factories were as evil as their opponents alleged. According to the Hammonds the Industrial Revolution obliged all those whom it affected to think about the problems that it raised, and by 1830 no aspect of life, society, politics, or economics looked the same to the working classes as it did to their rulers. A gradual disillusionment was giving risc to 'a strong and rapidly increasing political feeling', a working-class protest was born which was a moral revolt against prevailing concepts of society and a new concept involving 'a better standard for a race of men and women' was evolved.[57] Central to this was the issue of demolishing the claim of the capitalist to the uncontrolled exercise of his power, and as part of this cause was advanced the need for interference in the regulation of factories. Owen had written years before the 1833 Factory Act that the diffusion of manufactures would produce lamentable and permanent evils without legislative interference; without regulation of hours, for instance, the well disposed employer could never compete with his evilly disposed rival who worked long hours, and by demanding a shorter day Doherty and his Short Time Committees were voicing an 'affirmation of human rights by the workers themselves'.[58] The Factory Acts were then part of the inevitable working-class response to the new situation of exploitation and part of an alternative working-class morality that was being presented.

This is a highly popular view of how the Industrial Revolution developed social and political attitudes, but it is at once rather too superficial and rather too romantic a view. Against it is argued the fact that moments of greatest exploitation often failed to produce resistance, whereas times of diminishing exploitation appeared to produce the most violent worker opposition.[59] And a further weakness of the case is the apparent absence of working-class protest on the question of factory conditions before the relatively late period of the early 1820s. For a long time it was the philanthropic mill-owners, such as Sir Robert Peel senior, and doctors who led the agitation against child-labour and not members of the working classes, who appear to have joined when other issues were at stake.[60] Whatever the extent of working-class commitment to a higher morality, there can be little doubt of working-class desire to promote factory reform as a means of increasing wages; nor need this be in any sense an accusation of sharp practice as was sometimes suggested by those who opposed regulation. In the words of the Pudsey Short Time Committee, in 1836, the object of reducing hours was to make 'human labour prizeable and valuable': it seemed not unreasonable to suppose that labour would acquire a scarcity value if its availability were curtailed and Richard Oastler confirmed that increasing wages was an object in shortening hours.[61] The pursuit of leisure was also a legitimate aim which workmen sought to foster, for the working classes had, according to Dr Hook, vicar of Leeds, the same right to recreation and enjoyment as other classes. 'Was man only made to labour?' asked the same Pudsey Committee; time should also be put aside and bodily and mental energy conserved for the improvement of the mind. Robert Baker, a factory inspector, made the same point in 1854, that it had been necessary to fix a reasonable limit to hours of labour so that workers might not only have physical protection but time for mental and social improvement too.[62] This was the ideal of innumerable working men's organisations from the London Corresponding Society onwards.

The sentiments seem laudable enough but there has been some cynical questioning of the relationship between these aims, however worthy in themselves, and the moral outrage over child labour that occupied most of the public debate on the need for factory legislation. The campaign on behalf of the children was, perhaps, a less than honest way of promoting a shorter working day for adults, through the link between the two kinds of labour, and the 1833 decision to give the children an eight rather than ten hour day was unpopular because its excessive humanity compelled shift systems to be introduced and prevented the adults from benefiting from the children's gain.[63] Working-class humanitarianism was therefore, it is said, a fraud. Certainly the initial contest over state regulation had the appearance of being fought not so much on the rights of the capitalist as over the conflicting rights of children and their fathers.[64] Robert Peel made the basic observation in 1816 that small children coerced into factory labour by whatever pressures were hardly free agents to play an economic system to their maximum advantage and that many parents were simply not fulfilling their parental duty.[65] The same ground had all to be covered again in 1833, when the right of the father to control his own children's hours of work was supported by those who resisted the proposed legislation of that year. Leonard Horner, another factory inspector, argued that the child's natural rights were as important as the father's; that the state must become the guardian of these if the father sought to rob the child, and that alleged interference was a mere sophism.[66] The child must be protected against parents described elsewhere as monsters who enjoyed 'idleness through the sweat of their children'.[67] The Factory Commissioners who expounded the case for state regulation of children's hours in 1833 were still able to speak at this date of 'the pernicious notion of the propriety and necessity of legislative interference to restrict the hours of adult labour'; but it was not simply that the father's absolute rights had collapsed in 1833; the capitalist's had also been severely undermined and would be again effectively challenged in the 10 Hour Act of 1847 and its later amendments.[68]

The timing of the Factory Reform Movement is a matter of some significance. One modern authority observes somewhat sceptically that the landed interests acquired their sense of responsibility towards the industrial workers only when the manufacturing interests adopted an aggressive attitude towards the Corn Laws; and early nineteenth century social reform has been interpreted as a series of Factory Acts foisted upon the Whig manufacturers by Tory landowners and Mines Acts foisted upon the Tory landowners by the Whigs in return.[69] Cooke Taylor was one of the early exponents of this kind of interpretation when he wrote in 1841 that an outcry had been raised against factories to counteract the growing cry for repeal of the Corn Laws[70] Tory paternalism, it has been conceded, was 'doubtless mixed by some less worthy motives', yet even E. P. Thompson agrees that paternalism can be passionate and involved and not necessarily condescending.[71] What he does question is whether Oastler and Bull were in any way typical of the Tories or whether the country gentry, with a few exceptions, were anything but oblivious to the abuses around them. Richard Oastler's own awakening of conscience is a significant indication of what were probably prevailing attitudes of ignorance. It is similarly questioned whether the Anglican parsons who featured strongly in the leadership of the Factory Movement in the West Riding were typical of the Church of England as a whole, about which Shaftesbury had some very scathing remarks to make.[72]

It would seem that the Factory Movement, like the Industrial Revolution of which it was part, is not open to monocausal explanations, though a recent ingenious examination of the parallel development of technological innovations and the movement for factory reform in Lancashire has concluded that the real impulse behind the movement was the impact upon the family of new production techniques and employment patterns. As long as the cotton spinner was employing and supervising his own children, the outcry over factory children was little more than a philanthropic concern for the pauper apprentices, but from the middle 1820s, when the spinner might require the services of nine young assistants, the kinship link was broken and factory discipline, imposed from outside the family, became intolerable as non-factory classes sent their children into the mill to supply this new need. Similarly, with the mass introduction of powerloom weaving at the same time and the movement of women, in many cases the wives of the handloom-weavers, into the mills, the pattern of working-class family life was again severely disturbed. Factory legislation has been seen as an attempt to preserve family links intact and to call a halt to the process of 'differentiation'; in fact the opposite effect was achieved. The 1833 Act broke the kinship link finally by providing different working days for adults and children, establishing the latter as workers outside the family group who were protected by the law rather than by their father and who must begin to look for education to the schooling that the law was requiring rather than to the instruction that family labour might incidentally provide.[73]

The motivation behind factory reform was complex, and so too was that which inspired the resistance to it. On the surface it might appear that this was a straight conflict between good and evil, though there could be disagreement about the casting for the two roles. Sir James Graham's claim in 1818 that the petitioners were no other than a set of idle, discontented, discarded, good-for-nothing workmen suggests that he saw the conflict in simple enough terms.[74] So too did the 1833 Factory Commissioners when they described the men who led the 10 Hour Movement as notorious troublemakers who had been involved in all species of industrial disorder.[75] Other men attempted to argue the case less in personal terms and more on grounds of political theory or practical politics. The theory had had a chilling ring when the masters attacked the 1833 Factory Act on traditional liberty grounds; by infringing the liberty of the parent the government was saddling the operative with an idle and unprofitable family until they reached the age of nine.[76] Another liberty was that of the workmen to choose his own conditions of employment, a plausible pretext for non-intervention, and traditional theories of the state's role were also brought out to remind people that the government's duty was to protect property and not to resurrect paternalistic functions – that were even more traditional.[77] Though there was certainly present this element of ideological hostility to state intervention, it was long ago argued that philosophical reservations were less important than practical ones, and recent writings on the attitudes of the classical economists and the meaning and importance of laissez-faire ideas have suggested a need to see both thinkers and administrators as more flexible and pragmatic in their attitudes than was once supposed.[78] For the Hammonds the only principle that seemed to apply was the one that established order is its own justification. In the name of enlightened self-interest employers were exercising the freedom to take what labour they could get on whatever terms they thought fit to impose, thus perverting the teachings of Adam Smith and applying them only partially, to their own advantage.[79]

But practice was probably more important than theory. As a solution to alleged problems the 10 Hour Movement had, in Cooke Taylor's words, 'no parallel in the annals of quackery'.[80] Francis Place argued that it was in practice impossible to prevent manufacturers from carrying on their business in a way in which they thought most advantageous, whilst Samuel Smiles suggested that the value of legislation in promoting human advance was always exaggerated since the social evils of the days were mostly the outgrowth of perverted lives; for the factory worker the solution evidently lay within himself and his capacity for improvement rather than with the legislature.[81] Gaskell thought it impractical to legislate in the form of Factory Acts, but evidently thought it practical to legislate instead against the steam engine, whilst Cardwell worried about 'the blind impulse of humanity' which would lead to even worse evils than those it was attempting to cure.[82]

The main practical opposition was undoubtedly on economic grounds, from the general fears that profits would fall if hours were shortened to the specific fear later that the 10 Hour Bill would ruin the cotton trade. The factory commissioners quoted with approval in their report of 1833 the views of a millowner, Mr Ashworth, that over the past thirty years the rates of profit had been greatly diminished and his workpeople seriously disturbed by the interference of mischievous agitators; at the same time promoters of time bills had threatened still further inroads on profits by proposing to limit working hours along with many vexatious penalties and restrictions.[83] A 10 Hour Bill, in the view of another owner, Robert Greg, would result in the emigration of owners along with their machinery and capital, and would be a virtual surrender to the enemy.[84] Most famous of all was the ingenious theory of Nassau Senior that profit was made only in the final hour of a 12 hour day and that a 10 Hour Bill would be utterly ruinous; masters were tired of regulations and wanted only tranquillity.[85] The 'most dire prophecies of doom' included Daniel O'Connell's prediction that a Ten Hour Act would make Manchester 'a place of tombs', as rivals took over the commercial lead which Britain would be voluntarily relinquishing.[86]

In predicting the economic consequences of factory regulation the reformers almost certainly were more successful than the masters. The 10 Hour Bill did not impoverish the poor and cover the land with wretchedness as Vernon Royle of Manchester had predicted; instead shorter hours and improved conditions, accompanied by greater efficiency, raised wages as the men had predicted that they would.[87] Once state regulation of hours and conditions had been established, according to one authority, the new system advanced on lines 'immeasurably superior to the old domestic system'; this verdict ascribes to factory regulation a key role, as do the Hammonds in adjudging it one of the three contributions, along with trade unionism and the civil service, made by England to what they call 'creating society out of chaos'.[88] However acceptable this is as a long-term verdict, it must be remembered that law enforcement did not automatically follow from law enactment in spite of inspection; it is notorious that some employers in association with some parents connived at the disregard of the legal minimum age for child employment and that the schooling clauses were in many cases little more than a pious hope. In a report on factory schools in 1838 it was asserted that of 500 mills in the West Riding there were not 12 where educational provision was systematically good.[89] The 10 Hour Act of 1847 proved just as vulnerable; some Lancashire owners found a loophole in the Act and by operating an adapted shift system were able to work a 15 hour day, which prompted the reconstitution of the short-time committees who were able to secure their position by a new Act in 1850. In view of this willingness to undermine legislation it would be unrealistic to suppose that change might anticipate rather than follow legislation; factory inspector, Leonard Horner, reported on the recklessness with which dangerous machinery was left exposed in some mills, whilst his colleague, T. J. Howell, said it was obvious that millowners would not take the precaution of fencing off dangerous machinery until compelled to do so by a stringent enactment.[90] And when the enactments came a whole range of petty producers continued to resist this growth of regulation and attempted to avoid the scrutiny of the state in what has been called its role of industrial policeman.[91]

It is somewhat difficult to reconcile this with what has been termed the 'Tory interpretation' of social reform, which suggests that reform occurred when a situation of 'intolerability' had been reached and was almost a matter of consensus politics. It was 'inherently probable' in the circumstances of the time, a matter of necessity, 'the necessity of the factory', which was recognised by increasingly humanitarian sentiments abroad in society.[92] This kind of reasoning, a hindsight that dictates that something which happened was required to happen, helps very little in an understanding of causation. Factory hours which were intolerable to men who worked them were not so to Nassau Senior who did not; he believed that the very light work involved made them both possible and necessary.[93] Nor did the long and bitter struggles of the factory inspectors to enforce safety regulations suggest that they were anything but an unwelcome imposition on those whom it was proving necessary to coerce by law. Factory legislation involved violent opposition at all stages; it came not through any 'general awakening of conscience' but through the efforts of minorities who were prepared to contend for it, minorities who certainly included the factory inspectors themselves who contributed the 'administrative impetus' to reform that is now so highly valued.[94]

Extending the devaluation of the reformers to the Factory Acts themselves are others, apologists for the factory system, who argue that to a large extent the problems caused by industry were solved by industry and that the Factory Acts were not necessary to the disappearance of the early evils of the system; even without legislation an increase in real wages would have led to a fall in hours and an elimination of child labour. As the factory masters became more experienced and efficient the abuses died away; the passage of time took care of most things and the surest route to business success was a regard for workers' welfare. The Factory Acts were even counter-productive and inhibited those very developments which they sought to promote.[95] 'Lawgivers', wrote Buckle, 'are nearly always the obstructors of society instead of its helpers', and the givers of factory laws according to some exemplified this point; they caused working-class misery by reducing family incomes and suffering to the children put out of work; they encouraged workers, through the shorter hours, to waste even more of their income than formerly; they encouraged the survival of the small and isolated mills where conditions were worst since here the Acts could be most easily evaded; and they caused a sacrifice of national productive power through reduced hours and the loss of skill acquired by children who had been trained early and then forbidden to practise.[96]

The hypothetical alternative, this time of an England without Factory Acts, becomes attractive only through a highly optimistic faith in the capacity of employers to reform themselves and their practices, a capacity not always born out by events. The faith is challenged too by a rival view that the years of the early 'Forties marked a deterioration rather than improvement in factory conditions. As a result of the pressure of severe commercial competition, when many industries were experiencing real difficulties, stories of abuses were again on the increase and complaints of bad ventilation, long hours, high temperatures, and particularly the speeding up of machinery were to be heard.[97] There seems little ground for supposing either that the employers as a whole were so benevolent as to be willing to reform without pressure from the legislature and the chivvying of inspectors or that they were so enlightened in their pursuit of self-interest that business success led them voluntarily to adopt policies that would lead to a happy and contented work-force. A reaction against earlier exaggerations has probably caused some historians, it has been argued, to minimise unduly the brutal conditions of early factory life and in this way to reduce the apparent importance of factory legislation.[98] If it were possible to have written the Factory Acts out of nineteenth century history, the story would have been very different for their exclusion.

7 *The Trade Unions*

'. . . some looked on Trade Unions as a menace to order, but others on them as encouraging a false ideal and a false view of society.'

—*The Town Labourer*, p. 213.

Trade Unions remain a live issue because they somehow contain within themselves most of the ingredients of the eternal debate on how to reconcile freedom and organisation and how to permit liberty to the individual and at the same time control the social consequences that his free action might involve. The historical role of British trade unionism has a similar ambivalence and ambiguity that excite a love-hate response from those most sympathetic with the aims that the movement is supposed to have had and a patronising blessing from those with least sympathy. The very name of trade unionism evokes an almighty shudder of emotion from such as the Hammonds, for whom the early nineteenth-century trade unions were 'schools of heroism', in which the workers of Great Britain took their first steps towards becoming workers of the world.[1] But the militancy and anti-establishment stance that their role required were eventually to come up against that most debilitating of attainments, success, which caused the unions to become, unforgivably, part of the very establishment they had endeavoured to undermine. As a successful cause, trade unionism automatically became entitled to the patronage with which successful causes are endowed within the Whig tradition. And as they gained new friends for deflecting the working classes from direct action, industrial sabotage and revolutionary conspiracy, towards more acceptable modes of conduct, so did the unions lose old friends for precisely the same reason, selling out to the establishment and robbing the working-class movement of its revolutionary potential.

The function of trade-unionism has an ambiguity that is difficult to resolve. The Hammonds' ideal working man was he who tried to raise the status of his entire class and not he who tried to raise only his own status. Such a man would find a natural home within the trade union movement rather than within the ranks of the *nouveax riches* whom their rejected ideal was always aspiring to join.[2] Trade-unionism embodied altruism and selflessness, the pursuit of a common good which might necessitate personal sacrifice. At the same time it seemed to many to embody the opposite of these, being concerned with the material enrichment of selfish sectional interests whose plans encompassed no grand design for human amelioration, only the intention of exploiting a situation to the maximum immediate selfish advantage. Thus, the first humanitarian impulse to regulate child labour, the Factory Act of 1819 which was concerned with apprentices, was not, it has been argued, the achievement of the organised operatives but of a small group of philanthropic employers.[3] And in the role of typical trade unionists are seen the cotton spinners, whom Ure believed to be united in closed, exclusive societies from which they deliberately and cruelly sought to exclude the desperate hand-loom weavers who were vainly attempting to break into factory employment.[4] These men, 'proud of the power of malefaction', terrorised their fellows into strikes, and were themselves, in Gaskell's view, 'rolling in comparative wealth' and prone to committing 'outrages of the most wanton kind'.[5] These men evidently did not belong to the Hammonds' 'school of heroism and public spirit', and these very authors found the cotton spinners advancing in 1818 the precocious economics of business enterprise that if liberal wages were paid to workmen, home consumption of manufactured goods would increase accordingly, and proportionate economic growth would take place.[6]

The early craft unions of the pre-industrial age had employed a recipe of mixed ingredients, provision and protection for their members achieved by self-preservation as exclusive societies which regulated entry by means of rigorous apprenticeship requirements, possessing an 'aristocratic' flavour which remained typical of trade-unionism throughout the nineteenth century. In origin, they were not, as the Webbs admit, the result of intolerable oppression, but might, like the London tailors, have used the fair prosperity of the first half of the eighteenth century to better their wages and shorten their hours.[7] Until the 1820s they were usually the organisations of single crafts in single towns, mainly below 500 in membership, and in addition to their industrial interests might well serve the same social functions as friendly societies.[8] But if the Industrial Revolution was not the beginning of trade-unionism it certainly sharpened the need for its existence;

it acquired, according to the Webbs, a general purpose of preserving wage-earners from the new policies of buying labour like raw materials in the cheapest market, and in many industries it was the resort of workers whose livelihood was now threatened by the influx of new men and new machines.[9] By 1825, a Select Committee was reporting the existence of combinations 'in more or less objectionable form' in almost every part of the country where large bodies of men were gathered together for manufacturing purposes;[10] they were still pursuing conventional trade society policies of seeking to regulate wages, control apprenticeship, and restrict employment to society members, but activities were now on a scale and of an intensity that betokened a new importance to trade-unionism. New features were also emerging such as the more ambitious scale of many organisations; Francis Place's London tailors were arranged in what has been called 'martial organisation'; Yorkshire textile workers were being mobilised in the 1820s through a network of committees headed by a General Council; wool-combers and cloth-finishers had a national, if impermanent, organisation; the framework-knitters of Nottingham had in 1812 mobilised all other hosiery centres throughout the British Isles for the few months of their campaign to secure legislation for their trade; there had been experiments in 'general unions' in Manchester and London in 1818; and the period even saw the first attempts at independent trade union organisation among women.[11]

In early industries such as textiles and coal-mining an incipient trade-unionism had sought to achieve collective gains by riot and wrecking, an unlikely means of altruistic expression, and was frequently successful. This memorably described tactic of 'collective bargaining by riot' has been suggested as the power-basis of pre-Industrial Revolution trade-unionism, found in the workshop, the mine, or the home.[12] In times of scattered industrial units and officially proscribed combination, it could be the effective means of quickly pressuring individual employers into granting wage increases or altering conditions of employment, safeguarding the workers' interests against unemployment, the competition of new machinery, or threats to their standard of living. Whilst it is clear that such violence in industrial relations served a real purpose in workmen's lives and was not simply an emanation of savagery or high spirits, too little is known of the organisation and behaviour of pre-Industrial Revolution workers to warrant any sweeping generalisations that the known incidents of collective violence were characteristic of a whole tradition rather than perhaps the sum total of events of this kind. They would eventually be replaced after 1825 by more peaceful collective bargaining, by most criteria a preferable approach, though trade union members continued to resort to violence to discipline defaulters in their ranks and to deter threatening outsiders in times of strikes long after this date.

More peaceful activity that involved many more people was membership of friendly societies which was believed to involve almost a million people in 1815 and continued to run well ahead of trade union membership through the nineteenth century. Some trade societies undoubtedly took advantage of the one benevolent law, that of 1793, and registered as friendly societies after the Combination Laws of 1799–1800 had denied them a legitimate overt existence, thus providing some grounds for the suspicions that friendly societies were somehow revolutionary and might provide a cover for subversive activities.[13] Besides being legal, friendly societies also provided the same kind of facility and service that many looked for in a trade society; they offered members an insurance against the vagaries of the economic system in which they lived as savings were put by weekly to cover the possibilities of sickness and the eventuality of old age and death.[14] Despite the fears of a few, they were attractive to a government conscious of mounting poor-rates in the 1790s and they shifted responsibility for social provision from the community to the individual, who was encouraged to develop qualities of thrift and independence, qualities admired by his social superiors, to ensure his survival in a harsh world.[15] By helping themselves, the friendly society members were undoubtedly helping their rulers, but there were disadvantages in this particular means of self-help. The funds of the friendly societies were too committed to specific purposes, quite apart from what was dissipated on conviviality, to be of the required general use; and, above all, the friendly societies were inadequate trade union substitutes in that they were powerless, indeed not intended, to control those matters of trade, such as wage-levels and apprenticeship, which were of such importance to workmen.[16] If friendly society funds that should have gone on sickness or death benefits were being spent on strikes, this merely established the inadequacy of the friendly society to serve its ulterior purpose; although the societies retained a massive hold over working-class affections throughout the nineteenth century it was as a supplement to and not as a substitute for trade unions.

Perhaps the most fascinating phase of early nineteenth-century trade union development was the period of the experiments in general union of 1831–4 when the sectional interests of particular groups of skilled workers were apparently superseded by a concern for promoting the interests of the workers as a whole from different occupational groups. This seeming manifestation of a new solidarity and working-class consciousness has encouraged romantic description as the most glorious period in British trade-unionism and 'without question the finest episode in building trade union history', in that after the 1832 Reform Act there developed a 'determination to smash the government of the employers', a syndicalist programme of attack in which the Builders' Union made the first assault upon the employers.[17] Personal views will, of course, help to determine response to the developments of these years, but there are some grounds for supposing that they were less significant than is sometimes supposed. For one, policies of general unionism were probably not so rationally arrived at, not so purposefully designed that they had sound prospects of success. Cole suggests that they were inspired in part by the various teachings of Owen, Thompson and Hodgkin, but largely by the grievances felt against new machinery, the factory system, and general distress. Like the Charter, the General Union was to be 'an instrument of sudden and complete emancipation', but, as with Chartism, the links between the grievances and their removal were not clearly perceived.[18] The first attempts at general union in Manchester and London in 1818 were 'still-born'.[19] After the failure of the spinners' strike in 1829, John Doherty attempted to organise a general strike fund by means of a National Association for the Protection of Labour, but its lack of money made it little more than a name, and that name very misleading in view of its concentration of strength in the Lancashire area and its confinement to the textile trades.[20] Similarly, with the better known Grand National of 1834, its name was 'a propagandist device rather than an accurate description, it was based essentially on the crafts of London, and the main body of skilled trades remained aloof from it; the alleged membership of an 'incredible half a million' was incredible because untrue in that 16,000 subscribers was the real situation, and the presence of Robert Owen at its head supplied it with neither strength nor purpose.[21] He was interested in neither trade-unionism nor any other movement of working-class revolt but searched endlessly for an audience to whom his schemes for moral regeneration and social restructuring might be preached, an audience which, in this case, had little practical interest in the ideology of his message.[22]

Instead of the general unions being seen as the attempted fulfilment of some ideological commitment, they should be viewed rather as attempts made by the old sectional interests to pursue fairly traditional ends by this new means of general union. Trade groups were realising in the 1820s that their bargaining positions might be strengthened if they built up national unions as the Carpenters, Bricklayers, and Spinners attempted to do, and as the Operative Builders did by their Union of 1831. They might also strengthen their position by securing help from outside the trade, by appealing to groups from other industries, but the aims remained sectional and practical and were not inspired by some high-flown social philosohy. Individual unions had individual interests, usually wages or matters relating to labour supply; it was to pursue their sectional interests that they went on strike and it was on the failure of the sectional strikes that the general unions collapsed, leaving behind the local groups to pursue their specific aims by other, more traditional means.[23]

Yet the notion had been voiced that there was a working-class interest which could be expressed and achieved in a national trade union organisation and a working-class power that could be mobilised through general strike. This was a significant realisation because it offered an alternative route to political power for those who were aware of its possibilities. There had always been a tendency amongst spies and even those who employed them to confuse trade-unionism with political radicalism and machine-breakers with revolutionaries, and the new militancy which overtook trade-unionism in 1830 was bound to bring this confusion nearer to being a reality.[24] Doherty's declared wish to raise the working classes from a state of moral degradation caused the Hammonds to detect a 'strong and rapidly increasing political feeling' at this time and 'large and ambitious ideas in the air on the subject of the organisation of the working-class movement'.[25] The promise, or threat, according to viewpoint, was not, however, to materialise just yet, and if trade-unionism was acquiring a new potency at this time it was not through its political threat but through more aggressive claims, realisable in an industrial context, to restore to the labourer the products of his labour. Whether this constituted in practice a transition from 'amelioration to revolutionary' designs is very doubtful, since it was the rise of the efficiently organised skilled worker unions of the post-Owen period that effectively took trade unions out of the political sphere for another 30 years and secured for their own labourers at least a greater share of the products of their labour.[26]

According to Clapham there were in the early 1840s fewer than

100,000 paid-up trade unionists in the whole of the country, which gives some idea of the collapse that followed the 1834 break up of the general unions.[27] The fall used to appear very severe because of the apparent heights achieved in 1834, but now that these seem less than formerly, historians have been ready to pick up the trade union pieces and find greater comfort in these post-Owen years. It has been argued, for instance, that the trade union activity of 1835–6, the Glasgow strikes of 1837, and the English strikes of 1842 are all indicative of a far from moribund body, and that there are many signs of trade union growth to be detected in these years, amongst the printers and the miners, for instance. Also, many of the traditionally organised crafts remained after the 1834 débâcle and others quickly came back to life.[28] The pattern of growth in this period is one that urges cautious comment rather than sweeping generalisation. Emphasis should again be placed on the small local unions that remained a basic feature of nineteenth-century trade unions, the small trade societies which best survived the traumatic experiences of the early 'Thirties, and their steady growth 'town by town, craft by craft'. In the cotton trade, for instance, developments were intermittent rather than dramatic, localised rather than centralised, and central organisation came into being only for such *ad hoc* purposes as the promotion of a Ten Hour Act in 1847.[29] Another element of continuity from the 1820s was the build-up of wider district organisation, exemplified in the strong county units amongst miners in Northumberland, Durham, Lancashire, and Yorkshire, which made a short-lived national federation possible in the 1840s.[30]

National federations and associations had also been presaged in the 1820s, and it is the continuation of this trend, exemplified by the establishment of the Amalgamated Society of Engineers in 1851 with almost 12,000 members, which has usually been seen as the most significant development of the new period. This was a 'model' union of skilled artisans, central administration, high membership fees, and generous benefits in return for those qualifying for membership.[31] Perhaps the A.S.E. was the most successful fulfilment of old trends rather than anything essentially new. Other groups such as the iron-founders and building trades established organisations on a similar pattern, but it did not create a model for many other major groups such as coal-miners, cotton-workers, and cabinet-makers who made no attempt to follow the lead.[32] The real novelty, it has been suggested, lay in the stability and success of the new organisations;[33] it lay also in the new attitudes that were emerging inside trade-unionism towards employers and to the whole process of industrialisation. The relative absence of industrial and political protest in the middle decades of the nineteenth century, in part an indication of rising living standards enjoyed by the working classes, is reflected in the mood of reconciliation which seems to characterise these years. Just as the Lancashire mule-spinners came to accept the minders of self-actors in 1842 and barriers between groups of engineers were breaking down in the 1840s, so were the New Model Unions concerning themselves with 'peace and respectability', 'defence not defiance' and substituting 'industrial diplomacy for the ruder methods of class war'.[34] Industrialisation was becoming accepted, and within industry the unions sought 'to control the job, not production'.[35] The argument had narrowed down to one of how the unions could get the best possible deal for their members within an industrial system which they now agreed to accept. The argument was once again about wages, hours, and the restriction of labour supply, but for the purposes of driving a hard bargain, not of overthrowing the system. The unions of so-called 'labour aristocrats', for none but labour-aristocrats were organised in unions before the 1870s, have been heavily criticised for their sectional selfishness and spirit of exclusiveness. In agreeing to work the system with their employers, it has been suggested, they were almost converts to their economics, yet whatever view is taken of their narrow outlook it is hardly possible to argue a theoretical compatibility between the employers' wish to secure their labour as cheaply as possible and the determination of the trade unions to make them pay as dearly as they were able.[36]

The aspirations of trade unions were not, of course, without their opponents, and the Hammonds were able to show how the leaders of society were ready to select from contemporary writings on the new science of political economy whatever quotations and arguments fitted the case they wished to make. Adam Smith, who did not support a legal ban on trade unions, supplied the argument that trade, industry and barter would always find their own level and the doctrine of enlightened self-interest which determined that from pure selfishness, if for no other reason, the employer would ensure that his workforce was contented. Ricardo contributed the ideas that the cost of labour would be determined by the strength of competition, and McCulloch the notion that the market rate of wages is exclusively dependent on the proportion that capital bears to the number of labourers.[37]

Wages were dependent on the laws of supply and demand; when trade unions attempted to improve wages they interfered with 'natural' laws and were therefore harmful. They were even of wicked intent if the wage fund theory were accepted, for this meant that one group of workers could benefit only at the expense of another when the total sum available for wages was constant.[38] The influence of the economists was decisive; such convenient philosophers must be treated with respect, for they all seemed to suggest that trade unions had no legitimate role to play in the determining of wages. They had similarly unfriendly things to say about the Corn Laws too, but it was a selective use of their material that society's leaders chose to make. It has been pointed out that already by 1795 Pitt could state the general inexpediency of legislative interference on the question of wages without needing to present an argument.[39]

Where arguments were put forward they were often couched in the language of the political economists, in terms of the freedom and liberty of the two parties involved in wage agreements. On the employers' side, for instance, the 1839 Constabulary Commissioners were informed that strikes by trade unions robbed the employer of his free choice of workmen, and one particular employer proudly reported his own determination to ignore the union and insist on private bargains with individual workmen. Another translated this into practical terms by reporting: 'My business is now proceeding quietly on my own terms.' There was also a concern, real or pretended, for the liberty and freedom of the workman who was threatened by trade unions with the loss of his liberty to dispose of his own labour in his own way. A man's labour, said Lord Cockburn, was his principal property and to deny him the liberty to dispose of it would be to make him a beggar; it is not without irony that trade-unionism should be singled out as the cause of beggary and not without exaggeration that it should be described as a tyranny so disgraceful and intolerable that there was no despotism like it.[40] Gravener Henson attempted to suggest that it was not only the trade union that was potentially tyrannous when he defined laissez-faire as 'let us alone' but asked if the employers were prepared to let their workmen alone.[41] The legislation of 1825, following the trial period of Combination Law repeal, continued to allow trade unions to exist but denied them any power to bring the reluctant defaulters into line, thus embodying the principle of individual independence. This had been implicit in the campaign waged earlier by Francis Place for the repeal of the Combination Laws and explicit in some of the notes he made for his own and Joseph Hume's guidance, when he argued the need to leave workmen and their employers as much as possible at liberty to make their own bargains in their own way, and to settle disputes without regard to 'legal absurdities'. 'Make men depend on their honour and they will act honourably with very few exceptions' was his pious hope, which was not far removed from the view that affairs could safely be left to the masters to attend to them in a manner that would safeguard the interests of all.[42] Improvements in the attitudes of the masters, said Gaskell, were the best guarantee of improvement amongst the men.[43] They were not disposed to oppress their labour, ran another argument; wages would always rise when trade was good and there was no need to apply pressure for that purpose; in fact extorted increases never lasted since a 'factitious rise of wages obtained at the expense of the natural profits of the capitalist' diminishes the motive for capital investment and working prospects.[44] Masters and men should then act sensibly together, and this was eventually the view too of Gravener Henson, for long a militant trade union leader, who was totally disillusioned by trade-unionism by 1838 and who concentrated his later efforts on bringing the masters and men together and thereby avoiding the evil of combination.[45]

Like so many nineteenth-century arguments the case against trade-unionism was frequently presented in the terms of a moral crusade for personal reform. Gaskell urged the mill artisans to shake off the habits that were destroying them physically and morally, to discountenance agitations, combinations, and political quarrels, and to renounce gin shops, political clubs, and union rooms that they might be a contented population. Trade-unionism clearly belonged to a package of evils that were to be disavowed. Gaskell was indeed prepared to spell out the fact that their moral influence was pernicious in that they created barriers between masters and men and rendered workmen and their families improvident; it was almost a duty of masters to protect themselves against 'the unfounded and unreasonable demands of their workmen'. In this way the workmen would be saved from the results of their own folly, their lost wages through strikes and bad habits acquired in times of idleness and 'delusive excitement'.[46]

> '". . . facts have proved, and are daily proving, how much better it is for every man to be independent of help and self-reliant", said Mr Carson thoughtfully'[47]

and the treatment of trade unions by 'sympathetic' writers such as Elizabeth Gaskell and Dickens is a fair indication of the distance still to be travelled before acceptability and respectability would be reached.

In part the hostility to trade-unionism was probably the result of what might be termed the 'climate of opinion' arising from the French Revolution and the French Wars, when trade unions were seen as a threat to law and order and a further symptom of the Jacobin menace. In part it arose from the very low opinion that the governors of society held about working men; they were lazy and needed the spur of hunger to drive them to work and the force of discipline to keep them there, but they were at the same time, in Wilberforce's words, 'that valuable portion of the community whose labour was so essential to the social system under which we live', though their valuable function did not, in the Hammonds' words, render Wilberforce any the less reluctant 'to defend some particularly gross outrage on the poor'.[48] This low opinion of workmen and their characters was naturally translated into hostility towards their behaviour as trade-unionists, as from the employers who told a royal commission that it was always the highest paid workers who were the prime movers in strikes and combination and another who boasted to the same commission that he had informed his men that he knew of no Weavers' Committee with whom he was prepared to negotiate.[49] Union officials were, according to Ure, the fomenters of misrule; unions were conspiracies of workmen against the interests of their own order and they were responsible for the abrupt transition to mechanisation which the men themselves lamented, for science and mechanical ingenuity would inevitably come together to defeat 'every unjustifiable union which the labourers may form'.[50] Unions were led by mischievous agitators who disturbed the contentment and good order of the workers and diminished the profits of their employers, views strongly upheld by the Select Committee on Combination Laws, 1825.[51] The worst thing that the 1833 Factory Commissioners could say about the leaders of the 10 Hour Movement was that it was led by 'the same men who in every instance of rash and headlong strikes have assumed the command of the discontented members of the operative body, and who have used the grossest means of intimidation to subjugate the quiet and contented part of the workpeople'.[52] The worst thing that the Bishop of Oxford could say about the possible consequences of the failure of the 10 Hour Movement was that it would drive workmen into combinations, which it had been the main object of the movement to prevent![53]

If workmen and their unions should be so regarded it was natural that employers and the government should have been concerned to coerce the one and prevent the other, by law if necessary. And so the first half of the nineteenth century became, in one view, anything but laissez-faire in labour relations as the government lent its support to employers to enforce long-term contracts and provide heavy penalties for their breach, to outlaw trade unions and make striking illegal, and to assist labour recruitment by the New Poor Law, which drove men into employment under the threat of the workhouse alternative.[54] This process the Hammonds unequivocally described as 'the war on the Trade Unions', resisting any historians' inclination to find a non-committal title for their investigation. In one of their most fervent sections they censure the government for surrendering the power of the state to the discretion of an individual class, for allowing employers to pay their workmen whatever they thought fit, and for denying the workmen the power to defend themselves against the misery that this exploitation ensured. With the repeal of the wages and apprenticeship clauses of the Elizabethan Statute of Labourers in 1812–1814, following the 1799–1800 Combination Laws, which ensured that workers in combination did not threaten the 'free' labour market, paternalist protection in industrial affairs was at an end, and, in the Hammonds' words, the weight of the law was added to that of capital and unemployment to compound the burden that the working classes had to support.[55]

Of all these oppressive laws, those against Combinations have always had a central place in the popular view of the social consequences of the Industrial Revolution, the savage measures which were held by the Hammonds to be largely responsible for the degradation of industrial life, the laws which caused the working classes immeasurable loss in 'happiness, physical energy, and moral power', the legislation which put children as well as their parents at the disposal of their employers.[56] And even in recent times an academic study has described the laws as the 'first symptom of provocative change' by which governments and employers made their 'outrageous demand' to enforce discipline without exercising the protection that traditionally accompanied it.[57] One very cynical view dates the changing attitude from 1760 when the ruling classes, with an awareness and clarity of vision that has escaped most historians, noted the new industrial processes that were taking place and saw their 'opportunity for self-enrichment' if developments could proceed without restraint. Upper class greed is given the blame and Adam Smith exonerated.[58] Undoubtedly any growing mood was reinforced by the events and ideas generated by the French Revolution; the government of the 1790s was ready to confuse combination with Jacobinism and the London Millwrights' Petition of 1795 plus worrying reports about a powerful Weavers' Association in Lancashire made Pitt willing to listen to Wilberforce's proposals for comprehensive legislation to outlaw all combinations.[59] The Combination Acts did not, of course, proscribe existing lawful practice, but they did prohibit all combinations and they did introduce summary trial for alleged offenders. The penalty of up to three months' imprisonment for a convicted workman was mild compared with other punishments of the day, but the imposition of fines alone upon offending employers undermined any claim to the Acts' impartiality. It appeared 'an odious piece of class legislation' to a later commentator of scholarly detachment, and there is justification for other criticisms that the Acts forced trade unions into attitudes of secrecy and hostility towards the authorities and, by treating their members as rebels, drove them towards violence and sedition.[60]

Shortly after the Hammonds wrote their classic attack, the Combination Laws were reconsidered and grounds advanced for supposing that their villainous impact had perhaps been exaggerated.[61] Even severe critics of the Laws such as the Webbs and Raymond Postgate admitted their frequent non-enforcement; the Webbs quoted a contemporary pamphlet which suggested that the Acts had remained a dead letter for the shoemakers, printers, papermakers, shipbuilders, and tailors, artisan groups for whom it was primarily intended, whilst the Builders' societies were said to have enjoyed a 'relatively easy and carefree existence' under the Acts.[62] Whether this arose from the inefficiency of the machinery of law-enforcement or the willingness of magistrates to confine their activities to preserving the peace is not agreed. Local studies have tended to lend weight to the view of less than rigid enforcement. Nottingham, for instance, in the years of the Acts, experienced at least 50 illegal unions, at least 15 strikes, and no more than five prosecutions. Here there was clearly a magisterial policy of non-interference in an industry where patterns of wage negotiations were well established, and the municipal authorities even lent the local workmen the town hall for collecting signatures on behalf of repeal. In hosiery the movement of wages was determined by factors other than trade union organisation, which existed mainly in periods of acute depression and was usually powerless to do anything.[63] A similar picture emerges from Leicester, where the Corporation again operated a policy of salutary neglect, ignoring the laws on many occasions, passing lenient sentences when compelled to act, and being driven to more severe action under pressure from the central government, as in 1833.[64] These examples cast some doubt on the belief that repression was most severe where outwork was most extensive. Nor does the inactivity of the Lancashire magistrates during the great Cotton Spinners' strike of 1818 support the view that areas of factory industry and greatest technological change also experienced the greatest repression.[65] The Combination Laws did not represent the whole story, as Gravener Henson realised in 1824, for it was possible to charge workmen under other laws such as that against breach of contract and leaving work unfinished.

It is as yet not possible to supply the necessary quantitative evidence on the full extent of prosecutions under the various laws to establish or deny the claims made about the inhibiting effect of the law on workmen's combinations; nor will the psychological barriers set up by the law ever be amenable to any quantifying process. But what is certain is the fact that the years of the Combination Laws were years of a great variety of trade union activity despite the limitations that the law imposed. The London cabinet-makers and millwrights were believed to be better organised in the period 1800–20 than ever before, the engineers were believed to be in no way restrained by the Acts, and in Sheffield, it is claimed, the men were actually finding it easier to form unions than their masters.[66] There is plenty of evidence for the open existence of many trade unions during this period but much less for the revolutionary trade-unionism that waged an underground war and contributed to the mythology of the period, if not to the history.[67] These were also years of employers' combinations, which were never successfully challenged in law, though Henson did make a bold, fruitless attempt to indict combining hosiers in 1811.[68]

Despite having the power of the law behind them, employers still felt themselves severely threatened by the unions and still believed, or claimed to believe, that they were about to precipitate economic ruin for those masters confronted by trade unions. In a highly significant aside from their main purpose of showing the disordered state of the country and the need for a professional police force, the 1839 Constabulary Commissioners, presumably starting out with the intention of showing that industrial violence made policemen necessary, grossly overstated their case and indulged in a wholesale condemnation of trade unions and strikes, with or without violence, to which various employers were encouraged to contribute all their fears, prejudices, and special pleading. Trade unions were driving trade from particular towns and they were ruling employers and denying them any profit from their capital; in some cases were driving it abroad, because of the 'constant interruptions, annoyances, and insecurities in various shapes to which the capitalist is subject in England'. Sheffield, for instance, was thought to be on the verge of economic extinction because labour which cost 15/- or 20/- in that town could be had for 1/3d in Strasburg, whilst Austria was held up as a model country for industrial relations. The mill-owners there would soon have all combiners in prison; the government would give them all necessary backing and allow no interference with the masters; exemplifying this idea was a veritable employers' paradise near Vienna, an unregulated mill where the hours of labour were 5am – 9pm.[69] Such examples and arguments were hardly relevant to the case for a professional police force, but they are an entertaining example of what can slip out incidentally on one subject whilst another is ostensibly being discussed and are, as such, a fair indication of what people really believed when their defences were down.

This kind of overdrawn picture about the catastrophic effects of trade-unionism upon industry conveys an impression of devastatingly effective organisation which runs counter to the views formed as a result of detailed investigations of trade-unionism in the early nineteenth century. The enemy always seems more frightening than he is. Ure, for instance, attributed the growth of a Manchester silk-trade to the depopulation and decline of Macclesfield which the union there had caused by its restrictions on labour, but it was the cotton-spinners who particularly alarmed him. They had risen to such a degree of affluence and of power that they were able 'to maintain a stipendiary committee', an unforgivable crime, and to be dictators to an entire industry; in the Glasgow area, in particular, they had so completely organised their association that they had established a closed society, all-powerful to control the fortunes of their fellow-workers and the trade in general.[70] The spinners even led Gaskell to contradict himself by admitting that their interests were strictly guarded by combinations, as if combinations could actually be good for their members, and those of Glasgow have seemed to later investigators remarkable for the degree of organisation and stability which they were achieving in the 1820s and 30s, when some 90% of all spinners were enlisted in membership.[71] In fact even the spinners were showing the old friendly society concern for general welfare and insurance schemes and were still relying for support, in Lancashire, for funds from sympathetic masters, and were not yet the aggressively independent body that could concentrate on and achieve their industrial aims. Their strikes against self-acting mules, for instance, in the 1820s, were counter-productive in that they speeded up the introduction of the very machinery which they sought to oppose, and they lost their struggles against women workers and that to tie children's hours of labour to those of adult labour in addition to losing the battles over technology.[72] If the spinners were frequently unsuccessful, the weavers, when they did attempt to organise, as in 1818, were invariably so. In fact it has been recently argued, contrary to the commonly held view, that trade-unionism was generally weak in the textile regions during this period, reduced after the case of the Tolpuddle Martyrs, and able to make but little contribution to the 10 Hour Movement, with the exception of the Manchester based cotton-spinning organisation of John Doherty.[73] Even Engels conceded that trade unions could do nothing to alter the laws of supply and demand, though he thought they could exercise considerable influence by forcing manufacturers to put up wages more speedily when trade was good and also prevent them from cutting wages in an effort to compete with each other.[74]

An interesting argument recently advanced is that skilled workers who had the scarcity value to enforce their demands failed to do so, not simply from organisational failures, but because of an inability to appreciate the full-strength of their position. The so-called labour aristocracy, it has been argued, was slow to learn what the traffic would bear and calculated a 'fair wage' in relation to what labourers beneath them were earning and skilled men in other occupations rather than in terms of what they were worth. It was a calculation based on custom, not market values, and in consequence employers in the nineteenth century got their skilled labour at less than market cost, causing workers to work harder and for less money than they need have done. Examples of groups who failed to exploit the market are the ironfounders and engineers before 1840, who lived in a 'wonderful sellers' market' which they did not appreciate, and the Lancashire engineers who earned no more than 30/- per week in the 1850s when their value was much in excess of that. Altogether, it is suggested, workmen were slow to learn the rules of the game, and until they did employers would have far too easy a time.[75]

Such a process of learning must necessarily be a slow one and time would elapse before it was complete. And when it was, the effect of the lesson would be to make this labour aristocracy even more conscious of its superior position and anxious to press its sectional demands rather than agitate on behalf of the entire body of workers. It has been suggested, for instance, that in the 1830s and 40s status distinctions inhibited the growth of full-scale unionism among factory workers, and those of superior status were more concerned to perpetuate the gap between themselves and their fellows than to press for all-round improvements.[76] Mass unionism never seemed near to becoming a reality for most of the century. Trade-unionism remained the privilege of the skilled workers and the great body of unskilled remained unorganised until the closing decades of the century. There are many evident reasons why this should have been so; the inability of workmen to preserve list prices in declining industries and the repeatedly demonstrated futility of combination in such industries; the inability of unions to control country areas in scattered industries and the devices resorted to by masters in sending work into the country to get it done below list prices and beyond union influence; the difficulties in limiting labour availability in a period of fast-growing population which was perpetually feeding huge numbers of women and children into the labour market; the hostility of government and employer opinion on trade-unionism; and the difficulties in finding a race of local trade union leaders in an age which denied educational opportunity to most members of the working classes, for this was hardly an area where middle-class help would do: all these factors inhibited trade union development through the first half of the nineteenth century and beyond.

Instead of mass unionism a 'new model unionism' of better paid, skilled workers emerged from the ruins of the general unionism of the 1830s, a unionism of somewhat controversial historical role in nineteenth century society and politics. The repeal of the Combination Laws was, in the Hammonds' view, perhaps the most remarkable achievement in this period, and the writers of history have tended to confirm the view of one of Francis Place's correspondents from Leicester who wrote: 'Of your anxiety to promote the welfare of the working classes we cannot entertain a doubt.'[77] Doubts have, of course, now been entertained; what the Hammonds saw as one of the main achievements of nineteenth century trade-unionism, that it helped create society out of chaos and brought a steadying influence to bear upon the world of industry, the paradoxical growth of quiet and calm once the unruly unions had been allowed to exist, is now as likely to be seen as one of its great failures. If Francis Place is to be approved of for his success in 'handling and channelling' working-class protest into modes of conduct acceptable in terms of the values of his day, he is going to be disapproved of for precisely the same reason, for it is not necessarily regarded as a 'good thing' that the working classes were so contained. Various examples have been cited of how the working classes were diverted towards more acceptable forms of conduct and reconciled to the capitalist system rather than permanently alienated from it. The co-operative movement, for example, moving away from the community building of its founder Robert Owen, began to accept the industrial system and capitalism, and concentrated in exploiting this system to the maximum advantage of the working classes through co-operative shop-keeping.[78] Similarly, the friendly societies and the trade unions were working-class institutions within the capitalist state, seeking not to overthrow it but to work within it for the protection of the working-classes, again performing a reconciliation role. It has been suggested that the co-operative and trade union movements followed a parallel course, with the strength of each concentrated in the same trades and areas, the Amalgamated Society of Engineers playing the role of the Rochdale Pioneers, and both teaching the workers to live with capitalism.[79] And this picture is supported by the further illustration that as the skilled workers began to appreciate the market calculations that could determine wages, they themselves adopted the rules of capitalist society and exploited it to their own private advantage.[80]

Whether this was a question of the biter being bitten or hoist with his own petard or whether the infection of the workers themselves with capitalist morality was the ultimate triumph of capitalism must remain a matter of opinion. What is more certain is that the trade unions of the pre-1889 period were the preserve of those who had done best out of the capitalist system, that the unskilled remained non-unionised, and that union was a demonstration, as much as a cause, of strength. Union members, whether they were builders, engineers, miners, iron and steel workers, skilled textile operatives, or belonged to old crafts such as printing or brass working, defined their position and had their wages defined in relation to the much lower paid and unskilled labouring jobs, filled from the large surplus pool of low-paid labour. Thus the self-acting mule spinner would earn twice as much as the weaver and more than double the amount of the big piecer. With skilled wages rising faster than unskilled and rising prices affecting all in the middle decades of the century, the living standards of the labour aristocrats improved relatively even more than their earnings did and they might be said to have adjusted very comfortably to the opportunities that the nineteenth century industrial state offered them. Whether their ability to restrict recruitment to their trades was more important than the skill that they controlled, a further echo of the selfishness/altruism interpretation of trade-unionism, or whether it was the valuable commodity they had to sell that constituted their power to organise and their success in using their organisation, it seems clear that their relatively comfortable economic position enabled them, perhaps compelled them, to remain aloof from working-class radical movements which tempted their less successful comrades. Most of the unions had a conservative record and many were to be found investing their funds in the industrial concerns which employed their members.[81] Because of this the belief arose, not surprisingly, that the labour aristocrats acted selfishly throughout most of the nineteenth century, safeguarding their own position, and being willing largely to abandon the rest of the working classes in return for a place for themselves in the sun. As early as 1827 they had been accused of possessing the vices of all aristocracies and being full of social antipathies towards those less well paid than themselves.[82] And the process of divide and rule, by which the more prosperous elements of the working classes were detached from the mass and attached to the social and political system, has left the labour aristocracy prone to accusations of class-betrayal.

Yet it is hard on the labour aristocrats to appoint them guardians of a working-class consciousness of yet unproved existence and to hold them responsible for upholding social altruism when all other groups practised self-interest. Nor were their own gains without general significance for the working classes as a whole. In asserting their claims for higher wages the trade unions, it is argued, advocated an alternative and class view of industrial economics which prevented the uncontested triumph of the view that a natural harmony prevailed between employers and employed. They opposed laissez-faire economics, gained wage increases and hours cuts for their members, developed strong organisation, achieved secure legal status, and formed Trades Councils and the Trades Union Congress for the future. Also, their moderation and good sense entitled them to middle-class backing and some reward in political terms, which they achieved in part by playing off the major parties against each other to the advantage of themselves, a third party, in much the same way as the Irish at Westminster were to exploit the party struggle. In this way, it is argued, they helped achieve such legislative successes as the 1870 Education Act, the Public Health and Artisans Dwellings Acts, and the new trade union legislation of the 1870s.[83] How far the trade unions were really responsible for this legislation, how far it was a positive achievement, how far a sop to Cerberus from on high, how far an inevitable consequence of the 1867 Reform Act, are, of course highly debatable and insoluble issues.

It is also maintained that the trade unions in addition fulfilled an educational role, teaching employers and the government the 'art of viable class relations' and reconciling erstwhile foes with working-class institutions that had stood the test of time and could no longer be effectively opposed.[84] Again, what for one would be registered on the credit side, might for another require an entry in the debit column in the assessment of trade union achievements, since 'viable class relations' are not necessarily seen to be desirable. But however this is viewed, there is wide agreement that trade unions, from being a cause of class enmities, became a means towards improved industrial and class relations. Writers and thinkers at last appeared to justify trade-unionism to society as a whole, even to attempt to find a place for it within 'orthodox economic theory', and some large employers such as Mundella and Lord Elcho, the Scottish colliery owner, became virtual patrons of trade union leaders.[85] The triumph of the 'viable class society' must be measured against the cost of its achievement, and even the proponent of the case is able to build up a not insignificant argument against it in terms of one third of the country's population in a state of poverty at the end of the century, increases in real wages falling further behind increases in the national *per capita* income, opportunities for upward social movement on the decline amidst the poverty and inequality at the century's end, and educational opportunities falling away at the secondary level as they improved at the primary stage following the Forster Act of 1870.[86] Add to this the continued employment of vast numbers of children, the depressed standards of those not fortunate enough to belong to the unionised aristocrats, and the crunch that the aristocrats themselves were beginning to feel at the end of the nineteenth century and at the beginning of the twentieth with the rise of the managerial, white-collar worker, and the debit side of the achievement argument begins to look impressive.[87]

For all its limitations, trade-unionism and not politics was the route chosen by the working classes in the nineteenth century insofar as they chose a means to organise themselves and express an opinion within the newly formed industrial society. Trade societies were certainly prepared to employ the machinery of politics in the late eighteenth and early nineteenth century campaigns to secure Parliamentary protection for their trades, and the failure of these efforts has been suggested as one reason why trade union strength needed to be developed as an alternative approach.[88] But it was a big step from approaching parliament as petitioners to using the strength of organised labour for political ends, the achievement and use of power within the state. The ideal of a politically self-conscious labour movement arising from a half century of industrialisation has attracted some historians, but most are inclined still to accept the view that trade unions long sought to avoid political involvement and had little concept of a political role that they might play. It is usually possible to detect some links between trade unions and the political movements of the day, but these were invariably slight and not central to the union's purpose. Probably, as some suggest, depressed trades were more inclined to become involved in political campaigns in a desperate effort to find any solution for their problems.[89] And some artisans did, as individuals, become involved in reform campaigns with middle class allies, but for the first half of the century at least, political activity had a minor role. Perhaps politics bore the same relationship to trade unionism throughout most of the nineteenth century that trade-unionism had borne to food rioting throughout the previous ages, namely that it was one step further away from their immediate experience than working-class people were currently equipped to take.

8 *Standards of Living and the Quality of Life*

'For the revolution that had raised the standard of comfort for the rich had depressed the standard of life for the poor.'

—*The Town Labourer*, p. 47.

However much people disagree on some aspects of the Industrial Revolution they are united in the belief that it was a development of outstanding importance. In one modern view it marked the most fundamental transformation of human life of which we have written records in the whole of the world's history;[1] and if contemporaries were slow to appreciate what was happening around them in the eighteenth century, they were becoming increasingly appreciative of its importance by the end of the first quarter of the nineteenth. For Gaskell, writing in the mid-'Thirties, the conversion of a great people from agriculturists to manufacturers in little more than half a century was a phenomenon worthy of recording and comment.[2] It took longer for the full significance of the economic changes to be in any real sense apprehended, and present-day comparisons with non-industrialised, underdeveloped countries are still the most vivid indicators of how meaningful a change was accomplished in Britain by the process of industrialisation. Generalisation is now made about the condition of all countries that have not industrialised, which retain peasant-agriculture as their main industry, and poverty is seen to be their distinguishing characteristic. In the late seventeenth century there was simply not enough work available for people to do, and half of the population of the country were unable to live by their own incomes and had a pauper-existence. The problem was far too great to be solved by any redistribution of wealth, even had that been contemplated, and the only answer short of reducing the number of people was economic expansion. This occurred with the Industrial Revolution, since which times mass starvation has been unknown and the eternal poverty of half the nation has disappeared. Without the Industrial Revolution mainland Britain might well have suffered the same fate in the nineteenth century as Ireland and headed for a similar fate to that of modern India. In short, if population growth had taken place without industrialisation, as it can do, it would have perpetuated and exacerbated the desperate standards of poverty of the late seventeenth century and ensured mass inability to survive.[3]

There is not much point now in arguing in favour of a non-industrialised Britain when industrialisation has taken place. The historian must properly face the much more genuine issue of the relative advantages and disadvantages of the industrialisation process for those who were actually experiencing it. Difficult though it may be for him to enter imaginatively into the arguments that took place on the relative merits of the domestic system and factory production, what seems now almost a fairy-tale existence was once a real life for millions of people, and its disappearance was by no means universally welcomed as a solution to mass poverty and a necessary step towards economic growth. The Industrial Revolution destroyed the family unit as the basis of production, transforming the lives of all its members, and creating quite a new kind of society in which working became a separate function from living, it ceased to be a family affair, and all social relationships were transformed.[4] It is not surprising that this process should have been resented and that commentators should have been aware of a 'declension in the social and physical condition of the artisan', even if it did not really exist, that responsibility for this decline should be attributed to the break-up of households and separation of families, and that the old domestic system should have been idealised beyond recognition by the first generations to experience its disappearance.[5] In later years of academic detachment it is possible to appreciate the large element of romance that this process involved and to point to the severe poverty that persisted in those industries which retained a domestic structure well into the nineteenth century prior to their eventual collapse, an experience which allegedly 'gives the lie to critics who express hostility to the industrial world by painting an idealised romantic vision of rural life'.[6] Though the rural life close to nature was doubtless lived at or near the starvation level in weather that was by no means always sunny, people were prepared to argue that this was a preferable way of life to that introduced by the Industrial Revolution, and it is no help to historical understanding to dwell on the overall implications of industrialisation and ignore the immediate and short-term ones.

One such immediate consequence was the new economic relationship which developed between men as the domestic mixed economy broke up and the workman became a labourer, selling his only commodity, his labour, in return for a weekly wage from his employer, to whom he was related only by the financial bond of this transaction. The economy of peasant holding and workshop combined, the social relationship with squire, parson, and employer which conveyed protection as well as duties upon the workman, were exchanged for a simple relationship based only on money received for labour performed. The division of labour principle imparted to the workman a simple well-defined role in the economic and social structure, and he became, in the Hammonds' words, not so much a human being entitled to a voice in affairs as a unit of labour power within an impersonal system.[7] And he became part of an enormous labour force for the use of a limited number of employers who thereby acquired a vast power over the lives of their fellow creatures. This was not the power of industry, which Owen accepted, but the power of capitalism which he believed would bring misery and exploitation unless controlled, a power which has been illustrated through the town of Oldham by means of the 70 capitalist families who were said to buy the labour of 12,000 worker families.[8]

Power can, of course, be exercised benevolently and need not be oppressive. Ure argued that the constant aim and effect of the scientific improvement that it commanded was philanthropic and designed to save the workman's eye, his mind, and his frame.[9] Others have argued that it was necessarily in the interests of the employer to secure his labour at as little cost as possible, that his own welfare rather than that of his employees was his prime consideration, and that 'cheap and docile' labour was what best suited his requirements.[10] If profits were dependent on low production costs the employer's interest was to keep wages down, and if the power of capital over labour was as great as some have argued, the overwhelming mass of the working force were in a highly vulnerable and precarious position by 1830 since the majority of people were labourers for hire by this date. This vulnerability had many aspects to it. For instance, the family money-wage now stood between the family and distress; if it was threatened by the unemployment or sickness of its members, there could be no recourse to part-time farming or vegetable-gardening to supplement the weekly budget. The social disturbances of the first half of the nineteenth century such as bread-riots, machine-breaking, and political riots, were often the consequence of the dangerous coincidence of high food prices and unemployment, which were insupportable burdens for men who were purely wage-earners.[11] Conversely, excess cash in a pre-industrial society might well have been dissipated on drink and no harm caused; if the higher and more regular wages of town life, of necessity higher since they were the sole means of dependency, were similarly treated, a family might quickly find itself in desperate straits. Previous experience simply offered no useful guide to present conduct, and the management of a new money economy for the family would be fraught with all kinds of complications and possible pitfalls.[12]

It is clearly difficult to attempt any overall assessment of the many economic and social changes which are known collectively as the Industrial Revolution. Some have offered such generalised verdicts on 'a period as disastrous and terrible as any through which a nation ever passed', or 'a cruel experiment which was proving a calamitous failure';[13] the Hammonds, concerned to evaluate the new industrial civilisation, adopted a similarly catastrophic viewpoint in judging 'the complex of all the forms and conditions that inspire and govern imagination and conduct'.[14] Unfortunately for their reputation, this great disapproval they felt of the social consequences of industrialisation led them to accept too uncritically many of the adverse comments previously made about the economic consequences of the Industrial Revolution and to suppose that there were no economic gains for any of those people whose fate most concerned them. The real grievances felt by the Hammonds about the new society were not basically economic ones, but they allowed themselves to make many rash statements on matters about which they knew very little, thereby providing easy targets for their critics, and helping to provoke in its modern form the inconclusive standard of living debate, which is to some extent irrelevant to the many worries that they felt about industrial society. This was probably an inadvertent drift in their purpose; concerned with the quality of life, they committed themselves to many bold statements about quantities involved, were unable to defend these, and were left looking rather foolish, all unnecessarily.

It is not, perhaps, surprising that they should have made this mistake, for the political economists who had supported industrialisation had mainly believed that it would depress workmen's wages, not to mention the critics of industrialisation, who assumed that widespread poverty was its inescapable companion. In pre-industrial times, Cobbett believed, there had been no poor rates, and every labouring man was well clothed and well fed.[15] As riches increased, according to Southey, so did poverty in the same proportion.[16] The labouring classes had become the labouring poor, in what Coleridge chose to call 'an ominous but too appropriate change in our phraseology', and these views were only being confirmed and given the historian's stamp of authenticity by Toynbee when he spoke of a great increase of wealth accompanied by an enormous increase of pauperism.[17] Sharing the social attitudes of these critics, the Hammonds followed them into their verdicts on economic matters, but their own verdicts are little more than statements of faith with little pretence to having statistical backing. Occasionally reference was made to figures; they reported, for instance, an assertion that the artisan at the beginning of the nineteenth century found that the expenses of living had increased five fold since he began his life, but they supplied no information about the man's age, his occupation, or his geographical location; but even supposing these to have been the most favourable possible to support the Hammonds' case and the least favourable to support a tolerable life for the artisan, the estimate seems somewhat wild and woolly. On other occasions they resort to plainer, unsupported allegations that the cotton-workers, manning the industry of greatest alleged profit, had the mass of its members degraded to the deepest poverty, that the workers as a whole were experiencing a bitter conflict to maintain their standards of life against the power of capital, that no share of the increased wealth arising from industrialisation went to the workers, that the standard of life of the poor was actually depressed by industrialisation, that workers employed in the new industries failed to obtain any part of the new wealth, and that the industries making the new wealth were failing to support their own workpeople. The 50 years which followed 1792 at the same time marked an increase in national wealth and reduced the working-classes to deeper poverty.[18] On all these claims their factual information is minimal or non-existent and their interpretation a crude and emotional response to what they feel must have been the true situation. Not surprisingly, they got their fingers burnt; furthermore, they left the way open for the debate on industrialisation to be conducted in terms of the material benefits which it was able to convey upon participants, something far removed from their original purpose.

In 1926 J. H. Clapham launched the modern standard of living debate by attempting to demonstrate statistically the falsity of the Hammonds' belief that everything was getting worse for the working man during this period, thereby committing the historian to those 'riddles of quantification' that now threaten him wherever he turns.[19] Using the available wage series, food prices, and cost of living indexes, Clapham argued that for every class of urban or industrial worker about which information was available, except such dying trades as that of the common hand-loomweaver, wages had risen markedly in the period 1780–1850. For the fortunate classes they had risen well over 40% and for urban and industrial workers in general perhaps about 40%. As the cost of living was lower in 1850 than in 1780 he concluded, not unnaturally, that a general and marked improvement in working-class living standards must have taken place. So impressed were the Hammonds by this mobilisation of statistical evidence that they were ready to concede that 'so far as statistics can measure material improvement, there was improvement'.[20] This concession was certainly premature in view of the substantial undermining of Clapham's figures that has since occurred, but it gave some pretext for the assumption that wages and prices pointed clearly to one possible conclusion only. Supplemented by estimates of national production, *per capita* income, and consumption during these years, these figures have produced a strong conviction that the real wages of most workers were rising. High wages were what attracted men to the towns and their factories; the evidence of wage differentials and labour migration not only suggests improved standards for the urban workers but actually indicates a welcome from the workers for this changed way of life.[21]

In fact Clapham impressed the Hammonds more than he did later scholars, who began to see that he had told less than the whole story and that his statistical evidence was perhaps not substantial enough to justify the conclusions based upon it. Statistics on wages were not extensive or reliable enough to warrant generalisation. They represented only the wages of skilled trades, and so presented an over-favourable impression; they told nothing about casual labourers and the great army of men outside trade societies whose wages were determined by competition rather than agreement. Also, they represented wage-rates, not actual earnings, and took no account of unemployment or underemployment, suggesting a work-force of skilled men fully employed on agreed rates. We have still, in one view, no index of employment or means of establishing the social and income structure of the work force; without these we can only guess at the true situation.[22] Similarly on prices, knowledge is insufficient to permit more than a hazardous guess on the movement of real wages, and no generalisation would be accurate for the working classes as a whole. Unagreed estimates hardly constitute a satisfactory basis for authoritative statement. In the absence of adequate knowledge on earnings, unemployment, and retail prices, runs one argument, it is impossible to say whether there was an average gain or an average loss for the wage-earner.[23] Another indicates some of the main points of agreement, for instance the fact that wages were rising faster than food prices in the early years of industrialisation, 1760–90, and that real wages were unable to keep pace with steeply-rising food prices in the war years, 1793–1815, but concentrates then on high-lighting some of the apparently insuperable obstacles to complete elucidation and agreement: regional difficulties in both wages and prices so complex as to render impossible any national hypothesis from sectional evidence; the impossibility of acquiring figures on the volume of employment available, making wages as opposed to wage-rates impossible to calculate; the technical problems involved in compiling a cost-of-living index which make such an exercise impossible or meaningless. In short, it is admitted that there is no agreement on the conclusions that are possible from the evidence that is available and that the evidence used depends on which sector of the economy is being cited at what particular time.[24]

In the absence of information, speculation and theorising are inevitable, and there appear to be sound theoretical reasons for supposing that industrialisation would not go ahead to the accompaniment of substantial wage increases. The incentive that lay behind the whole process was not social welfare and philanthropy but profit, and so it would not be unreasonable to expect profits to rise more quickly than wages. Also, the need to produce cheaply seemed to require that wages should be the minimum that employers could get away with, since it was to be some time before it was generally realised that high wages might be an encouragement to higher productivity and that increased purchasing power would create a bigger domestic market for sale. Another factor which seems likely to have held back wages was that economic growth was occurring at the same time as a massive population explosion, which pushed up the numbers of competitors for jobs, who were also being supplemented by Irish immigrants, and thus undermined the bargaining position of workers. Until 1830, it has been argued, the tendency of population growth to outstrip subsistence-means seemed the biggest threat to the workman's standard of living and brought upon him the oft-repeated exhortation to exercise moral restraint.[25] This arose in part, perhaps, because early wage-improvements of the late eighteenth century encouraged workmen to marry earlier and have large families, so contributing to their own demise in that only the scarcity of labour could increase its value; the overabundant supply of labour has been held responsible for the stagnation or even fall in real wages during the 'Twenties and 'Thirties, for these were the decades of greatest population growth.[26]

Such speculations, supported by calculations that even under the most optimistic of estimates *per capita* income doubled in the years 1790–1850, whereas real wages rose only between a half and two-thirds, suggest that observers have been right to see these years as ones of increasing inequality with a clear movement away from wages in the distribution of the national income.[27] What they do not imply is that any redistribution or greater 'exploitation' was of such magnitude that the poor actually became poorer in consequnece. To ask if poverty increased in this period of economic expansion is to suggest a gloomy answer only to those who posed the gloomy question.[28] To ask if prosperity increased would be to suggest an encouraging answer to those who were already predisposed to receiving one from their framing of the question. Such a predisposition might be manifested in the expressed belief that, contrary to the above stated calculations, there was no trend in distribution against the workers in this period and that there is even some evidence to suggest 'that distribution of income in England in 1850 was less unequal than in 1800'.[29]

Predisposition might also be illustrated by conflicting attitudes towards the government's role in redistributing national income during this period. Whilst R. M. Hartwell detects 'no marked trend' in the 'collections and disbursements of government', he notes the income tax levies of the war and post-1842 periods and the 'humanitarian and legislative pressure' which 'increased the social-overhead cost of industry, directly benefiting the workers'.[30] A more common emphasis is on the government's heavy reliance on indirect taxation during this period and the mildness of Peel's income tax of 1842. The state's role in redressing inequality was in fact minimal; it was generally felt to be undesirable that the state should extend its role to include provision for those who failed to survive the harsh competition that change was imposing on people; failure was seen as personal failure, and social welfare provision was not envisaged. As a result of the state's failure to take a firm initiative in the provision of public services the working classes were necessarily the last to enjoy all the advantages that Industrial Revolution had made possible, whether in terms of personal consumption, housing, sanitation, water-supply, medicine, or education.[31] This is almost an argument that under a different political and social system the working classes might have enjoyed the benefits of industrialisation more speedily. It deals with a hypothetical situation. In the real one it suggests neither that things were getting better nor that they were getting worse, only that they were not so good as they could have been, which is the kind of argument that historians should employ only sparingly.

Similarly on the question of working-class consumption patterns a little information can be made to go a long way and to mean vastly different things according to who is looking at it. Consumption statistics before 1850 are admitted to be 'inadequate and unreliable' yet at the same time are said to indicate modest if fluctuating increases in the consumption of most foodstuffs and other goods.[32] After all, Adam Smith had wisely seen that mass production demands popular consumption and so it should be no surprise to find that economic growth was spreading its benefits around. Whether these benefits were anything more than soap, candles, cheap cottons, and learned articles has been recently contested, but it does seem probable that some working-class families were enjoying enough affluence to add non-essential goods to their homes at the same time as others in distress were pawning those that were essential.[33] But the 'inadequate and unreliable' evidence does not favour one side only; investigations of tea, sugar, tobacco, and, more controversially, meat consumption, have suggested no significant rise in the standard of living, and it has been further suggested that the years of rapid urbanisation were probably years of declining working-class consumption of perishables until problems of transportation had been solved.[34]

To complete the confusion in this exercise of guesswork which passes for one of quantification there can be added the other statistical arguments on non-measurable quantities, whether population was growing faster than national productivity and thereby preventing standards from rising, whether long-term investment was seriously affecting current consumption, and whether the terms of trade were such that it was England's customers who received the early benefits of industrialisation rather than England's workers. The inability of any party to mount an incontestable statistical case has left all participants assured of the veracity of their own inferences, yet there seems little reason why economic historians, like men on trial, should be presumed innocent until the contrary is proven. And they cannot all be innocent. Statements of faith remain statements of faith if the main reason for accepting them is that no one has contraverted them statistically. Such statements, when made by the Hammonds, did at least have the merit of making little pretence to having statistical backing.

The inconclusive nature of this debate is being recognised in two ways, one of which is the balancing exercise that is attempted in setting off those who gained from industrialisation against those who lost. There have been repeated reminders that the factory workers who symbolised and epitomised the Industrial Revolution and who, by common agreement, enjoyed a rising standard of living once they had recovered from the reverses of the French Wars, were hardly typical British workmen and were a minority of the working classes even by the middle of the nineteenth century. Nor can generalisation be made from the gains of engineers, builders, or other skilled groups about the whole working-class experience. Along with such groups must be considered enormous sections like the million agricultural labourers who had prospered in wartime but suffered deteriorating standards for half a century afterwards, during which time many were on the verge of starvation, the quarter of a million handloom-weavers whose wages were beginning to fall by the end of the eighteenth century and who died a long lingering death as an occupational group throughout the first half of the nineteenth century, as did the domestic framework-knitters, for whom a new life was created by the factory industry of the second half of the century, and other domestic workers who were to remain members of 'sweated' trades throughout the century. Even for the urban factory workers short-term cyclical unemployment, which seemed to gather momentum as the new industrial pattern was established, could produce short-term freakish situations, such as that at Bolton in 1842 when 60% were unemployed, whilst Oldham, in the years 1800–50, a town of cotton-workers, coal-miners, and engineers, is said to have suffered from regular mass unemployment and to have had over 40% of its population in primary poverty at any one time.[35] Even at the end of the century social investigations of London and York revealed 43% below the poverty line, at a time when inequality was increasing and social mobility on the decrease. The obviously deteriorating standards of large numbers of people and the obvious poverty that still existed at the end of the century should clearly inhibit any over-optimistic generalisations about rising standards for working people as a whole and reinforce the need to balance gains against losses, to note the beneficiaries of industrialisation but to offset against these the 'long agony of poverty, starvation, and degradation' of some groups, which constituted the social cost of the process.[36] It might well have been the case, it is argued, that until the middle of the nineteenth century the number of sufferers was greater than the number of beneficiaries.[37] Another view takes this argument a little further. Acknowledging that from the 1860s gain outweighed loss, the argument suggests that until then the number of those whose condition had improved, multiplied by the degree of improvement, was probably less than the number of those whose condition had deteriorated, multiplied by the degree of deterioration. This offers tentative support to the notion that average working-class standards declined, but it is no more than an opinion which others would wish to contradict.[38] T. S. Ashton, for instance, offered as a guess the view that those who shared in the benefits of economic progress were more numerous than those who were excluded and that their numbers were steadily growing.[39] Others have guessed otherwise.

The other acknowledgment of the inconclusive nature of the debate is the apparent wish of its participants to seem moderate in their claims and to occupy ground not far away from a central position. On one side E. J. Hobsbawm has reached remarkably 'mild conclusions', acknowledging the possibility of a modest rise in average living standards and taking a stronger line only on the likelihood that a substantial improvement could ever be demonstrated. On the other side R. M. Hartwell shows a similar willingness to be as accommodating as possible. Although he believes that average standards were rising he recognises that they were not high or rising fast, that many suffered from dire poverty, cyclical fluctuations, and technological unemployment, and that these sufferings cannot be ignored. There is apparent common ground in the acceptance of the fact that the full picture is unavailable; the difference exists in their decisions to take up positions on opposite sides of the central fence.[40] But all positions currently held are far removed from that implied by the Hammonds in *The Town Labourer*, when their enthusiastic denunciation of industrial society led them into quite insupportable claims about living standards.

Perhaps too the Hammonds were less than fair to overlook the fact that the economic growth of the period 1790–1850 was able to take place whilst the population of the country was rising from nine to 14 millions and was sufficient to prevent this rapidly increasing population dissolving in social anarchy through hunger and depression.

Although the optimistic interpreters are ready to concede that living-standards for the masses were not high, they were evidently high enough to prevent hundreds of thousands from dying of starvation and the rest from erupting in political rebellion. Large increases in population which are not accompanied by appropriate economic growth bring disaster to the people concerned, and this disaster was avoided in Britain. Perhaps the supporting of a vastly increased population without great political upheavals and a marked deterioration in standards was in itself a substantial achievement, obviating any need to push the achievement beyond provable limits.[41]

In recognising this, it is, however, important to note too the emergence of something akin to a gospel of economic growth amongst some historians.[42] It has been fairly asserted that today's economic historians are more interested in problems of economic growth than in those of inequality and unemployment, more concerned to demonstrate the economic miracle that took place between the middle of the eighteenth and nineteenth centuries than to quibble about the defects in the social system that supported it.[43] This is a legitimate emphasis. It becomes questionable only if it carries the implication that economic growth was of itself so important that its achievement justified all else that accompanied it, 'a commitment to the ideology of economic growth so blatant', it has been alleged, 'that it is in danger of reducing a discipline to a propaganda'.[44] Whether or not the emphasis does carry this implication is, of course, a matter that some would affirm and others stoutly deny. What does lend weight to the view that economic growth has been ascribed almost magical qualities is a willingness to list all the major social advances of the period as achievements of industrialisation. Given the early role of child labour in the Industrial Revolution it is heavily ironical that a reduction in child labour should be claimed as one of the blessings which it conferred. Similarly, the almost universal hostility to trade-unionism amongst employers and society's rulers hardly justifies the inclusion of trade union growth amongst the benefits that the working classes enjoyed because of industrialisation. If the Industrial Revolution produced or exacerbated evils which society eventually recognised and governments endeavoured to remove, there is an obvious lack of logic in ascribing such ameliorations to the Industrial Revolution which rendered them a necessity.[45] By such reasoning we might thank Hitler for the successful Normandy landings.

When the Hammonds opted out of the argument on statistics in the

1920s, when Clapham seemed to be having the better of the exchanges, the decision was not simply a matter of their technical limitations on the statistical side or their methodological limitations as social historians. It derived rather from a genuine desire to show that the quality of life is determined by many factors which are by their nature not able to be measured accurately or represented statistically. This was consistent with their earlier claim in *The Town Labourer* that the level of family earnings was not to be regarded as the chief test of the happiness of a society and the implication that the economic aspect of the argument was a subsidiary one and that the quality of a civilisation was to be evaluated in other ways, for which quantitative values were not appropriate.[46] This response to Clapham, an unnecessarily premature concession on the standard of living issue, did represent their judgment on priorities, and it is a judgment that has been shared by E. P. Thompson in spite of the latter's somewhat severe treatment of J. L. Hammond for his wish to talk about 'happiness' 'in his most cloudy and unsatisfactory manner'.[47] Happiness may well be a cloudy concept, difficult to define, identify, and locate, but it is the happiness, contentment, satisfaction (or some other synonym) of the working man with which E. P. Thompson is himself primarily concerned, and the pursuit of happiness for its members is arguably a higher ideal for society to pursue than wealth. Clapham himself agreed that 'statistics of material well-being can never measure a people's happiness', but it was left to social critics such as the Hammonds and E. P. Thompson to exercise a clear preference for the second rather than the first.[48] Hence the recent claims that all is not necessarily well with a society just because its total wealth is increasing and that people who were in fact enjoying a slight improvement in their material standards might actually feel to be undergoing a catastrophic experience, that statistical averages and human experience might impart opposite impressions.[49] What should be attempted is an understanding of the experiences of those who lived through the Industrial Revolution, not simply a measurement of their incomes and outgoings. What should be examined is not so much their standard of life as their way of life, the one a measure of quantities, the other of qualities, the one of material achievements, the other of happiness. And on these criteria, with which the Hammonds would have been very content, the working classes are believed to have suffered an 'experience of immiseration' in spite of small material gains.[50]

Of the qualitative changes in life perhaps the most frequently debated had been the change from rural to urban living. The argument is advanced on the one hand that whatever gains urban workers were enjoying in real wages were being obtained within the context of deteriorating town life, involving social loss not embodied in any index.[51] Against this it is maintained that rural life was just as appalling as that within towns, and that prejudice rather than science is dictating views on this issue, though there has yet to appear a reasoned and convincing exposition of the view that industrial towns of the first half of the nineteenth century were pleasant and healthy places in which to live.[52] Even those who regret the absence of scientific assessment of towns and who look for a 'new methodology' to supply objective criteria on such issues, are nonetheless prepared to concede that the 'failure to devote enough resources to social infrastructure, particularly in rapidly growing cities, was the cause of considerable suffering',[53] which suggests that the qualitative change induced by town-dwelling was probably not a change for the better. Others have argued that housing and sanitation probably deteriorated despite any upward movement of real wages, and stress that such commodities as smells, smoke, and disease cannot be so readily seen on graphs as wages and prices.[54] It is true that in comparisons between rural and urban living value judgments have provided some help in supplying the answers, but they have usually supplied the answer that the early nineteenth-century town must have been an intolerable place in which to live.

Another qualitative difference in life styles was the replacement of domestic labour with factory labour, and here again value judgments, nostalgia and sentiment have usually combined to produce the view that working at home was somehow 'better' than working in a factory; even if factory earnings could be shown to be higher than domestic earnings and factory hours shorter than domestic hours there was still a preference for a way of life that involved some measure of self-determination, even at the high price that it cost. Some of the bitterest conflicts were experienced, it has been argued, not on money matters but on traditions and concepts, for instance the notion of the family economy; wage-labour in the factory disturbed existing relationships within the family and created for the first time a sharp and unnatural distinction between work and life, the former being undertaken only to make the latter possible.[55] This was an incalculable social disruption. Industrialisation, it is allowed by its warmest defenders, must mean some suffering, some dislocation, and partial destruction of older ways of life before it creates the opportunity for the growth of new ones, and the problem is to measure the rewards of the experience against the cost involved. That sounds like the language of arithmetic, but, we are warned, 'a final calculation of welfare must compare different ways of life' and this exercise requires skills and knowledge which the historian does not as yet possess.[56]

Arising from this change in work patterns is another line of criticism of industrial society that has appeared in the work of nineteenth- and twentieth-century social critics, a concern for its effect on the individual as a human being, a suggestion that he became less free, less able to exercise options, less able to develop his own potential, and therefore less capable of realising happiness because of the restrictions placed upon him. Ruskin believed that industrial wage-labour gave no pleasure, was degrading, and turned workers into something less than men; William Morris felt that the new goal of modest material satisfaction denied to men the experience of what the pleasures of life might be; the Hammonds reinforced the wage-slavery metaphor; and E. P. Thompson listed the loss of independence amongst the bitterest experiences of industrialisation.[57] But the most penetrating insights and moving language on this subject have come from Tawney, who condemned the absence of liberty as a worse evil than poverty: the method of obtaining an income was as important as the income itself; gold could be bought too dearly, and if the way of earning a living involved loss of liberty then the living was not worth earning. This he believed to be the reason why so many working people continued to idealise the pre-industrial age, that they resented their dependence and subservience, their lack of opportunity for self-direction, and an economic status determined by compulsion rather than choice.[58] It could be argued that such an analysis idealises the working man, who is more concerned with full employment, good wages, and the cost of living than he is with liberty; but it is the accuracy of this retort which now constitutes the saddest justification of Tawney's position.

Perhaps the main reason why people have been ready to believe in the distress and unhappiness of the working population during the first half of the nineteenth century has not, however, been the break-up of the domestic system and the inconveniences and discontents arising from the workman's new role as a wage-labourer. It has been rather the disturbed nature of this period of history, the existence of a great volume of social protest which creates a *prima facie* case for believing that something was seriously wrong within society and that many people were experiencing much discontent and distress. From the middle of the nineteenth century the country appears to move into a very settled period socially; the fear of revolution dies away and the working classes cease to give any great concern. But by contrast, the first half of the century, or at least from the later stages of the Napoleonic Wars onwards, experienced a succession of disturbances and threats to social stability; after the Luddite crisis of 1811–12 there were the threatened revolutions of 1815–20, the rural riots of 1816 and 1830, the prolonged agitations and disturbances concerned with Parliamentary Reform and general unionism from 1829, and a decade of Chartism, 1838–48, with its three serious crisis points. However these movements have been individually interpreted, they have been collectively recognised as the manifestation of deep discontent within society, an indication that the process of industrialisation was creating many victims and that its social repercussions were posing a threat to the stability of the whole system, a recognition that successive governments were being confronted by an unsatisfied society that was prepared to resort to violence in many forms to convey the intensity of its feelings. The years of the 1830s and early 1840s have been described as the period at which the common people were most persistently and profoundly dissatisfied, with hopelessness and hunger uniting to produce an endemic discontent which frequently flared up in political and social disturbances and which kept the spectre of revolution always within the thoughts of those responsible for the law and order of the country.[59] From the middle of the century the situation changed. Political movements died out; trade unions settled into their task of preserving the differential advantages of their labour élites; and the co-operative movement ceased to worry about re-creating society and turned itself into an efficient retailing organisation. And all these developments are usually treated as an indication of the growing prosperity of the working classes, who were at last beginning to enjoy in large numbers the advantages which three-quarters of a century of industrialisation had made possible. By contrast, and on the same kind of inference, the earlier period must have been a period when the cost of industrialisation outweighed its benefits, when workers experienced only the growing pains of the new industrial system and felt nothing of the delights that economic growth was capable of spreading throughout the community. Indeed, it has been asserted that the popular discontent makes sense only on a gloomy interpretation of the period; on an optimistic interpretation the discontent becomes almost inexplicable.[60] This does not mean that attempts have not been made to interpret it on this basis, for discontent bred of rising expectations has always been a convenient hypothesis for interpreters who have been reluctant to acknowledge the faults of systems under threat from within.

But if the Hammonds were content to switch the debate to a discussion of happiness, they were equally content to talk in terms of the morality of the new industrial system and to explore concepts of justice, for they believed that the working classes of the early nineteenth century were in moral revolt against a conception of society, a revolt which Gravener Henson had described in 1823 as a wish 'to attack principles which we conceived to be wrong in governing society'.[61] Now if happiness is difficult to define and identify, how much more so is justice, as Socrates found when he attempted to lead his colleagues to an agreed definition. The important thing, however, in testing industrial society, is not to find an agreed interpretation of the term but to find different people, perhaps with different interpretations, who nonetheless believed it more important that society should be justly organised, however they saw this, than that it should be materially prosperous. Amongst contemporaries Richard Oastler was one such man who, according to his biographer, 'with his simple Christian standards . . . considered it nothing less than blasphemy that enlightened selfishness would prove to be the fulfilment of the laws of nature': and many of Oastler's fellow critics of the new political economy argued not about efficiency or wealth but about the rights and wrongs of a system.[62] The passage of time and material progress have blunted the edge of this kind of criticism, and social justice has come increasingly to be measured in terms of pounds on wages and pensions. The Hammonds never did settle for this equation of social justice with material well-being, and their radical social criticism was concerned with relationships rather than riches. In the same tradition, but with a tactical wisdom greater than the Hammonds, Tawney spurned the standard of living debate and, despite his own practical involvement in politics and deep concern for poverty, concentrated his criticism of industrialism on the principles involved. His chief criticism was the lack of a sustaining moral ideal or ethical doctrine to replace the notion of success as its own justification, a notion that produced a trail of human wreckage behind the conquerors and a workforce paid at the lowest price for which their labour could be had. And for their part the working classes and their leaders were also culpable in aiming at comfort when they should have been aspiring to rights, content to consider the question of more or less when they should have been considering that of right and wrong, efficiency and material well-being when they should have been seeking justice.[63] Again, if this seems an impossible idealisation of the working classes and an unthinkable programme for their leaders, this is perhaps a measure of the validity of the Hammonds' criticism and of the ultimately corrupting effect of industrialism.

9 *The Methodist Contribution*

'For resignation was the message of religion as it was the message of nature.'

—*The Town Labourer*, p. 238.

The mountain of controversy concerning the social and political importance of the Evangelical Revival in general and Methodism in particular has got to be climbed because it is there as a result of the many and conflicting claims made about this non-economic factor in working-class lives; yet any attempt to assess the importance of these movements for working men during the process of industrialisation is fraught with difficulty. Gibbon, examining the successful establishment of Christianity within the Roman Empire, wisely reminded historians that they should not explain causation in terms of 'true' or 'false' religions but should restrict themselves to those spheres of human activity, political, economic, and social situations, which they were competent to assess. The importance of Methodism for the historian cannot be that it was the true faith that vanquished the false ones; yet conflicting views on the rightness or wrongness of the Methodist position and the emotional commitment with which they are presented make detached comment difficult. It is simpler by far to exercise the license of a Cobbett, whose unambiguous views were that 'the truth is, these fellows (Methodists) have no power on the minds of any but the miserable'.[1] An eulogist of John Wesley who believes that 'strong humanitarianism' was 'so distinguishing a mark of the Methodist Revival' is hard to comprehend alongside those who condemn the Methodist ministers for their total lack of qualms concerning the social consequences of industrialism.[2] Nor can a sympathiser with the Evangelicals easily be comprehended alongside the Hammonds, who found William Wilberforce always ready to defend some particularly gross outrage upon the poor and Hannah More offering no single reflection on the persons or systems responsible for the social evils of her day when she had so much to say about working-class morals.[3] The Hammonds, it is said, rarely mention Wilberforce without sneering at his conservatism, and their conclusions are 'biased and innaccurate' and 'marred by preconceived hostilities'.[4] Perhaps preconceived affections on the other side too have marred the conclusions of those who see the Evangelical Churchmen and Wesleyan Methodists as 'great as humanitarian reformers' and who attribute to their Sabbatarian attitudes the working man's weekly day of leisure which encouraged the growth of popular education.[5] The gulf that separates the starting points and therefore the attitudes of commentators on this subject is too great to permit any simple reconciliation of viewpoints in some historians' compromise.

The starting-point of most modern interpretations of the political importance of the religious revival of the eighteenth and nineteenth centuries is Halévys's classic view of religion as a great social stabiliser during years of political ferment. He was able to quote the Methodist Conference itself in a declared intention of 'promoting loyalty in the middle ranks as well as subordination and industry in the lower orders of society' and developed his famous thesis that Methodism probably saved Britain from the revolutionary fate that overtook France at this time.[6] And it has been suggested elsewhere as one of the marvels of English social life that 'so many wild and unlearned people should be kept quiet and submissive in the days of intense suffering and agitation'.[7] How far Methodism should be credited with this achievement and how praiseworthy an achievement it was are both matters of argument. It is not without irony that such an alleged political triumph should have emanated from a society that began by practising a 'no-politics' rule; the desire to remain respectable and acceptable, the personal inclination of Wesley himself, and the dubious elements to be found on the radical side would all encourage the eighteenth century Methodists to render unto Caesar the things that were his, but loyalty, obedience, and support for the *status quo* do in fact presuppose a political decision in favour of conservatism. This became more explicit in the 1790s, as ministers more consciously sought to lower the political temperature of the working classes, who were receiving such a disturbing example from France, and in the post-war period of crisis when ministers tightened their hold on their working-class members, enforcing obligations of loyalty, opposing trade unions and political societies which might tempt them from their true obedience, and, on occasion, expelling Wesleyan Sunday School members for the offensive conduct of wearing radical badges.[8] In the period of Jabez Bunting's control, the 1820s, it has been said, a Methodist priesthood emerged, the 'active agencies of reaction and repression', and the battle with radicalism was unmistakably on.[9]

The Hammonds' criticism was directed against all the principal Evangelical groups. Drawing heavily on the writings of Hannah More, they found that religion was being used as a prop to support highly conservative social and political systems and that the Evangelical approach to social politics was well suited to the requirements of the upper classes. Their central injunctions were for obedience and resignation; the ability to ignore problems was a test of religious faith. Their Christianity provided not a standard for judging institutions but a reason for accepting them.[10] It must, of course, be acknowledged that these generalisations hardly encompass the personal behaviour of the movement's great political campaigners themselves such as Wilberforce or Buxton, whose own activity contrasts vividly with the passivity and quiescence that they advocated for the working classes. The latter were to be persuaded to seek their salvation in the after-life rather than in political action to reform the conditions of real life and received a valuable antidote to the poisonous injections of the French Revolution: they might even be persuaded that their present poverty and general misery were greater guarantees of future felicity beyond the grave. Immediate material satisfaction would thus be renounced and working men would settle for a temporal existence in which they displayed the virtues of a good slave. Nor did the Hammonds have to build up this kind of picture by selective quotation; it represents a unified view of life and one that is to be found commonly enough. Andrew Ure, for instance, in writing his account of the manufacturing trades, entered into what might appear, but was in fact not, a diversion by discussing the value of Methodism to the successful pursuit of business in producing correct attitudes amongst the work-force; men, that is working-men, must learn not to scramble for what he calls the 'idle phantoms of pleasure and ambition', which were responsible only for tumults and agitation; rather should they expect to find their chief happiness not in the present but in a future state of existence. For the present they should display the patience and resignation of the 40,850 former scholars of the Stockport Sunday School Union who, he believed, preserved the general decorum of that town and neighbourhood, in a period of political excitement when their less fortunate brethren were being tempted along vainglorious paths of political reform and industrial protest.[11] The politically conservative role of the period's religious leaders is well-known; they would all doubtless have agreed with Arthur Young's view that a true Christian would never be a leveller and Wesley would have been delighted to think of the credit he would later be given for saving Britain from revolution.[12] He would have been less happy with the later psycho-sociological theories that interpreted the enthusiasm and passion that went into the religious movement he led as the sublimation of frustrated desires which sought an alternative outlet when their natural one had been dammed up. More particularly he would have regretted the description of religious fervour as 'a ritualised form of psychic masturbation', whereby dangerous energies and emotions that might otherwise have changed the political or social fabric were released in harmless love-feasts, meetings, and campaigns.[13] Wherever this kind of interpretation will finally lead us, there will probably always be a tendency for some to see in religious fervour something more than a concern for salvation and to associate it with more mundane and secular purposes of immediate self-satisfaction which might also incidentally satisfy some political purpose such as the dislocation or preservation of a social system.

For whatever precise or imprecise motive men became Methodists, there is no doubt that it was a very convenient faith for the employers who adopted and adhered closely to it, for it renewed and reinforced the traditional Puritan virtues which have been regarded as so conducive to successful business enterprise in other times and in other places. Emphasising the need to work hard, be thrifty, and to exercise personal responsibility for individual success, Methodism encouraged the disciplined life and gave to business enterprise a sanctity which justified both its harsh competitiveness and the rich rewards which might otherwise have been thought likely to make entry into the kingdom of heaven difficult. Methodism was, in one view, 'an ideological self-justification' for the manufacturer and his retinue, justifying his activities, even necessitating them, for the penalties suffered by a master lax in his principles would be not only damnation but also business failure.[14] And yet, however plausible this argument in theory, it would be difficult to demonstrate that the Methodist manufacturers were any more 'hard-faced' than any others, which must cast some doubt on its alleged practical importance.[15]

If the manufacturers did need Methodism to drive themselves to supreme effort, which is by no means certain, it is arguable that they needed it for their workmen even more. It would be hard to imagine a more cynical discussion of the merits of Methodism than that undertaken by Ure, for he appears to reduce a religious faith to nothing more than a convenience of industry, a more sceptical attitude from a supporter of Methodism than ever an opponent succeeded in mounting. It was the interest of every mill-owner, he believed, to organise his moral machinery on equally sound principles to the mechanical ones on which his mill operated, and for the judicious manufacturer this meant the enforcement of religious discipline, since he would find it 'very efficacious' to keep his workmen in the paths of virtue. The value was not to be measured in terms of souls saved but in profit made, for he believed there to be no cause to which the 'Gospel truth' of 'Godliness is great gain' was more applicable than in the running of a large factory; without Godliness there would, he said, be wasted material from broken and pieced yarns. And only religion could save the workmen from themselves: highly paid as they were, they were now surrounded by opportunities of 'inflaming their passions and depraving their appetites by sensual indulgence of the lowest kind'. To stave off prejudice and vice they must be 'trained up' in moral and religious matters, and there could be no more sublime spectacle than crowds of factory children in Sunday School, who were not only being saved from prejudice and vice but who would also ensure the continued success of the cotton trade. In Stockport, for instance, there had been an unrivalled growth of factory establishments, thanks to the Sunday School movement and in spite of Luddism, so that Stockport was now working up as much cotton as Manchester itself. A population of more than 50,000 was quietly engaged in industry through the week and devoted to religious exercise on the Lord's day, and so rich a pay-off was coming from religion that Ure believed that ministers of the gospel in the factory districts had 'sacred responsibilities' to ensure that 'animated with a moral population, our factories will flourish in expanding fruitfulness'.[16]

In the light of such statements it would be difficult to accuse any modern historian of undue cynicism who sought to develop this same line of thought; the theme has in fact only been refined and sophisticated as the convenience of other aspects of Methodist teaching has been understood in relation to some of the precise problems that employers faced in the early days of the Industrial Revolution. The need, for instance, to wean the early factory labourer from his wandering disposition, his inclination to opt out of industrial labour for a few weeks at harvest time, his too easy a contentment with a wage that would allow him to take a rest or get drunk when the factory required more labour from him, in general his rebellion against disciplined labour and adherence to pre-industrial traditions, all these required a corrective which Methodism so admirably supplied. It demanded obedience from its followers, a fulfilment of their work-contracts with employers, and devoted toil, and it threatened with eternal damnation any breach of law such as the embezzlement of materials. It is easy enough to accept the image of 'God the most vigilant overlooker of all', if rather less easy to appreciate the 'Sabbath orgasms' which allowed workmen to pursue their work-day tasks with undivided attention and energy. And equally attractive from the employers' point of view was the doctrine that poverty was a blessed state. Arthur Young had stressed with more frankness than discretion the need to keep the lower classes poor so that they would remain industrious. Now they were required to remain industrious if they were to be saved and their poverty would be a positive asset to them in attaining this happy state.[17]

Methodism was a very useful creed for employers to encourage or even enforce. Paradoxically it was also the creed most popular with the workmen themselves, serving simultaneously the needs of parties whose interests were in many ways diametrically opposed; poor men were persuaded to practise virtues which enriched their masters rather than brought worldly success to themselves and to seek individual salvation when many of their leaders were urging the need for collective action.[18] For Methodism was a popular movement, 'one of the great "People's Movements"', which spread rapidly in the manufacturing districts and only slowly among rural occupations; it was the religion of factory-workers, handloom-weavers, coal-miners, perhaps because of their perpetual nearness to death, and tinners, and the chapel, in the opinion of the Hammonds, who had no great love for Methodism, occupied a central place in the affections and thoughts of poor people who had little to do with the government of anything else.[19]

Though the various churches were finding it increasingly difficult to make physical provision for the rapidly growing population of the first half of the nineteenth century, it was the Nonconformists in general and the Methodists in particular, who made the biggest bid to keep pace in that they built six times as many places of worship as did the Church of England in this period with accommodation for four times as many people.[20] Whereas in 1770 an estimated proportion of no more than one in 14 of the population was non-Anglican by 1851 over a half belonged to this category.[21] These figures indicate noncomformity as the popular religious position, with Methodism way ahead of all other nonconformist groups, having an estimated two million people under its direct influence.[22] The figures are not to be explained in terms simply of mill-owners who coerced their employees into chapel attendance for reasons already considered or even in terms of the 'intimate association between performance-centred economic behaviour and alignment to Methodism' which drove aspiring immigrant workers into the town chapels.[23] A wise warning has been given that our knowledge of the life of ordinary people in Britain during the Industrial Revolution is too slight to permit any confident statement about how they regarded their nonconformity, but some tentative suggestions must nevertheless be made.[24] It could be agreed, for instance, that Methodism was the first religion that attempted to embrace the working classes of Industrial Britain, and that this immediately gave it an advantage.[25] The early Evangelical Movement within the established Church had been very much concerned with manners and morals and had occurred within the upper reaches of society. The Church of England seemed to have no time for the working classes and nothing to offer them.[26] The Methodists by contrast dropped the social barriers and extended a general welcome, introducing religion to social groups who would never have come within the notice of the Anglicans. Salvation was offered to the poor as well as to the rich, and the life of the poor man acquired a new significance if he after all were eligible for the redemption that his social superiors had seemed likely to monopolise.

But it was not simply an equality of opportunity for salvation that Methodism offered but an opportunity for much else that was otherwise lacking from the lives of poor people. The Hammonds appreciated that Methodism had a particular attraction as an entertainment in which workers could become involved, a substitute for the theatres and galleries where they would have had their idealised working man spend his leisure hours.[27] A similar view is that the chapels offered the working man his first acquaintance with music, his first literature, and some kind of simple philosophy which would help him to face the hard life outside the chapel walls.[28] Above all the Methodist congregation offered him a community in which he would be accepted and involved, enjoying fellowship of other people, having the chance to take part in discussion or decision-making, and perhaps finding in this community some substitute and recompense, if he were a first generation town-dweller, for lost traditions of his earlier existence. Indeed fellowship has remained to the present day an important part of the offering that chapels make to their members. And in this context it is important to realise that many of the harsher, more rigorous attitudes adopted by Methodist leaders would undoubtedly be softened at the local level both by efforts to adapt doctrine and practice to the needs of the local community and by the presence of a strong lay element in local leadership who would be more flexible than the professional ministry.[29] For all these reasons Methodism was able to make a mass appeal, and it would perhaps be wise to concentrate on this everyday role of the chapels in the lives of urban workers rather than on the moments of conversion which brought working-class adherents to the ranks.[30] This social and educative role is confirmed by the frequency with which working-class writers were ready in later life to recognise the importance of Methodist influence upon them in their youth.[31]

This general recognition is easy enough, but infinitely more difficult is the task of establishing the precise timing and phasing of the growth of Methodism amongst the working classes and the identification of the causal link which many have believed to exist between the two phenomena of religious revival and political radicalism. The latest and most ingenious attempt to identify the nature of the link, a matter of highly speculative hypothesis rather than careful observation, arises from a confident assertion that the rapid growth of Methodism during the Revolutionary and Napoleonic Wars was 'a component of the psychic processes of counter-revolution', 'a Chiliasm of despair' among working people who hoped for political salvation, perhaps from revolution or at any rate from reform, and, in their frustration and disappointment, turned to revivalist religion and helped to erect Methodism 'on the ruins of political Messianism'.[32] Thus the sublimation thesis acquires its most precise and novel form and Halévy's view is refuted by being stood upon its head: the failed revolution was not the consequence of the rise of Methodism; rather was Methodism the consequence of the non-occurrence of the revolution. Where the political movement failed the religious movement took over, offering consolation and a substitute activity which allowed violent and potentially dangerous political passions to be channelled harmlessly into religious fervour where they could play themselves out without damage to state or society. Now this interpretation has yet to be accepted. It has received cautious support from the reminder that the

Wesleyan ministers themselves expected religious observance to revive as political movements amongst the working classes declined, though whether these rises and falls represented the transferred allegiance of the same people is unknown.[33] Indeed, even on the overall growth rate of Methodism, irrespective of the personnel involved, it has been argued that there is no significant association between this and political repression or failure. Far from offering a religious substitute the most revivalist Methodists were in fact politically the most radical and the Wesleyan hierarchy, far from exploiting frustrations, were increasingly suspicious of fanatics and enthusiasts within their midst.[34] This, together with the older view that Methodism and radicalism grew together rather than consecutively, suggests that the conflicts and ambiguities within Methodism preclude any simple generalisation on the Methodist relationship with politics.[35] Detailed local investigation and accurate measurement must certainly precede any firm conclusions, though a straw in the wind that might be worth grasping is contained within the classic account of the Swing Riots of 1830 which hints at a possible link between abortive rioting in that year and a subsequent turning to nonconformity.[36] A seemingly endless debate remains in prospect.

If religion, and particularly noncomformist religion, was believed to be and is still thought to have been of such importance inside the community, it is not surprising that Sunday Schools too should have constituted an important theme in contemporary writing, for it was the Sunday Schools that ensured that future generations would be guided along the paths that the parent institutions were mapping out for the adults and it was the Sunday Schools that provided the closest resemblance to an educational system that the early nineteenth century had to offer. 'Learning', quoted Andrew Ure with ominous approval, 'is intended to be put in its proper place, as the handmaid of religion', and it is in that role, almost alone, that it is to be seen in this period.[37] Gaskell had few illusions about the kind of function that the Sunday School fulfilled; it was conducive to cleanliness, it made a change from the daily routine of labour, and, whatever its limitations, it provided the only kind of instruction a factory child was likely to get.[38] This would involve the teaching of moral restraint and the proper treatment of the Sabbath, hardly subjects likely to stretch the mind, which they were specifically not intended to do, for, like their parent bodies, they taught humility and submission and helped to make their charges less dangerous to society and more useful as workers. One view is that they were the cheapest way of 'civilising' the poor; another that they represented a dreadful exchange even for the old dame schools, because of the poisoning belief of the Evangelicals that all education amounted to was the 'moral rescue' of the children of the poor.[39] The day-schools, established by factory-owner Henry Ashworth, taught children 'to be obedient and orderly and to restrain their passions', since mule-spinners were said to prefer obedient and docile children.[40] There was little suggestion that education should be concerned with matters beyond behaviour and indeed strong suggestions that it should not. Gaskell, a warm friend of the factory children, believed that the Sunday Schools produced little educational benefit but this did not disturb him since he thought it a mistake for infant schools 'to cultivate too much the intellect'; this was an error and an absurdity, for only morality was worth teaching.[41] Ure found a praiseworthy model in Prussian schools where he observed a contented poor, resigned to their indigence and obscurity, and educated only for lives of service, which he believed to be quite proper since he was very critical of the view that knowledge meant power and that learning helped man to better himself. In this way was the purpose of education being wrongly defined since it would set men above their station, disgust them with ordinary labour, and encourage them to be ambitious, envious, and dissatisfied, characteristics which only the well-to-do were allowed to possess.[42] Literacy was a very mixed blessing, and both the Methodist and Anglican Churches found it necessary to forbid the teaching of writing in their Sunday Schools. Jabez Bunting's extirpation of this practice, it has been said, in language not intended to betoken neutrality, was successful until the 1840s;[43] such instruction constituted a violation of the Lord's Day in that it might be turned to vocational and thereby secular advantage. Reading too was a great hazard for, as one modern commentator argues, those who were taught to read the Bible were also acquiring thereby the ability to read *Rights of Man*, a consequence there was no escaping.[44]

What does or does not constitute 'education' will always be a matter of dispute, and it is arguable if nineteenth century endeavours, designed in one view 'not to discover and develop the latent talent of the poor but to keep it safely slumbering', can be appropriately summarised under this heading.[45] A whole book has indeed been written on the educational ideas of John Wesley which illustrates the lack of common ground amongst those who employ the term. It is claimed for Wesley that he was probably the only man of importance in the eighteenth century who was practically interested in the education of children of all classes. The foundation of his educational work is said to have been 'primarily humanitarian', another word of more than one meaning, and it is claimed that Wesley's observation of the poverty and misery of the poor stirred his heart to give them a better existence. His complaint against existing schools was their total lack of religion and religious motive, and his educational precepts were designed to rectify that deficiency. They included the requirements that the will of the child should be completely subordinate to that of the teachers, that parents should begin to break the child's will from the first moment it appeared (perhaps Wesley shared Hannah More's view on the child's 'corrupt nature and evil dispositions'), that the child should not be allowed contact with language of beauty since it instilled into tender minds both obscenity and profaneness, and that all play-time, being abhorrent, should be banned. Again without irony it is suggested that Methodist education was a legacy left by Wesley to the whole world, a legacy which Britain was not able to inherit in full since Wesley did nothing about education nationally, being content to establish his own school and enunciate some principles for the running of it.[46]

Historical accident was largely responsible for giving the churches a control of education, which radicals tried unsuccessfully to break throughout the nineteenth century. The Sunday Schools were virtually the only educational opportunity, such as it was, open to the working classes for most of the Industrial Revolution, and when elementary education first began to receive government funds in 1833 the allocation was divided between the two church societies involved in school-building. And the national system of elementary schools which the Forster Act of 1870 attempted to create was a matter of filling the gaps that remained rather than providing an alternative or replacement system which some radicals called for. It would be no exaggeration to say that 'the religious debate bedevilled the matter from the outset';[47] every successive step required the approval or pacification of the religious interests involved and every Education Act ever passed in modern Britain has been a tinkering with a system built up by religious bodies rather than a purpose-built network to serve the purposes of the modern state. And when religious interests have existed, so too have religious rivalries, which throughout the nineteenth century inhibited the increasingly necessary involvement of the state in educational affairs to ensure that the country's system was meeting its requirements.

By 1870, after a century of industrialisation, there were places available in grant-aided schools for less than half of the country's children and of these about one seventh were unfilled. The explanation for this has been made partly in terms of the reluctance of the working classes themselves to send their children to school; for even free schooling could be a luxury beyond the pockets of many working-class families when it involved loss of earning capacity to the family.[48] And if education were to serve a purely functional role in indoctrinating working men in the ideals of their employers and governors, there could have been little of positive attraction in it. Furthermore, the acceptance of the need for education characterised a working man of long-term ambition for himself, his family, and perhaps his class, which few working men could be expected to have possessed when committed to the short-term struggle for survival. 'What the hell do we care about reading if we can get nought to eat?', was a not unreasonable rhetorical question asked at Cooper's Adult School in Leicester during the Chartist period, for it poses the eternal dilemma of the difficulty of pursuing long-term aims in conditions of short-term intolerability.[49] Some working-class leaders such as John Doherty were anxious that working men should go ahead and organise their own education, and educational activities had long formed part of reform societies such as the London Corresponding Society and later the Hampden Clubs.[50] The tradition was continued by the London Working Men's Association where such stalwarts as Francis Place and William Lovett saw in education the answer to working men's problems, and the pursuit of adult education was one of the many programmes on which the fragmented Chartists concentrated after the collapse of the national movement for parliamentary reform. The Benthamites contributed a professional element in government and administration which continued to press for an alternative system beyond the control of the churches but they failed in their attempt; instead they stimulated the churches to extend their own efforts and to attempt to outbid each other in the competition to provide elementary schools before the 1870 Act.

It has been widely suggested that the religious revival in England and the educational growth that it sponsored more or less consciously aimed to control working men in their political attitudes and to regulate their beliefs and behaviour that they would be quiescent co-operators in forwarding the industrialisation process as well as political inert in times when events in France and social developments at home might have prompted them to take a greater interest in public affairs. Whether or not these aims were achieved remains to be considered.

It can be said at the outset that although the Evangelical Revival started off inside the Church of England, it could not be contained there, and that Methodism, whatever the reluctance of its founders and their early followers, was, like Lutheranism in the sixteenth century, a breakaway rebellious movement, and therefore one inherently unsuited to perform an authoritarian role. Like Lutheranism it quickly assumed an authoritarian stance once it had itself broken with authority, but like Lutheranism it failed to prevent further breakaways from itself, for successful rebellion encourages successful rebellion and makes difficult a through-going autocratic stance and repressive spirit. On the same analogy Methodism became a popular movement, not only in its mass support but by freeing the individual eventually to seek salvation independently of any hierarchy, Anglican or Wesleyan, and again the very concept of authority is undermined. And with the individual feeling freer to interpret Scriptures and draw his own inferences, these might prompt Methodists, as they had prompted the South German peasants in 1525, towards radical social or political doctrines. Such a man was Griffith, one of the leaders of the agitation against the Wesleyan hierarchy in 1851, who proclaimed that if he was a Chartist it was his Bible that had made him so.[51] Bible knowledge was in general a useful weapon that former Wesleyans could wield on behalf of the radical cause, for it could be employed selectively to justify reform just as it could be used for contrary purposes.[52]

In practice the religious revival resulted in the proliferation of numerous competing sects, likened to a free trade system in religion and to stepping-stones away from orthodoxy on the road to disbelief, where radicals of varying degrees of rebellious inclination might take their stand, combine their religious rebellion with a political one, and exercise in their seceding sects an influence on working-class movements totally disproportionate to their physical numbers.[53] Thus the Rev. J. R. Stephens severed his brief connection with the Wesleyan body and launched himself as a popular orator in the North of England in such causes as the Factory Movement and the Anti-Poor Law Movement: thus the New Connexion Methodists severed their links with the parent body in 1797 and at the same time abandoned the conservative political attitudes of the Methodist leadership; thus the Primitive Methodists abandoned their leaders and their Church's hierarchical structure, the local preachers making the churches their own, and contributed large numbers of able leaders to subsequent working-class movements both political and industrial. Not that it was necessary for individuals to leave the Methodists before they became radical leaders, for it was clearly possible for many to reconcile their religion with political radicalism. This might have been because the lay readers were less doctrinaire than the clerical, as a result of which accusations were frequently made that their Sunday Schools were centres of sedition and actively promoting Radical ideas. Or it might have been the case that Wesleyanism had many tensions at its centre and that by villifying Tom Paine the Wesleyans built him up and kept his memory fresh in the public mind and their own, inviting a swift switch of allegiance in times of excitement such as Chartism when Methodism and radicalism might be seen hand in hand and religious leaders might call for action rather than for resignation.[54] This kind of observation has prompted the opinion that Methodism and Radicalism advanced simultaneously and perhaps even in some sort of alliance relationship rather than that they occurred consecutively, the one a reaction against the other.[55] At all events Methodists were often a source of concern to local magistrates, who feared their strengthening presence in working-class organisations, and many followers of Wesley turned to radical political action whatever the intentions of their leader and his successors.

For those potential radicals who were diverted into peaceful ways by their membership of a Methodist community, there were potential ministers who were diverted into working-class political and industrial activity. Part of the dilemma was their insistence sometimes on literal scriptural interpretation by which their Christianity compelled them to seek equality for those supposedly equal in the sight of God, to love their neighbours, and 'to apply God's commandments to the various institutions of the social system', as the Rev. J. R. Stephens wished, a set of aims heavy with menace for the social and political systems.[56] For some Methodists, a religion of commitment might engender a political life of commitment, for the carry-over from Methodist passion to reforming zeal could be considerable and easily occasioned.[57] And the kind of qualities that the zealous Methodist acquired, a sense of moral purpose, earnestness, sobriety, a sense of solidarity, would certainly be invaluable in the service of industrial or political campaigns should these attract him.[58] It was, however, most of all for their organising abilities that Methodists were valued in working-class ranks. Southey had objected to Methodism on the grounds that it familiarised the working classes with the idea of combination, and experience gained in public speaking, and the planning and administration of chapel activities was carried over into political affairs and employed with the dedication which Methodism had taught.[59] Methodism became, in the Hammonds' view, in fact though not in intent, 'a training ground for democracy' and helped to build up a democratic structure for society, remote though this intention was from the ideas of its founder.[60] As 'schools of practical democracy and self-government', Methodist communities contributed a model for working-class organisations, and scarcely any popular movement of the first half of the nineteenth century was without a debt to Methodism for its structure and techniques.[61] It provided the class meeting, the mass meeting in the open air, leaders for both the political and industrial sides of the labour movement, and a tradition of success through non-violent action.[62]

This last point is of vital importance, for, as J. F. C. Harrison observes about Chartism in Leicester, if working men borrowed their forms and techniques from Methodism, they also carried over its thought and attitudes into Chartism, which was modified accordingly.[63] This raises again the question of whether the influence of Methodism was to be found on the radical or on the conservative side, for it is clear that the political and industrial organisations which Methodists helped to create were reformist and not revolutionary organisations, concerned to change society and government not to overthrow them. Cobbett had believed the Methodists 'the bitterest foes of freedom in England', Francis Ward of Nottingham had called them 'an accursed set', and a modern scholar has concluded that they weakened the poor by adding the 'ingredient of submission' to the other trials that the poor had to bear.[64] For each magistrate worried by their presence there were more who were glad to have them around in troubled times, when they must have exercised a strong restraining influence. Altogether there seems little grounds for challenging the verdict that Methodism influenced the outcasts of society in 'a profoundly non-revolutionary direction'.[65] Perhaps Cobbett was right to be so bitter about the Methodists, a bitterness shared by some modern scholars, for perhaps they were taking over the working-class movement and ensuring that there would be no fundamental changes in society, no revolution, and no working-class consciousness. It has recently been argued that the conservative influence was two-fold; in the early part of the nineteenth century the working-class Wesleyans were a stabilising influence on large numbers not themselves Wesleyans who were diverted from political and industrial protest by the zealous few; later the ex-Methodists made an even greater contribution by leading the working classes in non-violent ways and helping to accommodate them to the existing system through their own reformist institutions.[66] In other words, the more effective job of rendering the working classes innocuous was done by befriending rather than by opposing them, a kind of operation done by others besides Methodists during the course of the nineteenth century. Halévy might well have been right to emphasise the conservative role of Methodism, but wrong in his timing of that contribution and his judgment of how it was made.

There is, of course, another possibility, which is that the whole emphasis placed upon Methodism and the concern shown for assessing its impact is misdirected. This line of argument was developed by E. J. Hobsbawm, who suggested that because there was no revolution in Britain and because Methodists were opposed to revolution this implied no necessary causal connection between Methodism and the non-occurrence of revolution; there were other factors in the situation besides Methodism, the flexibility of Parliamentary politicians, the work of the Utilitarians, and the weaknesses of the revolutionary movement itself, for instance, all possible causes over which Methodism had no influence. The real undermining was, however, done by estimates of numbers who subscribed to the cause. Except for Norfolk and Cornwall, Methodism was not a force of importance in the South of England, and even in the North it was really strong in only three areas, the industrial towns and villages of the Pennines, Durham, and Staffordshire, in the last two of which the Wesleyans were challenged by the Primitives. Altogether, it was thought unlikely that there were more than 150,000 Methodists out of a population of 10 millions in 1811, and unlikely that such a minority could have had a decisive political influence one way or the other. In fact observation of the correlation between Methodist and radical strength permitted several contradictory inferences to be drawn; Methodist strength in the West Riding seemed to have exercised no moderating influence there, and where Methodism was at its weakest, as in Sheffield, so too was radicalism. Similarly, in the East Midlands radicalism was no less strong for the success of Primitive Methodism after 1818. In general, it was argued that Wesleyanism was unlikely to have been able to prevent revolution had other conditions been favourable to it, and the stress laid upon its minority role has strengthened the case for supposing that religion's part in political affairs has probably been exaggerated, though this is not to deny that minorities often exercise influence out of all proportion to their size.[67] If the situation in the middle of the nineteenth century is examined and it is accepted that two million people were under Methodist influence by this point, this still represents only one tenth of the entire population. Many of these people were not working-class anyway, and the largest and presumably most influential body, the Wesleyans, had the smallest proportion of working-class members. Conversely, the most working-class body, the Primitives, had a mere 100,000 members, and had its strength outside the large towns.[68] The Wesleyan followers of the great evangelist were ready to concede by this point that they had not reached the poorest elements, the social outcasts, and Methodism, like Anglicanism, was well on its way to becoming a middle-class religion, had perhaps been moving in this direction from as early as 1821. And as its hold on working-class allegiance declined, so too, it has been suggested, did its political importance.[69] Perhaps the working-class Methodists were too few both to prevent revolution in Britain and to justify the attention that has been given to them.[70]

If the last two centuries are taken as a whole, a more remarkable feature of society than the rise of Nonconformity has been the decline of religion, which has actively engaged the thoughts and activities of a dwindling proportion of people with the passage of time. Paradoxically, the great religious revival of the eighteenth and nineteenth centuries was accompanied by the growth of indifference, which is the majority position today. It is possible that the Hammonds failed to bring out this development sufficiently and suggested too strong a bond between their town labourers and evangelical religion. Cobbett noticed that the labouring people had in great measure ceased to go to church, and Gaskell admitted that little heed was paid to religion by the mass of the manufacturing population in the towns and lamented that most of the mill-workers lived in practical heathenism.[71] These impressions were confirmed by the 1851 religious census, which showed that the working classes were little concerned with either church or chapel, especially the former which had very little to offer them. The Northern towns were the places where religious attendance was worst, and the bigger the town the greater its religious indifference: the 'most respectable' elements of the working classes persisted in religious worship but there were 'people beyond in the shadows with whom no contact had ever been made'.[72] The only disagreement today concerns the extent of this fall-off, not that it had taken place and established an irreversible pattern.[73] This religious decline has been variously interpreted. In sociological terms urbanisation might well have been a process of liberation from ties paternalist and religious, and Horace Mann suggested various aspects of the social divisions that discouraged the working man from attending church.[74] In philosophical ones, goodness for its own sake and for immediate social benefit was replacing goodness as a pursuit which would ensure salvation in the after-life; the secular need for right conduct was in itself sufficiently overwhelming to provide an immediately satisfying justification without any recourse to the supernatural.

The Church had possessed most influence in society when it had been a monolithic structure and, speaking with one voice, it had been listened to. By the nineteenth century the sects had proliferated as never before and the interpreters of Christianity were legion, all pretending to explain what was or what was not conduct appropriate to the Christian. The Factory reformers, for instance, explained that they were trying to bring factory labour under the control of Christian and constitutional principles, and many Anglican clergy were active in the movement. The opponents of factory reform were also Christians and doubtless found complete justification for their own position from their religious faith; if the nonconformist ministers of Manchester did not come forward to the help of the factory child, it was not because they did not regard themselves as Christian. It was not only on social reform that there was no single Christian position. The notion of wealth as the supreme object of human endeavour, a notion which the Hammonds believed to be dominating the years of the Industrial Revolution, has been described by Tawney, who believed that it dominated the establishment and its reformers alike, as 'the negative of any system that can be described as Christian'. He also quoted with approval the Keynes view that 'modern capitalism is absolutely irreligious'.[75] Tawney regretted the arrival of capitalism and the passing of Christianity. The Hammonds regretted the former but not the latter, for they believed that the religious teachings of the nineteenth century, with their emphasis on resignation, were basically incompatible with ideas of pursuing power through industrial and political organisation with a view to controlling wealth and using it to solve the problems of society of which they were acutely conscious.

Controversy must inevitably continue to surround such issues as the role of the churches during the Industrial Revolution, the part they played, the part they should have played. It is common practice on the one hand to berate the churches for their neglect and their failures. In response it is urged that the churches were after all religious bodies and not organised for secular purposes, however well they sometimes served them, that the primary interests of the Clapham Sect were not, of course, social reform and that they should not therefore be condemned for not pursuing it.[76] Some contemporaries, such as the redoubtable vicar of Leeds, Dr Hook (1836–59), did make deliberate attempts to make Christianity relevant to the needs of industrial society, but they were fighting a losing battle.[77] In the Hammonds' view the Methodist movement and the Trade Union Movement were necessarily rivals for the 'minds and hearts' of the industrial population, and the existence of trade-unionists or Labour politicians who were also Methodists does not invalidate this opinion, which derives from what they supposed to be a basic incompatability between those whose ultimate goals were attainable only after death and those who sought immediate power to fulfil immediate social purposes that resignation could never achieve.[78] Changes in society and the secular state would come inevitably and appropriately through secular organisations, and as these developed and extended their range and capacity to deal with social and political problems they would tend to displace the Churches rather than work with them, leaving them to an ever smaller minority who would continue to believe that there were more important matters than those relating to social and political organisation.[79] For the vast majority, however, aspirations and satisfaction would increasingly centre upon state schooling, political parties, trade unions, working men's clubs, or football clubs, the institutions of Kitson Clark's New Leviathan, the modern secular state.[80]

10 *The English Working Class*

> '. . . the Industrial Revolution obliged everybody whom it affected to think about the problems it raised . . . By the end of this period scarcely any aspect of life or society or politics or economics looked the same to the two worlds.'
>
> —*The Town Labourer*, pp. 275, 289.

It is a commonplace that the English working class owed its origin to the Industrial Revolution and that it appeared in the first half of the nineteenth century. Some have been content to state generally that the Industrial Revolution gave birth to a working class, others to offer a period, 1780–1840, for instance, when this event or development occurred. Such claims might be accompanied by doubts whether 'a proletariat in the developed sense' had emerged by this time and by an expressed preference for vaguer concepts of 'working people' or 'labouring poor' down to 1840.[1] At other times such caution is ignored, and fairly precise dates, the years 1816–19, for instance, are offered as the time at which the 'working class almost sprang into existence'.[2] A preference for the descriptive 'working classes' over the more precise 'working class' continues to characterise the cautious approach, especially since the thesis of 'the making of the English working class' put forward the argument that in the years 1780–1830 a working-class consciousness emerged of interests separate from and conflicting with those of other classes.[3]

This proposition is easier to make than to demonstrate. It is not difficult to show, as historians have shown, the creation of a social gulf between rich and poor which troubled contemporaries and to supply the other ingredients which might have been expected to produce working-class consciousness and a working-class response. The new towns, it was realised, physically separated the rich from the poor. Cobbett noted daily advancement towards a society containing but two classes of men, the masters and their 'abject dependants', and Disraeli saw the same dichotomy between the privileged orders and the working classes, at enmity with each other and nowhere more clearly so than in

Manchester where Prentice observed a situation of mutual hostility.[4] This was the raw material of class-consciousness. The urban working classes would, Cobbett hoped, in 1816, give him mass support for they were the only hope of better things.[5] In the cities, Alton Locke was told, social intercourse would breed combination and 'power irresistible', the same power that Sydney Webb was to suggest in his metaphor of 'Samson . . . feeling for his grip on the pillars'.[6] It is perhaps significant that Webb's giant was still not fully roused, for in this context the wish has often proved to be father to the thought and the working class to be a force that should have emerged rather than one that clearly did emerge.

It is all too easy to assume, as the Hammonds did, that eventually the terrible conditions imposed by industrialisation and the accompanying repressive government evoked a political and industrial response that finally put things to right. They talk of a class struggle between rulers and workers, and of a society which was different in all its aspects for members of the respective worlds. They argue that the working classes, abandoned by those who might have given them help, began to move slowly towards finding their own salvation in trade-unionism, a 'school of heroism and public spirit', in Methodism which held out a rival philosophy but in fact encouraged them to learn the techniques of industrial and political organisation, and in the birth of a social and political consciousness which would lead them on to the political campaigns of Chartism and other movements in the future.[7] Through these would society be regulated and civilised. This argument carries a strong implication that by 1840 a working-class breakthrough into political activity had been achieved and that more triumphs were to follow Chartism. *The Town Labourer* ends on a note of optimism not unlike that generated in more recent times by E. P. Thompson, who makes even stronger claims about the new social and political consciousness of the working class, yet it is by no means clear that later nineteenth-century history was the promised fulfilment that earlier developments made possible or that earlier developments were as far advanced as might be supposed.

It is a moot point how far the development of a working-class consciousness was dependent on an awareness of the economic changes that were taking place in the late eighteenth and early nineteenth centuries. Though individual working men were capable of registering the changes in their own lives, there must be some doubt about any collective recognition that an Industrial Revolution was taking place and creating a whole new role for working men within it. Occasional statements such as the much quoted Cotton Workers' Address of 1818 suggest an appreciation of the change, but most contemporary speeches and writings are remarkable for their lack of awareness of the industrialisation process, their inability to recognise quickly and clearly the working-class predicament, and to identify the enemy against whom future struggles should be waged.[8] A long-continued willingness to see the landed aristocracy as the principal foe of the working classes, a readiness of working-class leaders to adopt middle-class slogans and phrase their grievances at Peterloo in such traditional terms as 'Taxation without Representation is Tyranny' and 'Liberty or Death', the old language of men not attuned to a new situation, the persistence of men on strike in canvassing contributions from friendly employers, all these suggest the slow development of any working-class consciousness in relation to the employing class.[9] Robert Owen was the first to talk to working men as working men, and not as political animals, but their response remained clouded with ambiguity in Owen's time and well beyond.[10] There remained throughout the nineteenth century an inability to decide whether 'the landed oligarchy or the manufacturing capitalist' or perhaps simply 'the government' constituted the main enemy of labour and an equal inability to determine whether the enemy, whatever his identity, should be tackled by working men or by political animals.[11] Ideally, class-conscious workers should have been co-ordinating both roles, yet the most comprehensive collection of working-class documents for this period illustrates a political reform movement, with some working-class contributions, and a trade union movement which involved other working men. It does not illustrate a unified working-class movement.[12] Those who were interested in politics were not apparently aware of labour questions; those who were interested in trade unions and labour questions were on the whole not aware of politics or were opposed to political involvement.

The 'collective self-consciousness' of working men which has been suggested as the 'great spiritual gain' of the Industrial Revolution was allegedly the product not only of economic developments but of the political and cultural experiences of the working classes during the counter-revolutionary years of Pitt and his successors.[13] It underwent a 'sudden leap forward' in 1818–19, found expression in collectivist ideas and specifically working-class institutions such as trade unions, co-operative societies, and Chartist lodges, and produced not only a growth of community feeling but a real feeling of identity of interests amongst working men from a great diversity of occupations.[14] The workers became conscious of the fact, as Engels had argued a century earlier, that they formed a separate class, with their own interests, policies, and attitudes which were contrary to those of 'capitalist property owners', which presumably encompassed both manufacturers and landed aristocracy.[15] These claims can to some extent be examined empirically. It would be difficult to show whether Bamford's weavers at Peterloo were experiencing a greater sense of community, but it is at least possible to note the language in which their complaints were voiced. It is similarly possible to note some of the political and industrial campaigns of the nineteenth century in which working men were involved and to judge these, along with other social developments, as evidence on behalf of some of the claims made concerning the new working-class consciousness. And if it is difficult to come to grips with workers *en masse* it is easier to examine them in limited numbers in particular towns, where observations on the differing structures of employing groups and the varying occupational make-up of the local labour force have already suggested a variety of political response and varying degrees of class-consciousness.

One empirical test of working-class consciousness can be carried out by examining the political ideas that emanated from the working classes in the first half of the nineteenth century, and the policies that their leaders pursued, for this should establish whether there is a recognisable working-class political position, a recognisable ideology giving expression to the new consciousness. E. P. Thompson has advanced the view that an 'alternative system' was being increasingly advocated and has quoted O'Brien's statement of 1833 that the working classes were contemplating an entire change in society which would involve a total subversion of the existing order.[16] This is a vague and purely negative attitude. It is given a more positive and constructive side by E. P. Thompson's own claims that by the early nineteenth century 'collectivist values' were dominant in many industrial communities and that by the early 'Thirties 'the battle for the minds of English trade-unionists between a capitalist and socialist political economy' had already been won, if only temporarily.[17] But whatever qualification is made about the duration of the victory, it still remains a most extraordinary claim that the trade unions had clearly appreciated these alternatives open to them and had made this particular choice of options.

Historians have indeed been impressed by the exact opposite of this, namely the almost total absence of an alternative system from the thoughts of working-class leaders who attempted to channel discontents, the lack, even amongst the Chartists, of a clearly defined alternative social system that political power would be used to achieve. Throughout the middle decades of the century labour leaders advocated no specifically working-class position, working-class politics had no clear ideological basis, and only the Positivists ascribed to working men a distinctive political role and at the same time possessed some influence over working men.[18] In the absence of a working-class ideological position, the workers were open to the rival bids of the Liberals and the Conservatives and the Reform League's agreement with Gladstone in 1868 was to inaugurate the era of Lib-Labism in English politics, leaving poor Engels to lament the willingness of the English working class to perform the unworthy role of a Liberal tail and the absence of any genuine labour movement save for those men who were willing to take part in strikes.[19] The less fortunate members of the working classes, according to Beatrice Webb, sank into brutalised apathy whilst the more fortunate settled for 'administrative nihilism', so that when the alternative system of socialism was advocated at the end of the century it came from other social groups than the workers.[20] Now Beatrice Webb was undoubtedly being tendentious in the role she was ascribing to herself and her fellow intellectuals, but her analysis of the earlier void is fair enough. With Lovett advocating a union of capital and labour in production as the great social need of the time and O'Connor seeking to establish communities of independent peasant proprietors, there was little in the way of an alternative working-class ideology in existence to form the basis of working-class action in politics or industry in the middle of the century.[21]

The difficulties involved in identifying the enemy and the absence of a clear ideological position which would indicate long-term goals ensured further difficulties in the build up of any long-term working-class strategy and the elucidation of short-term tactics. Food rioting or machine-breaking were only short-term solutions and the future lay with those who directed working-class effort towards political and industrial organisation, which were to hold some of the answers in the long run but never enough of the answers sufficiently quickly to justify the high hopes placed upon each in turn. Parliamentary reform highlights the dilemma. The readiness of large groups of workers such as the cotton weavers, the woollen workers, and the stocking-knitters to petition Parliament in the early nineteenth century shows a familiarity with political techniques and a willingness to use them; and in spite of the failure of these excursions into politics there was substantial working-class involvement in the post-war reform movement and the events of 1830–32 which finally achieved the breakthrough.

Some have welcomed this working-class participation as evidence of maturity and clear-thinking, a conversion to the doctrine of 'first things first', yet it could alternatively be argued that parliamentary reform was a mirage that inhibited the formation of a working-class consciousness.[22] By co-operating in the denunciation of borough-mongers and sinecurists, working men were very much playing the middle-class game and failing to appreciate the significance of those economic changes that were making such combined political campaigning a totally unrealistic exercise in terms of the acquisition of power for the working classes or the tackling of their own economic problems. If the machine-breakers and the revolutionaries propagated the myth of a short-cut to salvation, so too did Cobbett and Bamford create the myth of parliamentary reform as the grand panacea. Not even the disappointments of the 1830s could restrain a massive commitment to Chartism from working men who believed that political power could be achieved as a means of tackling the various economic and social grievances that they felt. Yet it is inconceivable that the ruling classes should have indulged in such an act of collective altruism as the passing of the Charter, abdicating power and exposing themselves to the multitude of solutions to society's problems with which they had been threatened. However wise a commitment to parliamentary politics might ultimately turn out to be, it offered no prospect of immediate working-class power. Not surprisingly was there political disillusionment after Chartism and a switch of emphasis towards industrial and social action; influence was the most that working men could hope to exercise, influence through co-operation with established political forces rather than power by attempting to replace them. This does not mean that those who advocated trade-unionism were necessarily right to avoid for so long any political involvement or that the advocates of general unionism were not creating a further myth in suggesting that by general union the workers 'might provide themselves with every species of power'.[23] The unions were slow to develop any concept of the political role which they might play in government and were in fact beginning to play by the 1870s. And the sustaining myth of 'general strike' continued to exercise a strong periodic charm until

1926. Neither politics nor industrial organisation on its own held the complete answer, and so it is not surprising that the working classes floundered helplessly between the two for so long.

There is no blame attached to this failure, but the failure does undermine seriously those claims that have been made about the political consciousness of the working classes by 1830 and their importance in British political life by this time.[24] It is quite possible to accept a new maturity or sophistication in working-class behaviour which permitted 100,000 to assemble without provoking a riot, even though the Nottingham and Bristol Reform rioters were to display 'backward-looking behaviour'.[25] But this is quite different from political consciousness. The London Boot and Shoe Operatives, declaring their support for Chartism in 1842, remarked on the general view of the working classes that politics had nothing to do with them, and perhaps Robert Owen had been only realistic in believing the working classes incapable of their own emancipation and mistaken to pursue it via politics, for, as their politically conscious leaders recognised, they lacked both the education and the leisure necessary for the successful practising of this art.[26] The national working-class reform campaign of 1816–19 did not prove that the working class had sprung into existence; no more did the brief triumphal gesture, the Chartist convention of 1839, establish the working-class political movement as a settled and effective force in British politics.[27] The high water-marks indicate only the potential of the situation not the actuality. Chartism concludes a period of working-class failure rather than triumph and represents the last dismal throw for a long time rather than the flowering of working-class political consciousness. The disintegration of Chartism into its various component parts in the 1840s indicated a highly fragmented working-class and illustrated the nature of working-class politics for the next half-century. Although there are plenty of examples to be cited of a working-class presence in national politics, and this in itself was something new, a politically conscious working class could hardly leave proof of its existence by the half century of quiescence and inactivity that followed the collapse of Chartism.

The great gap that occurred between the process of industrialisation and the emergence of a political labour movement at the end of the nineteenth century, however understandable, remains the biggest weakness in the case for accepting the existence of a working-class political consciousness at a much earlier date. The failure to see this is in part a failure of imagination. In spite of Aristotle, man continues to give ample evidence of his wish not to be a political animal, and experience of modern-day Labour politics at the ward level is a much more accurate guide to the nineteenth century than romantic dreams of frustrated revolution. Massive apathy and what is to their would-be political leaders an infuriating willingness of real working men in bulk to respond favourably to those who suggest that their true enemies are to be found in racial or religious groups rather than capitalist employers, both cast doubt on the validity of the concept of working-class political consciousness at today's advanced stage of working-class development, let alone in the early nineteenth century. Enthusiasm then as now was likely to be luke-warm and short-lived and politics a minority activity. It is essential to remember Richard Hoggart's warning that histories of the working classes are usually histories of the activities of a minority within them.[28] The failure of Chartism exemplified all the weaknesses of the working class as a political force, a basic lack of interest in politics, fragmentation, and a preoccupation with sectional economic interests; and between the Chartists and the late-century Socialists political activity was very sparse. What activity there was concerned itself less with attempts to control the political machine at the centre, as Chartism had done, than with voluntary organisations such as co-operative societies that would bring their benefits irrespective of who controlled the political machine. The 1868 election, following the enfranchisement of the urban workers, simply revealed for Engels 'the disastrous political ineptitude of the English working-class', which fell victim to the power of the parson and the 'cringing to respectability'.[29]

If the political ineptitude of the workers betrayed a low degree of class-consciousness, it could be argued that politics was one step removed from the everyday lives of working men, who were more likely to display their sense of class in their trade-unionism. But the failure of the working class to emerge as a political force occurred in part because it contained within itself a great diversity of economic interests which made effective political action impossible, and this same diversity was to have a similarly inhibiting effect in industrial affairs. The attempt of early twentieth-century Syndicalists to replace the hundreds of small craft unions by a few large industrial unions was a recognition of the need to abandon the sectional interest for the sake of the greater body, but it is unrealistic and romantic to suppose that a working-class ideal has generally carried more weight and influence than the more immediate realisation of individual satisfactions. In a large industry like cotton it cannot be supposed that the élitist spinners would have shown an undue concern for the fate of the depressed handloom weavers as long as there were weavers, hand or power-loom operators, to weave the yarn that they were spinning. There could be no cotton worker interest, and therefore no working-class interest, unless it be supposed that it was easier for men to share a common identity with workers from another industry than with workers from their own. Similarly, in the much smaller textile branch of silk-ribbon weaving, it has been shown that the interests of the outdoor country-weavers who operated hand-machines were not those of the factory operatives on power-looms, or even the town-dwellers who used the same machinery as the country-weavers.[30]

The divisive impact on labour of separate, if not conflicting, economic interest is best seen on the issue of the so-called aristocracy of labour who were, in effect, those skilled working men who were able to organise themselves into trade unions during the middle decades of the nineteenth century.[31] Just as the co-operative movement, turning from community-building to shop-keeping, accepted capitalism, imitating and exploiting it to improve the position of working-class co-operators under it, so too did the trade union organisations of the workers. Though slow to appreciate their market worth, it has been argued, skilled workmen eventually built up their organisations and began to understand that market calculations rather than custom could determine their personal return; they accepted the rules of the capitalist system, exploited them to their own advantage, and thereby accepted the morality of capitalism.[32] This labour aristocracy depended for its position on the scarcity value of the commodity it had to sell and consequently resorted to the traditional and unfraternal tactic of restricting entry to the occupation, for which the cotton-spinners, for instance, were much criticised. And so the gap was widened between the best-paid, most skilled and the worst-paid, least skilled workmen. This might have been a rational and expected development; it certainly accorded with current values, but it did little to encourage working-class homogeneity and any sense of class solidarity. The London Working Men's Association had made ominous reference to its wish to cater for 'the intelligent and useful parts of the working classes', and these people were conscious of the gap that separated them from the ordinary mass of the labouring population, a gap that grew larger after 1850 as distinctions within the working classes sharpened.[33] Even E. P. Thompson has to admit that the artisan was as much concerned to maintain his status against his unskilled brethren as he was to put pressure on his employers and to concede that in the London of the 'Forties and 'Fifties the distinction between artisans and labourers was greater than it had been during the Napoleonic Wars.[34] It was the labour aristocrats who were unionised and made whatever political contribution came from the working classes in the quarter century which followed the demise of Chartism.[35]

This period has been described as one of 'mature class conflict', a term which some would undoubtedly wish to challenge, when those workmen who were organised into trade unions kept alive the 'working-class ideal' of a fair day's work for a fair day's pay as the only working men sufficiently well organised to extract their appropriate dues from the employers.[36] It might be argued against this that they were less concerned with keeping alive any working-class ideal than they were in selfish, sectional advancement that paid little heed to those enormous groups of unskilled men who were not organised and not well-paid but who were very much 'working-class'. If the labour aristocrats thought at all of the desirability of organising the labourers, it was the agricultural workers, it has been suggested, not the town labourers they had in mind.[37] The growth of trade-unionism was clearly inhibited by status consciousness, as a result of which mass unionism was very long delayed. And without mass unionism there was hardly an organised working class. At the present time, wrote Toynbee in 1884, each class of workmen cared only for the wages of its own members.[38] The collective concern was lacking. But if the labour aristocrats are to be heavily criticised for their abandonment of the less fortunate it must be remembered that they did not ask to be appointed guardians of the working-class consciousness, even if it did on occasion suit their convenience to represent themselves as spokesmen for the workers as a whole when governments had to be impressed. In their political dealings the trade unions of labour aristocrats have been shown to have had a conservative record, and their interest in Labour politics, when it did arise, has been argued as the further consequence of selfish action on their part.[39] Apart from the old craft unions, the labour aristocrats held aloof from the Labour Representation Committee until frightened into action by the Taff Vale judgment, though what really shook their complacency, it has been argued, was the rise of the white collar worker at the end of the nineteenth century, which closed off opportunities of career and social advancement and threw them back towards the hundreds of thousands of unskilled workers who were now at last organising industrially and taking the political initiative too.

In addition to these factors associated with separate economic interest which inhibited working-class unity, historians have noted other impediments. It is easy enough to talk generally about industrialisation and its consequences, but it is the common practice today to stress rather the diversity of local experience than its uniformity as different areas at different times and in different ways passed through their phase of the Industrial Revolution. The typical experience is no longer being sought, and local studies are highlighting the problem of meaningful generalisation. One such study has suggested that the economic structure of Oldham produced a highly developed class-consciousness at a very early point in the nineteenth century, whereas in Northampton, where poverty and evil social conditions were just as easily identifiable, a different structure left the work-force of the town quite without such a sense of identity. An interesting follow-on from this is the suggestion that early nineteenth-century patterns remained far from constant; that whereas the Oldham workmen were conscious of being working-class early in the century and the Northampton workmen were not, by end of the century it was Northampton that was providing the Socialists whilst the Oldham workers were voting Tory and expressing solidarity only in resistance to incoming Catholic Irish.[40] This kind of confusion suggests the need for a cautious approach towards both the acceptance of class as a principal determinant of nineteenth-century urban history and as a concept for explaining the political behaviour of large numbers of working men in national as well as local affairs.[41]

Another interesting phenomenon observable in Lancashire was the perpetuation of semi-independent communities on the outskirts of industrial towns whose members felt a strongly particularist rather than urban loyalty, and this doubtless inhibited class development in these areas. Similarly, many cotton operatives persisted in feelings of loyalty towards a mill-community and an individual mill-owner, accepting the latter's political tutelage rather than striking out politically on class lines. These complications have resulted in what has been described as the unexplained 'political orientation of mid-Victorian Lancashire mill-operatives', an orientation which adds no weight to the thesis of a politically self-conscious class.[42] And further undermining this thesis has been the attack of historians, not always opposed to the thesis, on the industrialisation process for destroying working-class traditions and culture patterns associated with pre-industrial life. As modes of life and recreation long familiar were abandoned for the joyless stereotype of urban life, the ability of working men to construct new patterns of life and build up new traditions must have been limited and ensured a lengthy process that would delay the emergence of any working-class consciousness.

The alternative to the creation of a working-class consciousness was the assimiliation of the working classes, by which they would be persuaded that they shared a common interest with their rulers and social superiors rather than a separate interest of their own. And it would be rash to assume that this approach, very consciously pursued at times, did not have considerable success. The Mechanics Institutes, started in the 1820s, were favoured by Gaskell for the moral restraint that members voluntarily imposed upon themselves rather than for any mental improvement they encouraged, but they failed to become mass educators because they quickly became the preserve of tradesmen, clerks, and respectable artisans;[43] their alleged success in diverting some intelligent and energetic working men from political radicalism to social ambition was perhaps not all that far removed from the purpose of those who had always intended them for a socialising role. The 1826 Society for the Diffusion of Useful Knowledge was hoped to reach a wider audience for propagating middle-class views on economic and political questions and again socialising possible radicals by persuading them to aim at material success by means of self-education.[44] If the workers could be persuaded to want what the middle classes wanted, to share the middle-class ethic in pursuit of material progress, they would be much less of a problem to their rulers. Aping the bourgeoisie was an occupation that must militate against working-class consciousness and solidarity. There is nothing specifically middle-class about wanting to possess the artefacts of modern civilisation, a nineteenth-century clock or a twentieth-century refrigerator, and Felix Holt saw no reason to want to join the middle classes because he possessed some learning.[45] Yet he realised that his kind were inclined to forsake their comrades in pursuit of a high door-step and brass-knocker. And when Thomas Cooper returned to Lancashire after his Chartist days were over, he was appalled to find working men not only betting on dogs and pigeons but also on horses 'like their masters', a debilitating pastime as far as class-consciousness was concerned.[46]

And if slogans of progress and self-help helped to disseminate a common social philosophy throughout the popular ranks, the working-class position within society became stabilised and institutionalised by the success of those specifically working-class institutions such as the friendly societies, the co-operative societies, and the New Model Unions, which were both acceptable within the current value system of the capitalist state and gave their members a strong vested interest in wishing to preserve it. The unions became institutions of social reconciliation and respectability and they strengthened both the workers who joined them and the existing political and social structure which they were no longer endeavouring to undermine.[47] Tolerance, even encouragement, of the trade unions was supplemented by a growing political tolerance, accommodation, and assimilation. The workers failed to get the vote in 1832 and again during the Chartist period, but in 1867 urban workers were enfranchised and five of the Charter's six points were eventually conceded.[48] Continued political exclusion would doubtless have enhanced a sense of working-class consciousness; political assimilation undoubtedly weakened any such feeling.

If class-consciousness and political-consciousness were not so important to the workers as might be supposed and if, as Hoggart argues, the place of political activity in working-class lives tends to be overrated, the question must be posed of what was thought to be important.[49] There is no lack of modern evidence to suggest that material affluence invariably drives ideological content from the political debate, and historians have observed a similar process at work in the nineteenth century. As early as 1847 Feargus O'Connor lamented that the Nottingham framework-knitters were no longer interested in what he had to say the moment they had a shilling in their pockets, whilst another Chartist leader, Thomas Cooper, could find no audience for himself and no political arguments among the well-dressed working men of Lancashire, only talk of co-ops, building societies, and their shares in them.[50] Beatrice Webb had a similar experience in the 'Eighties; the revolutionary tradition had become little more than a romantic memory as workers enrolled in their friendly societies, organised their trade unions, or managed their co-operative stores.[51] It is significant that the Reform League were prepared to canvass support for their franchise campaign on the grounds that the vote would enable working men to rise in the social scale; it was being sought as a social convenience or expedient rather than as a right.[52] The workers were settling, as Tawney was to say, for material well-being rather than their rights, for modest comfort rather than a concept of justice.[53] In Royden Harrison's words, the dream of the new society was abandoned for a prosperity sufficient to mask the perpetuation of inequality.[54] To observe this development is not necessarily to regret it, though Tawney was both observant and regretful. What the observation does, however, compel is a questioning approach to notions of working-class consciousness of interests distinct from and opposed to those of other classes.

As a postscript it is of interest that historians are now inclined to argue that it is at the end of nineteenth century and the beginning of the twentieth century that new working-class traditions are becoming established and recognisable. It is then that not only political organisations and trade unions for unskilled workers begin to flourish but also a working-class sub-culture begins to appear with its various identifiable features such as the working-men's club, the Saturday football match, and the rites and celebrations associated with family occasions.[55] Family bonds strengthen and community solidarity becomes possible as the state begins to assume some of the burdens associated with old age, relieving the strain on the family and local community.[56] The term 'working class', it has been argued, might more properly be applied to the year 1900 than to the year 1800; the case for this is stronger both in terms of the emergence of new political and industrial organisations, a political labour movement for the first time, and in terms of working-class life and behaviour with characteristic features that carry its members beyond the simple unit of factory labour and into a social existence. This is not to suggest that the working-class ideal of 1900 is not as susceptible to an over-romantic interpretation as that of the early part of the nineteenth century; it would be possible to undermine the concept with much the same arguments that can be advanced for the earlier period, but they would be slightly less applicable and do slightly less damage to the thesis at this later point in time.

References

1 The Town Labourer: Historians and Social Critics

1. Hammond, J. L. and B., *The Town Labourer,* 1966 edit., 1917, hereafter referred to as *The Town Labourer.*

2. Toynbee, A., *The Industrial Revolution,* 1969 edit,, 1884, p. 84; Southey, R., *Letters from England,* 1951 edit., 1807, p. 212.

3. Cole, G. D. H. and Postgate, R. W., *The Common People,* 1946 edit., 1938, p. 274.

4. Carr, E. H., *What is History,* 1964 edit., 1961, pp. 75-9; Thompson, E. P., *The Making of the English Working Class,* 1968 edit., 1963, pp. 485-6.

5. Postan, M. M., *Fact and Relevance, Essays on Historical Understanding,* 1971, p. 66.

6. Hartwell, R. M., *Interpretations of the Industrial Revolution in England,* and *The Rise of Modern Industry in The Industrial Revolution and Economic Growth,* 1971.

7. Tawney, R. H., *Religion and the Rise of Capitalism,* 1938 edit., 1926 p. 280.

8. *The Town Labourer,* pp. 213-4.

9. Gallie, W. B., *Philosophy and Historical Understanding,* 1964, p. 181.

10. Thompson, E. P., *The Making of the English Working Class,* p. 225.

11. Tawney, R. H., *Equality,* 1931 edit., 1929, pp. 132-3, 141-3.

12. Webb, B., *My Apprenticeship,* 1971 edit., 1926, pp. 344-5.

13. Thompson, E. P., *The Making of the English Working Class,* p. 13.

14. Hayek, F. A. ed., *Capitalism and the Historians,* 1954, preface.

15. Hill, C., *Reformation to Industrial Revolution,* 1969 edit., 1967, p. 260.

16. *Ibid*., p. 264.

17. Hartwell, R. M., *Interpretations of the Industrial Revolution, op. cit.*

18. *The Town Labourer,* pp. 83-88.

19. Quoted by Hartwell, R. M., *The Rise of Modern Industry, op. cit., The Town Labourer,* p. 242.

20. Hartwell, R. M., *The Rise of Modern Industry, op. cit.*

21. Thompson, E. P., *The Making of the English Working Class,* eg. pp. 629, 632, 636, 647-50.

22. *The Town Labourer,* pp. 114, 146.

23. Clapham, J. H., *An Economic History of Modern Britain; The Railway Age*, 1963–4 edit., 1926, preface to 1939 reprint.

24. Postan, M. M., *Fact and Relevance, op. cit*., p. 67.

25. Thompson, E. P., *The Making of the English Working Class,* p. 229.

26. Hart, J., *Nineteenth Century Social Reform: A Tory Interpretation of History, Past and Present,* 31, 1965.

27. eg. Hartwell, R. M., *The Rise of Modern Industry, op. cit.*

28. Hutt, W. H., The Factory System of the Early 19th Century, in Hayek, F. A. ed., *Capitalism and the Historians, op. cit.*

29. *The Town Labourer,* pp. 171, 214.

30. Quoted by Hobsbawm, E. J., *Industry and Empire*, 1968, p. 49.

31. Hammond, J. L. and B., *The Rise of Modern Industry,* 1966 edit., 1925, pp. 217, 244.

32. Hartwell, R. M., *The Rise of Modern Industry, op. cit.*

33. Hammond, J. L. and B., *The Rise of Modern Industry,* p. 216.

34. *The Town Labourer*, pp. 43, 116, 206, 226, 289.

35. Marwick, A., *The Nature of History,* 1970, p. 66.

36. Toynbee, A., *The Industrial Revolution,* p. 93; Tawney, R. H., *Commonplace Book* ed., J. M. Winter and D. M. Joslin, 1972, p. 41.

37. Toynbee, A., *The Industrial Revolution,* p. 93.

38. Hobsbawm, E. J. and Rudé, G. F. E., *Captain Swing,* 1969, p. 14.

2 *Law and Order in Industrial England*

1. *The Town Labourer,* pp. 101, 87.

2. Mather, F. C., The Government and the Chartists, in Briggs, A., *Chartist Studies,* 1959, p. 386.

3. Mather, F. C., *Public Order in the Age of the Chartists,* 1959, p. 43.

4. Thompson, E. P., *The Making of the English Working Class,* p. 213.

5. Tobias, J. J., *Crime and Industrial Society in the 19th Century,* 1967, pp. 156-186.

6. Thompson, E. P., *The Making of the English Working Class,* p. 73.

7. *Ibid.*, pp. 207, 709.

8. White, R. J., *Waterloo to Peterloo,* 1963 edit., 1957, p. 107.

9. Mather, F. C., *Public Order in the Age of the Chartists,* p. 57.

10. Patterson, A. T., *Radical Leicester,* 1954, pp. 92, 170, 222.

11. Hobsbawm, E. J. and Rudé, G. F. E., *Captain Swing,* pp. 253-5.

12. White, R. J., *Waterloo to Peterloo,* p. 108.

13. Thomis, M. I., *The Luddites,* 1970, pp. 129-30.

14. Darvall, F. O., *Popular Disturbances and Public Order in Regency England,* 1934, p. 257.

15. Mather, F. C., *Public Order in the Age of the Chartists,* pp. 33-4.

16. *Ibid.*, p. 226.

17. 1839 Constabulary Commissioners' Report, p. 75.

18. Mather, F. C., *Public Order in the Age of the Chartists,* p. 64, *The Government and the Chartists, op. cit.*, pp. 386-7.

19. 1839 Constabulary Commissioners' Report, p. 83.

20. Thompson, E. P., *The Making of the English Working Class,* p. 752; *The Town Labourer,* p. 99.

21. Thompson, E. P., pp. 749-50; Walmsley, R., *Peterloo: The Case Reopened,* 1969, pp. 22, 37, for his own and Donald Read's views.

22. Mr Walmsley's book is perhaps the gentlest treatment they have been given.

23. White, R. J., *Waterloo to Peterloo,* p. 92.

24. Hobsbawm, E. J. and Rudé, G. F. E., *Captain Swing,* p. 254.

25. Critchley, T. A., *A History of Police in England and Wales,* 900 – 1966, 1967, pp. 80-5.

26. Mather, F. C., *Public Order in the Age of the Chartists,* p. 43.

27. White, R. J., *Waterloo to Peterloo,* p. 98.

28. Thomis, M. I., *Politics and Society in Nottingham,* 1785 –1835, 1969, p. 232.

29. Mather, F. C., *The Government and the Chartists, op. cit.,* pp. 373-6.

30. Mather, F. C., *Public Order in the Age of the Chartists,* p. 27.

31. Mather, F. C., *The Government and the Chartists, op. cit.,* pp. 399-405.

32. *The Town Labourer,* pp. 91-2.

33. Thompson, E. P., *The Making of the English Working Class,* pp. 85, 88.

34. Fortescue, J. W., *A History of the British Army,* 1906, Vol. IV, Part 2, pp. 903-7; Western, J. R., *The English Militia in the Eighteenth Century,* 1965, pp. 379-80, 420; Radzinowicz, L., *History of English Criminal Law and its Administration from 1750,* Vol. IV, 1968, pp. 120-122; *Hansard's Parliamentary History,* Vol. 30, 22 February, 1793, 475-95, 8 April, 1796, 930-5; Mather, F. C., *Public Order in the Age of the Chartists,* p. 164.

35. *Ibid.,* pp. 164-70.

36. White, R. J., *Waterloo to Peterloo,* p. 112.

37. Thomis, M. I., *The Luddites,* p. 148.

38. Reith, C., *Short History of the British Police,* 1948, p. 21.

39. White, R. J., *Waterloo to Peterloo,* p. 188.

40. Mather, F. C., *Public Order in the Age of the Chartists,* p. 132.

41. Critchley, T. A., *A History of Police in England and Wales*, 900 – 1966, p. 95.

42. Mather, F. C., *Public Order in the Age of the Chartists*, p. 95.

43. Darvall, F. O., *Popular Disturbances and Public Order in Regency England*, p. 250; Hart, J., Reform of the Borough Police, 1835 – 56, *English Historical Review*, Vol. 70, 1955.

44. 1839 Constabulary Commissioners' Report, pp. 83-4.

45. Reith, C., *Short History of the British Police*, p. 18, employs the 'broken reed' metaphor.

46. Thomis, M. I., *The Luddites*, pp. 144-5.

47. Hobsbawm, E. J. and Rudé, G. F. E., *Captain Swing*, p. 257.

48. Mather, F. C., *Public Order in the Age of the Chartists*, pp. 159-60

49. *Ibid.*, p. 177.

50. Thomis, M. I., *Politics and Society in Nottingham*, p. 207.

51. Darvall, F. O., *Popular Disturbances and Public Order in Regency England*, pp. 266-7.

52. *Ibid.*; Thomis, M. I., *The Luddites*, pp. 151-2.

53. eg. Correspondence in H. O. 42/123.

54. Mather, F. C., *Public Order in the Age of the Chartists*, pp. 59, 39.

55. Walmsley, R., *Peterloo: The Case Reopened*, p. 111.

56. Mather, F. C., *Public Order in the Age of the Chartists*, pp.154, 147, 63, 184, 67.

57. White, R. J., *Waterloo to Peterloo*, p. 154.

58. *Ibid.*, p. 12; Mather, F. C., *Public Order in the Age of the Chartists*, p. 215; Darvall, F. O., *Popular Disturbances and Public Order in Regency England*, pp. 275-7.

59. eg. White, R. J., *Waterloo to Peterloo*, pp. 164-6.

60. Mather, F. C., *Public Order in the Age of the Chartists*, p. 210.

61. White, R. J., *Waterloo to Peterloo*, p.107.

62. Mather, F. C., *Public Order in the Age of the Chartists*, pp. 184-215.

63. Critchley, T. A., *A History of Police in England and Wales*, 900 – 1966, pp. 45-6, 92, 54.

64. Mather, F. C., *Public Order in the Age of the Chartists,* p. 131.

65. 1839 Constabulary Commissioners' Report, p. 85.

66. Critchley, T. A., *A History of Police in England and Wales,* 900 – 1966, pp. 58-63.

67. *Ibid.,* pp. 76-88, 115-124.

68. 1839 Constabulary Commissioners' Report, pp. 68-80, 82-8.

69. Reith, C., *Short History of the British Police,* p. 52.

70. Hart, J., *Reform of the Borough Police,* 1835–56, *op. cit.*

71. *Ibid.*; Mather, F. C., *Public Order in the Age of the Chartists,* pp. 114-120.

72. Critchley, T. A., *A History of Police in England and Wales,* 900 – 1966, pp. 97-105.

73. *Ibid.,* p. 52.

74. Reith, C., *Short History of the British Police,* pp. 54, 57-8.

75. *Ibid.,* p. 89; Mather, F. C., *Public Order in the Age of the Chartists,* p. 104.

76. *Ibid.,* p. 98.

77. *Ibid.,* pp. 124-5.

78. *The Town Labourer,* pp. 72-80.

79. Coats, A. W., The Classical Economists and the Labourer, in Jones and Mingay eds., *Land, Labour, and Population,* 1967, p. 108.

80. 1839 Constabulary Commissioners' Report, p. 76.

81. Thomis, M. I., *Politics and Society in Nottingham,* p. 41.

82. Tobias, J. J., *Crime and Industrial Society in the 19th Century,* pp. 57-8.

3 *The New Towns*

1. Tobias, J. J., *Crime and Industrial Society in the 19th Century,* p. 35; Hobsbawm, E. J., *Industry and Empire,* p. 40;
Briggs, A., *Victorian Cities,* 1968 edit., pp. 88-9, 140.

2. *Ibid.*

3. Hobsbawm, E. J., *Industry and Empire*, p. 40.
Briggs, A., *Victorian Cities,* p. 12 quotes from *Bentley's Miscellany,* 1840.

4. Kellet, J. R., *The Impact of Railways on Victorian Cities,* 1969, pp. 150, 296; Disraeli, B., *Coningsby,* Penguin edit., p. 131.

5. Checkland, S. G., Towards a Definition of Urban History, in Dyos, H. J. ed., *The Study of Urban History,* 1968, p. 359.

6. Briggs, A., The background of the parliamentary reform movement in three English cities, 1830 – 32, *Cambridge Historical Journal,* Vol. 10, 1952.

7. Barker, T. C., and Harris J. R., *A Merseyside town in the Industrial Revolution: St Helens,* 1750 – 1900, 1959, pp. 314, 323.

8. Briggs, A., *Victorian Cities,* p. 106.

9. *Ibid.,* p. 115.

10. Mumford, L., *The City in History,* 1966 edit., 1961, pp. 515-7.

11. Briggs, A., *Victorian Cities,* p. 21.

12. Hammond, J. L. and B., *The Rise of Modern Industry,* p. 220.

13. *Ibid.,* p. 217.

14. *Ibid.,* p. 226.

15. Briggs, A., *Victorian Cities,* p. 18.

16. Checkland, S. G., *The Rise of Industrial Society in England,* 1815 – 85, 1964, p. 262.

17. eg. Mathias, P., *The First Industrial Nation,* 1969, pp. 33-4.

18. Hartwell, R. M., The Standard of Living Controversy : A Summary, in Hartwell, R. M. ed., *The Industrial Revolution,* 1970.

19. Mumford, L., *The City in History,* p. 539; Jones, F. M., The Aesthetic of the 19th Century Industrial Town, in Dyos, H. J., *op. cit.,* pp. 171-82.

20. Engels, F., *Condition of the Working Class in England,* trans, and ed. Henderson and Chaloner, 1958, p. 60.

21. Checkland, S. G., *The Rise of Industrial Society in England,* 1815–85, p. 253.

22. Mumford, L., *The City in History,* pp. 532, 534.

23. Barker, T. C. and Harris, J. R., *A Merseyside Town in the Industrial Revolution*, p. 178.

24. Quoted in Cole, G. D. H. and Filson, R. W., *British Working Class Movements, Select Documents*, 1789–1875, 1967 edit., 1965, p. 195; Ward, J. T., *The Factory System*, Vol. 2, 1970, pp. 40, 34.

25. Pollard, S., *A History of Labour in Sheffield*, 1959, p. 13.

26. Hobsbawm, E. J., *Industry and Empire*, p. 40.

27. Mumford, L., *The City in History*, p. 538.

28. Briggs, A., *Victorian Cities*, p. 89.

29. Mumford, L., *The City in History*, pp. 509, 522.

30. *The Town Labourer*, pp. 50, 54.

31. Chapman, S. D. ed., *History of Working Class Housing*, 1971, p. 12.

32. Briggs, A., *Victorian Cities*, p. 17.

33. Tames, R., *Economy and Society in 19th Century Britain*, 1972, pp. 40-1.

34. Checkland, S. G., *The Rise of Industrial Society in England*, 1815–85, p. 242.

35. Ward, J. T., *The Factory System*, Vol. 2, pp. 152, 40.

36. Beresford, M. W., The Back-to-Back House in Leeds, 1787–1937, in Chapman, S. D., *History of Working Class Housing*, pp. 95-121.

37. Treble, J. H., Liverpool Working Class Housing, 1801–1851, in Chapman, S. D., *History of Working Class Housing*, pp. 168-199; Gaskell, P., *Artisans and Machinery*, 1968 edit., 1836, p. 82.

38. Gill, C., *History of Birmingham*, Vol. 1, 1952, p. 367.

39. Chambers, J. D., *Modern Nottingham in the Making*, 1945, pp. 24-5.

40. Prest, J., *The Industrial Revolution in Coventry*, 1960, p. 26.

41. Patterson, A. T., *Radical Leicester*, p. 3.

42. Chapman, S. D., Working Class Housing in Nottingham, in Chapman, S. D., *History of Working Class Housing*, p. 146.

43. Ward, J. T., *The Factory System*, Vol. 2, p. 30.

44. Engels, F., *Condition of the Working Class in England*, p. 70.

45. Galt, J., *Annals of the Parish*, 1821, pp. 189-190; Southey, R., *Letters from England*, 1951 edit., 1807, p. 210.

46. Ward, J. T., *The Factory System*, Vol. 2, p. 40; Hennock, E. P., *Fit and Proper Persons*, 1973, p. 189.

47. Flinn, M. W., Introduction to Chadwick's *Report on the Sanitary Condition of the Labouring Population of Great Britain*, 1842, 1965, p. 58.

48. Thompson, E. P., *The Making of the English Working Class*, p. 365.

49. Flinn, M. W., Introduction to Chadwick's Report, pp. 4-11.

50. Mumford, L., *The City in History*, p. 532.

51. *Ibid*., p. 531; Thompson, E. P., *The Making of the English Working Class*, p. 364.

52. Mrs Gaskell, *North and South*, 1967 edit., p. 376.

53. Gaskell, P., *Artisans and Machinery,* p. 214.

54. Patterson, A. T., *Radical Leicester*, p. 142.

55. Thomis, M. I., *Politics and Society in Nottingham*, p. 24.

56. Briggs, A., *Victorian Cities*, p. 147.

57. Hammond, J. L. and B., *The Rise of Modern Industry*, p. 227.

58. Southey, R., *Letters from England*, p. 213; Hammond, J. L. and B., *The Rise of Modern Industry*, p. 219.

59. *The Town Labourer*, pp. 50, 58.

60. Mumford, L., *The City in History*, p. 527; Pollard, S., *A History of Labour in Sheffield*, p. 98.

61. *The Town Labourer*, p. 59; *The Rise of Modern Industry*, p. 229.

62. Disraeli, B., *Coningsby*, p. 111.

63. Cobbett, W., *Rural Rides*, 1967 edit., 1830, p. 316.

64. Harrison, J. F. C., *Learning and Living*, 1961, p. 40.

65. Barker, T. C. and Harris, J. R., *A Merseyside Town in the Industrial Revolution*, p. 314; Pollard, S., *The Genesis of Modern Management*, 1968 edit., 1965, p. 228; Gatrell, V. A. C., ed. Robert Owen, *A New View of Society*, etc., 1969, p. 50.

66. Ward, J. T., *The Factory System*, Vol. 2, p. 37.

67. Gaskell, P., *Artisans and Machinery*, p. 124; Briggs, A., *Victorian Cities*, p. 117.

68. Hobsbawm, E. J., *Industry and Empire*, pp. 71, 68.

69. Checkland, S. G., *The Rise of Industrial Society in England*, 1815–85, p. 265; Perkin, H. J., *The Origins of Modern English Society*, 1780–1880, 1969, p. 166.

70. Marshall, J. D., Model Communities, in Dyos, H. J. ed., *The Study of Urban History*, p. 216. Ward, J. T., *The Factory System*, Vol. 2, p. 40.

71. Engels, F., *Condition of the Working Class in England*, pp. 54-6.

72. Checkland, S. G., *The Rise of Industrial Society in England*, 1815–85, p. 265. Perkin, H. J., *The Origins of Modern English Society*, 1780–1880, p. 173; Kellett, J. R., *The Impact of Railways on Victorian Cities*, p. 358.

73. Harrison, J. F. C., *Learning and Living*, p. 38.

74. Hobsbawm, E. J., *Industry and Empire*, p. 68.

75. Prest, J., *The Industrial Revolution in Coventry*, pp. 79-80, 90.

76. Briggs, A., *Victorian Cities*, pp. 90-1.

77. *Ibid*., p. 88.

78. Foster, J., 18th Century Towns – A Class Dimension, in Dyos, H. J. ed., *The Study of Urban History*, pp. 281-99.

79. Briggs, A., *Victorian Cities*, Ch. 5.

80. Pollard, S., *A History of Labour in Sheffield*, pp. 41-2.

81. Barker, T. C. and Harris, J. R., *A Merseyside Town in the Industrial Revolution*, pp. 288, 412.

82. Marshall, J. D., Model Communities, in Dyos, H. J. ed., *The Study of Urban History*, pp. 224-30.

83. Dyos, H. J., Agenda for Urban Historians, in Dyos, H. J. ed., *The Study of Urban History*, p. 19.

84. Strange, G. R., The Victorian City and the Frightened Poets, *Victorian Studies*, 1968, Vol. XI, Supplement.

85. Williams, R., *Culture and Society*, 1963 edit., 1960, p. 146.

86. Morris, W., *News from Nowhere*, 1901, p. 99.

87. Briggs, A., *Victorian Cities*, pp. 22-3.

88. Coats, A. W., *The Classical Economists and the Labourer, op. cit.*, p. 109; Cobbett, W., *Rural Rides,* p. 118.

89. Hammond, J. L. and B., *Rise of Modern Industry,* p. 250.

90. Clapham, J. H., *The Railway Age, op cit.*, p. 541.

91. *Ibid.*, p. 545.

92. Pollard, S., *A History of Labour in Sheffield,* p. 14; Hennock, E. P., *Fit and Proper Persons*, p. 191.

93. Mathias, P., *The First Industrial Nation*, p. 13.

94. Checkland, S. G., in Dyos, H. J. ed., *The Study of Urban History*, p. 358.

95. Thompson, E. P., *The Making of the English Working Class*, p. 355.

96. Gaskell, P., *Artisans and Machinery*, pp. 17, 194, 313, 353.

97. Ward, J. T., *The Factory System*, Vol. 1, p. 67.

98. Ward, J. T., *The Factory System*, Vol. 2, pp. 22-3.

99. Briggs, A., *Victorian Cities*, p. 67.

100. Kingsley, C., *Alton Locke*, 1884 edit., p. 339.

101. Cobbett, W., *Rural Rides*, pp. 495-7.

102. eg. Banks, J. A., Population Change and the Victorian City, *Victorian Studies*, 1968, Vol. XI, 3.

103. Briggs, A., *Victorian Cities*, p. 24.

104. Anderson, M,. *Family Structure in Nineteenth Century Lancashire*, 1971, is a pioneer work in this area; Hoggart, R., *The Uses of Literacy*, 1957, remains a highly entertaining introduction to the subject.

4 *The New Machines*

1. *The Town Labourer*, pp. 28-9.

2. Hammond, J. L. and B., *The Skilled Labourer*, p. 5.

3. Driver, C., *Tory Radical, The Life of Richard Oastler*, 1946, p. 426.

4. Thompson, E. P., *The Making of the English Working Class*, p. 224.

5. Driver, C., *Tory Radical*, p. 136; Kydd, S. H., *The History of the Factory Movement*, 1966 edit., 1857, p. 92.

6. Cobbett, W., *Rural Rides*, pp. 317-8.

7. Hobsbawn, E. J., *Industry and Empire*, p. 49.

8. Gaskell, P., *Artisans and Machinery*, pp. 173, 288.

9. Tupling, G. H., *The Economic History of Rossendale*, 1927, p. 214.

10. Thompson, E. P., *The Making of the English Working Class*, p. 599.

11. Webb, B., *My Apprenticeship*, p. 344.

12. Toynbee, A., *The Industrial Revolution*, p. 192; Hammond, J. L. and B., *The Skilled Labourer*, p. 194.

13. *Ibid.*, p. 4; Thompson, E. P., *The Making of the English Working Class*, p. 220.

14. Ward, J. T., *The Factory System*, Vol. 2, p. 43; Gaskell, P., *Artisans and Machinery*, p. 5.

15. Mrs Gaskell, *Mary Barton*, p. 92.

16. *Leeds Mercury*, 2 May 1812.

17. *Manchester Commercial Advertiser*, 21 April 1812.

18. Disraeli, B., *Coningsby*, p. 131.

19. Bythell, D., *The Handloom Weavers*, 1969, pp. 180, 198-9.

20. Hobsbawm, E. J., *The Machine-Breakers*, *Past and Present*, 1, 1952.

21. *Ibid.*, and *The Age of Revolution*, 1962, p. 38; Thompson, E. P., *The Making of the English Working Class*, pp. 569-659; Rudé, G. F. E., *The Crowd in History*, 1964, Ch. 5.

22. Bronte, C., *Shirley*, 1965 edit., p. 108.

23. Hammond, J. L. and B., *The Skilled Labourer*, p. 53.

24. Pamphlet, *From Bishop Blaize to the Misguided Men who destroy Machinery*, 1812.

25. Ure, A., *The Philosophy of Manufactures*, 1967 edit., 1835, p. 8.

26. Webb, B., *My Apprenticeship*, p. 346.

27. Engels, F., *Condition of the Working Class in England*, *op. cit.*, p. 253.

28. *Manchester Commercial Advertiser*, 21 April, 1812.

29. Ure, A., *The Philosophy of Manufactures*, pp. 7-8, 40-1, 365, 369.

30. 1839 Constabulary Commissioners' Report, pp. 71-6.

31. Hammond, J. L. and B., *The Skilled Labourer*, p. 190.

32. *Ibid.*

33. Habakkuk, H. J., *American and British Technology in the 19th Century*, 1962, p. 153.

34. *Ibid.*, pp. 155-6

35. Thomis, M. I., *The Luddites*, p. 16 and *Politics and Society in Nottingham*, p. 35.

36. Smith, W. J., The Architecture of the Domestic System in South East Lancashire and the Adjoining Pennines, in Chapman, S. D. ed., *History of Working Class Housing*, 1971, pp. 261-2.

37. Ure, A., *The Philosophy of Manufactures*, p. 23.

38. Kydd, S. H., *The History of the Factory Movement*, p. 127. Thomis, M. I., *The Luddites*, pp. 63-4.

40. Hobsbawm, E. J., *The Machine Breakers*, *op. cit.*

41. *Ibid.*

42. Patterson, A. T., *Radical Leicester*, p. 41.

43. Thomis, M. I., *The Luddites*, p. 41.

44. Smelser, N. J., *Social Change in the Industrial Revolution*, 1959, espec. p. 321.

45. Thomis, M. I., *The Luddites*, pp. 56-9.

46. Pinchbeck, I., *Women Workers and the Industrial Revolution* 1750–1850, 1969 edit., 1930, pp. 153-4; Hammond, J. L. and B., *The Skilled Labourer*, p. 149.

47. *Ibid.*, p. 194.

48. Patterson, A. T., *Radical Leicester*, p. 41.

49. Prest, J., *Industrial Revolution in Coventry*, p. 47.

50. Hammond, J. L. and B., *The Skilled Labourer*, p. 302; *Leeds Mercury*, 25 January 1812.

51. Thomis, M. I., *The Luddites*, pp. 63-4.

52. 1839 Constabulary Commissioners' Report, p. 76.

53. Hobsbawm, E. J., *The Machine-Breakers, op. cit.*

54. Gaskell, P., *Artisans and Machinery*, p. 323.

55. Hobsbawm, E. J. and Rudé, G. F. E., *Captain Swing*, pp. 362-3.

56. Their views are discussed in Bythell, D., *The Handloom Weavers*, p. 6.

57. 1839 Constabulary Commissioners' Report, pp. 74-6, 88; Hobsbawm, E. J., *The Machine-Breakers, op. cit.*; Cooke Taylor, W., *Notes of a Tour in the Manufacturing Districts of Lancashire*, 1968 edit., 1842, pp. 171-4.

58. Ure, A., *The Philosophy of Manufactures*, pp. 69-76; Thomis, M. I., *The Luddites*, pp. 165-6.

59. Hammond, J. L. and B., *The Skilled Labourer,* p. 243.

60. Hobsbawm, E. J., *The Machine-Breakers, op. cit.*

61. Prest, J., *The Industrial Revolution in Coventry*, p. 118.

62. Gaskell, P., *Artisans and Machinery*, pp. 275, 283.

63. Hobsbawm, E. J., *The Machine-Breakers, op. cit.*

64. Habakkuk, H. J., *American and British Technology in the 19th Century*, p. 142.

65. *Ibid.*, p. 147.

66. Smith, W. J., *The Architecture of the Domestic System in South East Lancashire and the Adjoining Pennines, op. cit.*, pp. 261-2, 272.

67. Habakkuk, H. J., *American and British Technology in the 19th Century.*

68. *Manchester Commercial Advertiser*, 21 April 1812.

69. Cole, G. D. H. and Postgate, R. W., *The Common People*, p. 307.

70. Hammond, J. L. and B., *The Rise of Modern Industry*, p. 205.

71. Morris, W., *News from Nowhere*, pp. 66-7.

72. Thompson, E. P., *The Making of the English Working Class*, p. 327; *The Town Labourer*, p. 28.

73. *Ibid.*, p. 38.

74. Ward, J. T., *The Factory System*, Vol. 2, p. 147.

75. Gaskell, P., *Artisans and Machinery*, pp. 313, 359.

76. Hammond, J. L. and B., *The Skilled Labourer*, p. 147.

77. Bythell, D., *The Handloom Weavers*, p. 139; Gaskell, P., *Artisans and Machinery*, p. 42.

78. *Ibid*., pp. 327-8.

5 *The Handworkers*

1. eg. Pinchbeck, I., *Women Workers and the Industrial Revolution*, 1750–1850, 1930.

2. Perkin, H. J., *The Origins of Modern English Society*, 1780–1880, p. 146.

3. Kydd, S. H., *A History of the Factory Movement*, p. 135.

4. *The Town Labourer*, p. 28.

5. *Ibid*., preface.

6. Coats, A. W., *The Classical Economists and the Labourer*, *op. cit*., p. 104; Flynn, M. W., Introduction to Chadwick's Report, *op. cit*., p. 4.

7. Bythell, D., *The Handloom Weavers*, p. 271.

8. Court, W. H. B., *The Rise of the Midland Industries*, 1600–1838, 1938, pp. 196-7.

9. Hammond, J. L. and B., *The Skilled Labourer*, p. 154.

10. Bythell, D., *The Handloom Weavers*, p. 40.

11. *Ibid*., pp. 41-8.

12. Thompson, E. P., *The Making of the English Working Class*, p. 304.

13. Report of Select Committee on Handloom Weavers, 1835, p. XI. Bythell, D., *The Handloom Weavers*, p. 270.

14. Mathias, P., *The First Industrial Nation*, p. 206.

15. Court, W. H. B., *The Rise of the Midland Industries*, 1600–1838, p. 202.

16. Ure, A., *The Philosophy of Manufactures*, p. 336. Prest, J., *The Industrial Revolution in Coventry*, p. 52.

17. Ure, A., *The Philosophy of Manufactures*, p. 333.

18. Report of Select Committee on Handloom Weavers, 1835, p. XV.

19. Report of Commission on Handloom Weavers, 1841, pp. 98-118.

20. Perkin, H. J., *The Origins of Modern English Society*, 1780–1880, p. 345; Hobsbawm, E. J., *Industry and Empire*, p. 43.

21. Thompson, E. P., *The Making of the English Working Class*, p. 331.

22. Thomis, M. I., *Politics and Society in Nottingham*, p. 38.

23. Prest, J., *The Industrial Revolution in Coventry*, p. 51.

24. *Ibid.*, p. 140.

25. Thomis, M. I., *The Luddites*, pp. 59-61.

26. Hammond, J. L. and B., *The Skilled Labourer*, pp. 200-204.

27. Prest, J., *The Industrial Revolution in Coventry*, p. 66.

28. Smelser, N. J., *Social Change in the Industrial Revolution*, pp. 141, 143.

29. Church, R. A. and Chapman, S. D., Gravener Henson and the Making of the English Working Class, in *Land, Labour, and Population*, *op. cit.*

30. Gaskell, P., *Artisans and Machinery*, pp. 12-14.

31. Report of Commission on Handloom Weavers, 1841, p. 39.

32. Thompson, E. P., *The Making of the English Working Class*, p. 305.

33. Smelser, N. J., *Social Change in the Industrial Revolution*, p. 185.

34. Thomis, M. I., *Politics and Society in Nottingham*, p. 15.

35. Hammond, J. L. and B., *The Skilled Labourer*, p. 58.

36. Patterson, A. T., *Radical Leicester*, p. 284.

37. Ure, A., *The Philosophy of Manufactures*, pp. 328, 336.

38. eg. Pinchbeck, I., *Women Workers and the Industrial Revolution*, *op. cit.*

39. Report of the 1833 Factory Commissioners, p. 51.

40. Patterson, A. T., *Radical Leicester*, p. 283.

41. Thomis, M. I., *Politics and Society in Nottingham*, pp. 18-26.

42. Pinchbeck, I., *Women Workers and the Industrial Revolution*, p. 177; Prest, J., *The Industrial Revolution in Coventry*, p. 65.

43. *Ibid.*, p. 220.

44. Hammond, J. L. and B., *The Skilled Labourer*, p. 204.

45. *Ibid.*, p. 220.

46. Court, W. H. B., *The Rise of the Midland Industries*, 1600–1838, pp. 211, 215.

47. Hobsbawm, E. J., *Industry and Empire*, p. 73.

48. Bythell, D., *The Handloom Weavers*, pp. 106, 137, 139.

49. Clapham, J. H., *The Railway Age*, p. 551; Thompson, E. P., *The Making of the English Working Class*, Ch. 9.

50. Prest, J., *The Industrial Revolution in Coventry*, p. 15.

51. Thomis, M. I., *Politics and Society in Nottingham*, p. 33.

52. Prest, J., *The Industrial Revolution in Coventry*, pp. 112-13.

53. Smelser, N. J., *Social Change in the Industrial Revolution*, p. 260.

54. *Ibid.*, p. 251.

55. Thomis, M. I., *Politics and Society in Nottingham*, p. 103.

56. Hammond, J. L. and B., *The Skilled Labourer*, pp. 218-9.

57. Prest, J., *The Industrial Revolution in Coventry*, p. 62.

58. *Ibid.*, p. 118.

59. Hammond, J. L. and B., *The Skilled Labourer*, pp. 78-9, 91, 94-6.

60. eg. Bythell, D., *The Handloom Weavers*, p. 176.

61. Hammond, J. L. and B., *The Skilled Labourer*, p. 89; Cole, G. D. H. and Postgate, R., *The Common People*, p. 214.

62. Hammond, J. L. and B., *The Skilled Labourer*, p. 113.

63. Thompson, E. P., *The Making of the English Working Class*, p. 331.

64. Bythell, D., *The Handloom Weavers*, pp. 211-29.

65. White, R. J., *Waterloo to Peterloo*, p. 191.

66. Stephens, W. B. ed., *History of Congleton*, 1970, p. 185.

67. Report of Commission on Handloom Weavers, 1841, p. 120.

68. A favourite concept of Smelser, N.J., *Social Change in the Industrial Revolution, op. cit.*

69. Clapham, J. H., *The Railway Age*, p. 556.

70. Bythell, D., *The Handloom Weavers*, pp. 251-263.

71. Prest, J., *The Industrial Revolution in Coventry*, p. 130.

72. Perkin, H. J., *The Origins of Modern English Society*, 1780–1880, p. 345.

73. Hobsbawm, E. J., The Labour Aristocracy in 19th Century Britain, in *Labouring Men*, 1968 edit., 1964.

74. Pinchbeck, I., *Women Workers and the Industrial Revolution*, p. 308; Perkin, H. J., *The Origins of Modern English Society*, p. 146.

75. Bythell, D., *The Handloom Weavers*, p. 161; Thompson, E. P., *The Making of the English Working Class*, pp. 331-46.

6 *The Factory Workers*

1. *The Town Labourer*, p. 26.

2. Hill, C., *Reformation to Industrial Revolution*, p. 272.

3. Mathias, P., *The First Industrial Nation*, pp. 60-3; Perkin, H. J., *The Origins of Modern English Society*, 1780–1880, pp. 129-31; Chambers, J. D. and Mingay, G. E., *The Agricultural Revolution*, 1966, pp. 98-104.

4. Chambers, J. D., Enclosure and Labour Supply in the Industrial Revolution, *Economic History Review*, 2nd Ser., Vol. V, 1953. Marwick, A. J., *The Nature of History*, p. 228.

5. Perkin, H. J., *The Origins of Modern English Society*, 1780–1880, pp. 129-31.

6. Ward, J. T., *The Factory System*, Vol. 1, p. 80.

7. Hill, C., *Reformation to Industrial Revolution*, pp. 261-2.

8. Laslett, P., *The World we have lost*, 1968 edit., 1965, p. 165.

9. Thompson, E. P., *The Making of the English Working Class*, p. 599.

10. *Ibid.*, p. 210; Hammond, J. L. and B., *The Rise of Modern Industry*, p. 232.

11. Chapman, S. D., *The Early Factory Masters*, 1967, pp. 179-99.

12. Prest, J., *The Industrial Revolution in Coventry*, p. 48.

13. *Ibid.*, p. 94.

14. Hill, C., *Reformation to Industrial Revolution*, p. 262.

15. Kydd, S. H., *The History of the Factory Movement*, p. 19.

16. Smelser, N. J., *Social Change in the Industrial Revolution*, p. 103.

17. *Ibid.*, p. 105; Pinchbeck, I., *Women Workers and the Industrial Revolution*, 1750–1850, p. 184.

18. *The Town Labourer*, pp. 145-6.

19. *Ibid.*, p. 31; *The Rise of Modern Industry*, pp. 206, 198.

20. *The Town Labourer*, pp. 24, 44, 171; Kydd, S. H., *The History of the Factory Movement*, p. 22.

21. Hutt, W. M., *The Factory System of the Early 19th Century*, *op. cit.*; Stephens, W. B. ed., *History of Congleton*, p. 185.

22. Ure, A., *The Philosophy of Manufactures*, pp. 310, 353.

23. Ward, J. T., *The Factory System*, Vol. 2, p. 64.

24. Hutt, W. M., *The Factory System of the early 19th Century*, *op. cit.*

25. Ward, J. T., *The Factory Movement*, 1962, pp. 62-3.

26. Hartwell, R. M., *Interpretations of the Industrial Revolution in England*, *op. cit.*; Hutt, W. M., *The Factory System of the early 19th Century*, *op. cit.*; Fraser, D., *The Evolution of the British Welfare State*, 1973, p. 21.

27. 1833 Factory Commissioners' Report, pp. 7-15.

28. Tawney, R. H., *Commonplace Book*, *op. cit.*, p. 12.

29. Pollard, S., *The Genesis of Modern Management*, p. 191.

30. Gaskell, P., *Artisans and Machinery*, p. 162. Ure, A., *The Philosophy of Manufactures*, pp. 290, 231.

31. Hartwell, R. M., Children as Slaves, in Hartwell, R. M., *The Industrial Revolution and Economic Growth*, 1971.

32. 1833 Factory Commissioners' Report, pp. 18-24.

33. Cooke Taylor, W., *Notes of a Tour in the Manufacturing Districts of Lancashire*, p. 163.

34. Ure, A., *The Philosophy of Manufactures*, p. 379.

35. Ward, J. T., *The Factory System*, Vol. 2, p. 27.

36. Kydd, S. H., *The History of the Factory Movement*, pp. 10-11.

37. Hutt, W. M., *The Factory System of the early 19th Century*, *op. cit.*; Smelser, N. J., *Social Change in the Industrial Revolution*, p. 277; Southey, R., *Letters from England*, p. 208.

38. Perkin, H. J., *The Origins of Modern English Society*, 1780–1880, p. 154.

39. 1833 Factory Commissioners' Report, pp. 25-32; Hutt, W. M., *The Factory System of the early 19th Century*, *op. cit.*

40. Smelser, N. J., *Social Change in the Industrial Revolution*, concentrates on this theme.

41. Cobbett, W., *Rural Rides*, p. 395.

42. eg. Hutt, W. M., *The Factory System of the early 19th Century*, *op. cit.*

43. 1833 Factory Commissioner's Report, p. 32.

44. Driver, C., *Tory Radical, The Life of Richard Oastler*, p. 556; Shelley, P. B., A Philosophical View of Reform, in White, R. J. ed., *Political Tracts*, *op. cit.*, p. 234; Southey, R., *Letters From England*, p. 208; Thompson, E. P., *The Making of the English Working Class*, p. 835.

45. Hutt, W. M., *The Factory System of the early 19th Century*, *op. cit.*

46. Hartwell, R. M., *Children as Slaves*, *op. cit.*

47. Hutchins, B. L. and Harrison, A., *A History of Factory Legislation*, 191, p. 90.

48. 1843 2nd Report of the Commissioners on the Employment of Children, p. 205.

49. Ure, A., *The Philosophy of Manufactures*, p. 15; Smelser, N. J., *Social Change in the Industrial Revolution*, p. 105.

50. Hutt, W. M., *The Factory System in the early 19th Century*, *op cit.*

51. *Ibid.*

52. Smelser, N. J., *Social Change in the Industrial Revolution*, pp. 397-8.

53. Hutt, W. M., *The Factory System in the early 19th Century*, *op. cit.*

54. Fraser, D., *The Evolution of the British Welfare State*, p. 17.

55. Hammond, J. L. and B., *The Rise of Modern Industry*, p. 198.

56. *Ibid*., p. 206.

57. *The Town Labourer*, pp. 297, 213.

58. Hutchins, B. L. and Harrison, A., *A History of Factory Legislation*, p. 50; Thompson, E. P., *The Making of the English Working Class*, p. 374.

59. Smelser, N. J., *Social Change in the Industrial Revolution*, pp. 391-2.

60. Mathias, P., *The First Industrial Nation*, p. 203.

61. Ward, J. T., *The Factory System*, Vol. 2, pp. 130-1; Kydd, S. H., *The History of the Factory Movement*, Vol. 2, p. 79.

62. *Ibid*., p. 213; Ward, J. T., *The Factory System*, Vol. 2; pp. 131, 182.

63. Smelser, N. J., *Social Change in the Industrial Revolution*, pp. 297 etc.

64. Ward, J. T., *The Factory System*, Vol. 2, pp. 128-9.

65. Kydd, S. H., *The History of the Factory Movement*, Vol. 1, p. 47.

66. Ward, J. T., *The Factory System*, Vol. 2, pp. 128-9.

67. Kydd, S. H., *The History of the Factory Movement*, Vol. 1, pp. 157-8.

68. 1833 Factory Commissioners' Report, p. 50.

69. Checkland, S. G., *The Rise of Industrial Society in England*, 1815 – 1885, p. 245.

70. Cooke Taylor, W., *Notes of a Tour in the Manufacturing Districts of Lancashire*, p. 249.

71. Ward, J. T., *The Factory Movement*, p. 416; Thompson, E. P., *The Making of the English Working Class*, p. 378.

72. *Ibid*., p. 384.

73. Smelser, N. J., *Social Change in the Industrial Revolution*, pp. 190-210, 294.

74. Kydd, S. H., *The History of the Factory Movement*, Vol. 1, p. 70.

75. 1833 Factory Commissioners' Report, p. 47.

76. Ward, J. T., *The Factory System*, Vol. 2, p. 142.

77. *Ibid*.

78. Hutchins, B. L. and Harrison, A., *A History of Factory Legislation*, 1911, p. 87; Taylor, A. J., *Laissez-faire and State Intervention in Nineteenth-century Britain*, 1972.

79. *The Town Labourer*, pp. 193, 207, 209.

80. Cooke Taylor, W., *Notes of a Tour in the Manufacturing Districts of Lancashire*, p. 131.

81. Ward, J. T., *The Factory System*, Vol. 2, pp. 157, Vol. 1, p. 83.

82. Gaskell, P., *Artisans and Machinery*, p. 173; Hammond, J. L., and B., *The Rise of Modern Industry*, p. 204.

83. 1833 Factory Commissioners' Report, p. 50.

84. Ward, J. T., *The Factory System*, Vol. v, p. 144.

85. *Ibid*., pp. 146-51.

86. Ward, J. T., *The Factory Movement*, p. 412.

87. Ward, J. T., *The Factory System*, Vol. 2, p. 142.

88. Pinchbeck, I., *Women Workers in the Industrial Revolution*, p. 307; Hammond, J. L. and B., *The Rise of Modern Industry*, p. 255.

89. Ward J. T., *The Factory System*, p. 165.

90. 1841 Special Reports of the Inspectors of Factories, x, p. 8; Ward, J. T., *The Factory System*, Vol. 2, p. 166.

91. Checkland, S. G., *The Rise of Industrial Society in England*, 1815 – 1885, pp. 250-1.

92. Hart, J., *19th Century Social Reform: A Tory Interpretation of History, op. cit*; Roberts, D., Jeremy Bentham and the Victorian Administrative State, *Victorian Studies*, Vol. 2, No. 3, March 1959.

93. Ward, J. T., *The Factory System*, Vol. 2, p. 147.

94. Thompson, E. P., *The Making of the English Working Class*, p. 384. Thomas, M. W., *The Early Factory Legislation*, 1948, for role of inspectors.

95. Hartwell, R. M., *The Rise of Modern Industry*, *op. cit*; Hutt, W. H., *The Factory System of the early 19th Century*, *op. cit*.

96. Driver, C., *Tory Radical: The Life of Richard Oastler*, p. 431; Hutt, W. M., *The Factory System of the early 19th Century*, *op. cit*.

97. Checkland, S. G., *The Rise of Industrial Society in England*, 1815 – 1885, pp. 247-9.

98. Ward, J. T., *The Factory Movement*, p. 404.

7 *The Trade Unions*

1. *The Town Labourer*, p. 249.

2. *Ibid.*, pp. 213-4.

3. Smelser, N. J., *Social Change in the Industrial Revolution*, p. 270.

4. Ure, A., *The Philosophy of Manufactures*, p. 338.

5. *Ibid.*, p. 282; Gaskell, P., *Artisans and Machinery*, p. 291.

6. *The Town Labourer*, p. 287.

7. Webb, S. and B., *History of Trade Unionism*, 1920, p. 44.

8. Musson, A. E., *British Trade Unions*, 1800 – 1875, 1972, p. 17; Fraser, W. H., Trade Unionism, in Ward, J. T., *Popular Movements*, 1830 – 50, 1970, p. 99.

9. Webb, S. and B., *History of Trade Unionism*, pp. 46-7; Fraser, W. H., *Trade Unionism*, *op. cit.*, pp. 97-8.

10. 1825 Report of Select Committee on Combination Laws, p. 3.

11. Pelling, H., *History of British Trade Unionism*, 1969 edit., 1963, pp. 33, 36;
Musson, A. E., *British Trade Unions*, 1800–1875, p. 17;
Thomis, M. I., *Politics and Society in Nottingham*, pp. 102-4;
Thompson, E. P., *The Making of the English Working Class*, p. 454.

12. Hobsbawm, E. J., *The Machine-Breakers*, *op. cit.*

13. Gosden, P. M. J. H., *The Friendly Societies in England*, 1815 – 75, pp. 16, 156.

14. Fraser, W. H., *Trade Unionism*, *op. cit.*, p. 99.

15. Perkin, H. J., *The Origins of Modern English Society*, 1780 – 1880, pp. 381-3.

16. Smelser, N. J., *Social Change in the Industrial Revolution*, pp. 315-20.

17. Postgate, R. W., *The Builders' History*, 1923, pp. 55, 59.

18. Cole, G. D. H., *Attempts at General Union*, 1818 – 34, 1953, p. 155.

19. *Ibid.*, p. 11.

20. Musson, A. E., *British Trade Unions*, 1800–1875, pp. 30-2; Pelling, H., *History of British Trade Unionism*, p. 37.

21. Oliver, W. M., The Consolidated Trades' Union of 1934, *Economic*

History Review, 2nd Ser., Vol. XVII, 1, August 1964;
Fraser, W. H., *Trade Unionism*, p. 105;
Postgate, R. W., *The Builders' History*, p. 105.

22. Musson, A. E., *British Trade Unions*, 1800 – 1875, p. 33.

23. Fraser, W. H., *Trade Unionism*, *op. cit.*, pp. 100-107;
Musson, A. E., *British Trade Unions*, 1800–1875, pp. 30-2.

24. eg. Patterson, A. T., *Radical Leicester*, p. 106.

25. *The Town Labourer*, pp. 296-7.

26. Perkin, H., *The Origins of Modern English Society*, 1780 – 1880, pp. 235-6.

27. Clapham, J. H., *The Railway Age*, p. 594.

28. Musson, A. E., *British Trade Unions*, 1800 – 1875, pp. 34-5, 49;
Fraser, W. H., *Trade Unionism*, pp. 110-111.

29. Pelling, H., *History of British Trade Unionism*, pp. 42, 46-7.

30. Williams, J. E., *The Derbyshire Miners*, 1962, p. 89.

31. Pelling, H. *History of British Trade Unionism*, p. 50.

32. Musson, A. E., *British Trade Unions*, pp. 53-4.

33. Fraser, W. H., *Trade Unionism*, *op. cit.*, p. 113.

34. *Ibid.*, p. 111; Jefferys, J. B., *The Story of the Engineers*, 1800 – 1945. 1945, p. 25.
Harrison, R., *Before the Socialists*, p. 10;
Webb, S. and B., *History of Trade Unionism*, p. 179.

35. Harrison, R., *Before the Socialists*, p. 10.

36. Perkin, H. J., *The Origins of Modern English Society*, 1780 – 1880, pp. 404-5.

37. *The Town Labourer*, pp. 195-201.

38. Pelling, H., *History of British Trade Unionism*, p. 55.

39. Perkin, H. J., *The Origins of Modern English Society*, 1780 – 1880, p. 186.

40. 1839 Constabulary Commissioners' Report, pp. 69-70, 73.

41. White, G. and Henson, G., *A few remarks on the state of the laws at present in existence for regulating masters and work people*, 1823, p. 109.

42. Place MSS, BM Add. MSS, 27803, Place's comments on Peter Moore's Bill, 1823.

43. Gaskell, P., *Artisans and Machinery*, p. 285.

44. 1839 Constabulary Commissioners' Report, p. 70.

45. Thomis, M. I., *Politics and Society in Nottingham*, pp. 73-4.

46. Gaskell, P., *Artisans and Machinery*, pp. 279-90.

47. Mrs Gaskell, *Mary Barton*, p. 374.

48. *The Town Labourer*, pp. 236, 233.

49. 1839 Constabulary Commissioners' Report, pp. 69, 73.

50. Ure, A., *The Philosophy of Manufactures*, pp. 280, 40-1.

51. 1825 Report of Select Committee on Combination Laws, pp. 10-12.

52. 1833 Factory Commissioners' Report, p. 47.

53. Kydd, S. H., *The History of the Factory Movement*, p. 274.

54. Hobsbawm, E. J., Custom, Wages, and Work-load in 19th Century industry in Hobsbawm, E. J., *Labouring Men*, 1968 edit., 1964.

55. *The Town Labourer*, Ch. VII, pp. 118-9, 132, 143-4;
Perkin, H. J., *The Origins of Modern English Society*, p. 189.

56. *The Town Labourer*, pp. 143-4.

57. Perkin, H. J., *The Origins of Modern English Society*, p. 188.

58. Postgate, R. W., *The Builders' History*, pp. 12-13.

59. Aspinall, A., *The Early English Trade Unions*, 1949, p. x.
Pelling, H., *History of British Trade Unionism*, p. 25.

60. Aspinall, A., *The Early English Trade Unions*, pp. x, xiii, xvii.
Webb, S. and B., *History of Trade Unionism*, p. 63.

61. George, M. D., The Combination Laws reconsidered, *Economic History*, 1927.

62. Webb, S. and B., *History of Trade Unionism*, p. 77;
Postgate, R. W., *The Builders' History*, p. 28.

63. Thomis, M. I., *Politics and Society in Nottingham*, pp. 60, 63-7.

64. Patterson, A. T., *Radical Leicester*, pp. 125, 139, 287.

65. Aspinall, A., *The Early English Trade Unions*, p. xxi.

Musson, A. E., *British Trade Unions*, 1800 – 1875, p. 24.
Thompson, E. P., *The Making of the English Working Class*, p. 552.

66. Webb, S. and B., *History of Trade Unionism*, p. 83.
Jeffreys, J. B., *The Story of the Engineers*, p. 12.
Pollard, S., *A History of Labour in Sheffield*, pp. 67-8.

67. Thompson, E. P., *The Making of the English Working Class*, pp. 199, 658.

68. Thomis, M. I., *Politics and Society in Nottingham*, p. 41.

69. 1839 Constabulary Commissioners' Report, pp. 70-80.

70. Ure, A., *The Philosophy of Manufactures*, pp. 284-5, 298.

71. Gaskell, P., *Artisans and Machinery*, p. 132;
Smelser, N. J., *Social Change in the Industrial Revolution*, p. 326.

72. *Ibid*., pp. 326, 329-30.

73. Ward, J. T., *The Factory System*, Vol. 2, p. 85.

74. Engels, F., *Condition of the Working Class in England*, *op. cit*., pp. 246-7.

75. Hobsbawm, E. J., Custom, Wages, and Work-load in 19th Century industry, *op. cit.*

76. Smelser, N. J., *Social Change in the Industrial Revolution*, p. 329.

77. *The Town Labourer*, p. 137; Place MSS, BM Add MSS 27803, Fol. 384.

78. Pollard, S., 19th Century Co-operation; From Community-building to shop-keeping, in Briggs, A. and Saville, J. eds., *Essays in Labour History*, 1967 edit., 1960.

79. *Ibid.*

80. Hobsbawm, E. J., Custom, Wages, and Work-load in 19th Century industry, *op. cit.*

81. *Ibid. The Labour Aristocracy in 19th Century Britain, op. cit.*

82. Thompson, William, *Labour Rewarded*, 1827, in Cole, G. D. H. and Filson, R. W., *British Working Class Movements*, *op. cit*., p. 202.

83. Perkin, H. J., *The Origins of Modern English Society*, pp. 395-6, 403-5.

84. *Ibid*., p. 407.

85. Harrison, R., *Before the Socialists*, pp. 15, 17-18, 37-8.

86. Perkin, H. J., *The Origins of Modern English Society*, pp. 421, 423, 426.

87. Hobsbawm, E. J., The Labour Aristocracy in Nineteenth Century Britain, in Hobsbawm, E. J., *Labouring Men*, 1968 edit., 1964.

88. eg. Pollard, S., *A History of Labour in Sheffield*, p. 66.

89. Musson, A. E., *British Trade Unions*, 1800 – 1875, p. 47.

8 *Standards of Living and the Quality of Life*

1. Hobsbawm, E. J., *Industry and Empire*, p. 1.

2. Gaskell, P., *Artisans and Machinery*, p. 7.

3. Mathias, P., *The First Industrial Nation*, pp. 5-7, 26-27; Laslett, P., *The World we have lost*, pp. 31, 47.

4. Thompson, E. P., *The Making of the English Working Class*, pp. 455, 486.

5. Gaskell, P., *Artisans and Machinery*, p. 6.

6. Mathias, P., *The First Industrial Nation*, p. 219.

7. Hammond, J. L. and B., *The Rise of Modern Industry*, p. 196.

8. Foster, J., 19th Century Towns – A Class Dimension, in Dyos, H. J. ed., *The Study of Urban History*, p. 284.

9. Ure, A., *The Philosophy of Manufactures*, p. 8.

10. *The Town Labourer*, p. 119.

11. Perkin, H. J., *The Origins of Modern English Society*, 1780 – 1880, p. 345.

12. Hobsbawm, E. J., *Industry and Empire*, p. 68.

13. Toynbee, A., *The Industrial Revolution*, p. 84; Webb, B., *My Apprenticeship*, p. 345.

14. *The Town Labourer*, Preface.

15. Cobbett, *Rural Rides*, p. 254.

16. Williams, R., *Culture and Society*, p. 41.

17. Coleridge, S. T., A Lay Sermon, in White R. J. ed., *Political Tracts, op. cit.*, p. 103.
Toynbee, A., *The Industrial Revolution*, p. 84.

18. *The Town Labourer*, pp. 28, 47, 102-3, 108, 143.

19. Clapham, J. H., *An Economic History of Modern Britain: The Railway Age*, pp. 548-565.
Checkland, S. G., *The Rise of Industrial Society in England*, 1815 – 1885, p. 227.

20. Clapham, J. H., *The Railway Age*, Preface to 1939 reprint, p. x.

21. Hartwell, R. M., *The Standard of Living Controversy: A Summary*, Hartwell, R. M. ed., *The Industrial Revolution*, 1970, p. 170.

22. Hobsbawm, E. J., The British Standard of Living 1790 – 1850 and The Standard of Living Debate: A Postscript, in *Labouring Men*, 1968 edit., 1964.

23. Hobsbawm, E. J., *Industry and Empire*, p. 74.

24. Taylor, A. J., *Progress and Poverty in Britain*, 1780 – 1850, History, February, 1960.

25. Coats, A. W., *The Classical Economists and the Labourers, op.cit.*, p. 116.

26. Perkin, H. J., *The Origins of Modern English Society*, 1780 – 1880, p. 140.

27. *Ibid.*, p. 138.

28. eg. Hobsbawm, E. J., *Industry and Empire*, p. 72.

29. Hartwell, R. M., The Rising Standard of Living in England, 1800–1850, *Economic History Review*, Vol. XIII, No. 3, 1961.

30. *Ibid.*

31. Mathias, P., *The First Industrial Nation*, pp. 209, 212;
Perkin, H. J., *The Origins of Modern English Society*, 1780 – 1880, pp. 141, 143-4.

32. Hartwell, R. M., *The Rising Standard of Living in England*, 1800 – 1850, *op. cit.*

33. Thompson, E. P., *The Making of the English Working Class*, p. 351.

34. Hobsbawm, E. J., *The British Standard of Living*, 1790–1850, *op. cit*;

Taylor, A. J., *Progress and Poverty in Britain*, 1780–1850, *op. cit.*

35. Hobsbawm, E. J., The British Standard of Living, 1790 – 1850, *op. cit*; Foster, J., *19th Century Towns – A Class Dimsension, op. cit.*, p. 285.

36. Perkin, H. J., *The Origins of Modern English Society*, 1780 – 1880, pp. 146, 421, 423, 427-8.

37. *Ibid.*, p. 148.

38. Checkland, S. G., *The Rise of Industrial Society in England*, 1815 – 1885, p. 229.

39. Ashton, T. S., The Standard of Life of the Workers in England, 1790–1830, in Hayek, F. A. ed., *Capitalism and the Historians, op. cit.*

40. Hobsbawm, E. J., The British Standard of Living, 1790 – 1850 and The Standard of Living Debate: A Postscript, in *Labouring Men, op. cit*; Hartwell, R. M., The Rising Standard of Living in England, 1800 – 1850, op. cit., and the Standard of Living: An Answer to the Pessimists, *Economic History Review*, Vol. XVIII, No. 3, 1965.

41. Mathias, P., *The First Industrial Nation*, pp. 223-4.

42. Marwick, A., *The Nature of History*, p. 66.

43. Hartwell, R. M., *The Rise of Modern Industry, op. cit.*

44. Thompson, E. P., *The Making of the English Working Class*, p. 916.

45. Hartwell, R. M., *The Standard of Living: An Answer to the Pessimists, op. cit.*

46. *The Town Labourer*, preface.

47. Thompson, E. P., *The Making of the English Working Class*, p. 227.

48. Clapham, J. H., *The Railway Age*, preface to 1939 reprint, p. 4.

49. Thompson, E. P., *The Making of the English Working Class*, pp. 230-231.

50. *Ibid.*, pp. 230, 486.

51. Checkland, S. G., *The Rise of Industrial Society in England,* 1815–1885, p. 228.

52. Hartwell, R. M., The Rising Standard of Living in England, 1800–1850, and The Standard of Living Controversy: A Summary, *op. cit.*

53. *Ibid.*

54. Mathias, P., *The First Industrial Nation*, p. 215.

55. Thompson, E. P., *The Making of the English Working Class*, pp. 222-3, 455.

56. Hartwell, R. M., The Standard of Living Controversy: A Summary, *op. cit.*

57. Williams, R., *Culture and Society*, pp. 145-7, 161; Hammond, J. L. and B., *The Rise of Modern Industry*, pp. 195, 232; Thompson, E. P., *The Making of the English Working Class*, p. 222.

58. Tawney, R. H., *Commonplace Book*, *op. cit.*, pp. 34, 40-1, 75.

59. Hobsbawm, E. J., *Industry and Empire*, p. 55.

60. Hobsbawm, E. J., The Standard of Living Debate: A Postscript, *op. cit.*

61. Thomis, M. I., *Politics and Society in Nottingham*, p. 107.

62, Driver, C., Tory Radical, *The Life of Richard Oastler*, p. 430.

63. Tawney, R. H., *Equality*, pp. 140-1, and *Commonplace Book*, *op. cit.*, pp. 9, 12, 18, 70, 80, 83.

9 *The Methodist Contribution*

1. Cobbett, W., *Rural Rides*, p. 182.

2. Body, A. H., *John Wesley and Education*, 1936, p. 40; Thompson, E. P., *The Making of the English Working Class*, pp. 354-5.

3. *The Town Labourer*, pp. 221, 233.

4. Howse, E. M., *Saints in Politics*, 1971 edit., p. 133.

5. Cowherd, R. G., *The Politics of English Dissent*, 1959, p. 166; Howse, E. M., *Saints in Politics*, p. 123.

6. Halévy, E., *England in 1815*, 1961 edit., 1924, pp. 424-8, 590-1.

7. Wearmouth, R. F., *Methodism and the Working Class Movements of England*, 1800–50, 1947 reprint, p. 52.

8. Harrison, J. F. C., *The Early Victorians*, 1971, p. 127; Taylor, E. R., *Methodism and Politics*, 1791–1851, 1935, p. 113; Stigant, P., *Wesleyan Methodism and Working Class Radicalism in the North*, 1792–1821, *Northern History*, Vol. VI, 1971; Wearmouth, R. F., *Methodism and the*

REFERENCES

Working Class Movements of England, 1800–50, pp. 140, 147-8.

9. Currie, R., *Methodism Divided*, 1968, p. 38; Wearmouth, R. F., *Methodism and Working Class Radicalism in the North*, 1792–1821, 148.

10. *The Town Labourer*, pp. 218-38.

11. Ure, A., *The Philosophy of Manufactures*, p. 423-4, 410.

12. Perkin, H. J., *The Origins of Modern English Society*, 1780–1800, p. 285.

13. Thompson, E. P., *The Making of the English Working Class*, p. 368.

14. *Ibid.*, p. 355.

15. Thompson, D. M. ed., *Nonconformity in the 19th Century*, p. 16.

16. Ure, A., *The Philosophy of Manufactures*, pp. 408-428.

17. Thompson, E. P., *The Making of the English Working Class*, pp. 359-369.

18. *Ibid.*, pp. 355-6.

19. Taylor, E. R., *Methodism and Politics*, 1791–1851, p. 61; Harrison, J. F. C., *The Early Victorians*, 1832–51, p. 127; Smelser, N. J., *Social Change in the Industrial Revolution*, pp. 69-71; Inglis, K. S., *The Churches and the Working Classes in Victorian England*, 1963, p. 4. *The Town Labourer*, p. 262.

20. Kitson Clark, G., *The Making of Victorian England*, 1965 edit., 1962, p. 171.

21. Perkin, H. J., *The Origins of Modern English Society*, 1780–1880, p. 199.

22. Wearmouth, R. F., *Methodism and the Working Class Movements of England*, 1800–50, p. 4.

23. Smelser, N. J., *Social Change in the Industrial Revolution*, p. 71.

24. Hobsbawm, E. J., Methodism and the threat of the Revolution in Britain, in *Labouring Men*, *op. cit.*

25. Hill, C., *Reformation to Industrial Revolution*, p. 276.

26. *The Town Labourer*, p. 264.

27. *Ibid.*, p. 262.

28. Kitson Clark, G., *The Making of Victorian England*, p. 196.

29. Checkland, S. G., *The Rise of Industrial Society in England*, 1815-1885, p. 270; Thompson, E. P., *The Making of the English Working Class,* pp. 378-9. *The Town Labourer*, p. 260; Harrison, J. F. C., *The Early Victorians*, p. 171; Hartwell, R. M. and Currie, R., The Making of the English Working Class? in Hartwell, R. M., *The Industrial Revolution and Economic Growth,* p. 372.

30. *Ibid.*

31. Harrison, J. F. C., *The Early Victorians*, p. 128.

32. Thompson, E. P., *The Making of the English Working Class*, pp. 381, 388.

33. Stigant, P., Wesleyan Methodism and Working Class Radicalism in the North, 1792–1821, *op. cit.*

34. Hartwell, R. M. and Currie, R., *The Making of the English Working Class?*, *op. cit.*

35. Hobsbawm, E. J., *Methodism and the threat of revolution in Britain*, *op. cit.*

36. Hobsbawm, E. J. and Rudé, G. F. E., *Captain Swing*, pp. 186-7.

37. Ure, A., *The Philosophy of Manufactures*, p. 410.

38. Gaskell, P., *Artisans and Machinery*, p. 244.

39. Smelser, N. J., *Social Change in the Industrial Revolution*, p. 76; Thompson, E. P., *The Making of the English Working Class*, p. 377.

40. Ure, A., *The Philosophy of Manufactures,* p. 423.

41. Gaskell, P., *Artisans and Machinery*, p. 250.

42. Ure, A., *The Philosophy of Manufactures*, p. 426-7.

43. Thompson, E. P., *The Making of the English Working Class*, p. 389.

44. Brown, F. K., *Fathers of the Victorians*, 1961, p. 125.

45. Tames, R., *Economy and Society in 19th Century Britain*, 1972, p. 119.

46. Body, A. H., *John Wesley and Education*, pp. 40, 42, 47, 50-1, 64, 86, 133.

47. Checkland, S. G., *The Rise of Industrial Society in England*, 1815–85, p. 257.

48. Kitson Clark, G., *The Making of Victorian England*, pp. 193, 196; Hill, C., *Reformation to Industrial Revolution*, p. 278.

49. Patterson, A. T., *Radical Leicester*, p. 327.

50. *The Town Labourer*, p. 242.

51. Taylor, E. R., *Methodism and Politics*, 1791–1851, p. 206.

52. Stigant, P., Wesleyan Methodism and Working Class Radicalism in the North, 1792–1821, *op. cit.*

53. Perkin, H. J., *The Origins of Modern English Society*, 1780–1880, pp. 203, 354.

54. Thompson, E. P., *The Making of the English Working Class*, pp. 378, 391-2.

55. Hobsbawm, E. J., *Methodism and the threat of revolution in Britain*, *op. cit.*

56. Kydd, S. H., *The History of the Factory Movement*, Vol. 2, p. 100.

57. Thompson, D. M. ed., *Nonconformity in the 19th Century*, p. 17.

58. Howse, E. M., *Saints in Politics*, p. 123.

59. Thompson, E. P., *The Making of the English Working Class*, p. 46.

60. *The Town Labourer*, p. 272.

61. Harrison, J. F. C., *The Early Victorians*, 1832–51, p. 129.

62. Wearmouth, R. F., *Methodism and the Working Class Movements of England*, 1800–50, pp. 171-6, 225; Perkin, H. J., *The Origins of Modern English Society*, 1780–1880, pp. 354-361.

63. Harrison, J. F. C., Chartism in Leicester, in Briggs, A. ed., *Chartist Studies*, 1967 edit., 1958, p. 8.

64. Perkin, H. J., *The Origins of Modern English Society*, 1780–1880, p. 356; Thomis, M. I., *Politics and Society in Nottingham*, p. 137; Thompson, E. P., *The Making of the English Working Class*, p. 355.

65. Hill, C., *Reformation to Industrial Revolution*, p. 276.

66. Perkin, H. J., *The Origins of Modern English Society*, 1780–1880, pp. 354-361.

67. Hobsbawm, E. J., *Methodism and the threat of revolution in Britain*, *op. cit.*

68. Inglis, K. S., *The Churches and the Working Classes in Victorian England*, p. 13.

69. Stigant, P., *Wesleyan Methodism and Working Class Radicalism in the North*, 1792–1821, *op. cit.*

70. Thompson, E. P., *The Making of the English Working Class*, p. 49; Hartwell, R. M. and Currie, R., *The Making of the English Working Class, op. cit.*

71. Inglis, K. S., *The Churches and the Working Classes in Victorian England*, p. 2; Cobbett, W., *Rural Rides*, p. 180; Gaskell, P., *Artisans and Machinery*, p. 253.

72. Kitson Clark, G., *The Making of Victorian England*, pp. 163-4, 167; Perkin, H. J., *The Origins of Modern English Society*, 1780–1880, pp. 199-200.

73. Best, G. F., *Mid-Victorian Britain*, 1851–75, 1971, p. 192; Pelling, H., *Religion and the 19th Century British Working Class, Past and Present*, 27, 1964.

74. Perkin, H. J., *The Origins of Modern English Society*, 1780–1880, p. 202.

75. Tawney, R. H., *Religion and the Rise of Capitalism*, p. 280.

76. Kitson Clark, G., *The Making of Victorian England*, p. 197; Howse, E. M., *Saints in Politics*, p. 136.

77. Harrison, J. F. C., *The Early Victorians*, 1832–51, p. 126.

78. *The Town Labourer*, p. 271.

79. Kitson Clark, G., *The Making of Victorian England*, p. 197.

80. Inglis, K. S., *The Churches and the Working Classes in Victorian England*, pp. 335-6; Kitson Clark, G., *Churchmen and the Condition of England*, 1973, p. XXI.

10 *The English Working Class*

1. Hobsbawm, E. J., *The Labour Aristocracy in 19th Century Britain, op. cit.*

2. Perkin, H. J., *The Origins of Modern English Society*, 1780–1880, p. 209.

3. Thompson, E. P., *The Making of the English Working Class*.

4. Williams, R., *Culture and Society*, p. 33; Disraeli, B., *Sybil*, p. 222; Briggs, A., *Victorian Cities*, p. 91.

5. Cobbett, W., Address to the Journeymen and Labourers, 1816, in Cole, G. D. H. and Filson, R. W., *British Working Class Movements, op. cit.*, p. 122.

6. Kingsley, C., *Alton Locke*, p. 339; Williams, R., *Culture and Society*, p. 185.

7. *The Town Labourer*, pp. 43, 249, 289-90.

8. Thompson, E. P., *The Making of the English Working Class*, p. 218.

9. Cole, G. D. H. and Filson, R. W., *British Working Class Movements, op. cit.*, p. 164; Smelser, N. J., *Social Change in the Industrial Revolution*, p. 326.

10. eg. Cole, G. D. H. and Filson, R. W., *British Working Class Movements, op. cit.*

11. Harrison, R., *Before the Socialists*, p. 55.

12. Cole, G. D. H. and Filson, R. W., *British Working Class Movements, op. cit.*

13. Thompson, E. P., *The Making of the English Working Class*, pp. 913, 213.

14. *Ibid.*, pp. 454, 462, 488, 887.

15. Engels, F., *Condition of the Working Class in England, op. cit.*, p. 273.

16. Thompson, E. P., *The Making of the English Working Class*, pp. 883, 888.

17. *Ibid.*, pp. 463, 912.

18. Harrison, R., *Before the Socialists*, p. 3.

19. Engels, F., The English Working-Class Movement in 1879, in Engels, F., *Selected Writings*, ed., Henderson, W. O., 1967, p. 97.

20. Webb, B., *My Apprenticeship*, p. 191.

21. Lovett, W., *Life and Struggles*, 1920 edit., 1876, p. 442.

22. White, R. J., *Waterloo to Peterloo*, p. 191.

23. The Crisis, 3 May, 1934.

24. Thompson, E. P., *The Making of the English Working Class*, p. 12.

25. *Ibid.*, pp. 451, 81.

26. Cole, G. D. H. and Filson, R. W., *British Working Class Movements, op. cit.*, p. 394.

27. Perkin, H. J., *The Origins of Modern English Society*, p. 209.

28. Hoggart, R., *The Uses of Literacy*, pp. 15-16.

29. Engels, F., The General Election of 1868, in Engels, F., *Selected Writings, op cit.*, p. 97.

30. Prest, J., *The Industrial Revolution in Coventry*, pp. 47, 51-2, 68, 80, 117.

31. Hobsbawm, E. J., *The Labour Aristocracy in 19th Century Britain, op. cit.*

32. Hobsbawm, E. J., *Custom, Wages, and Work-load in 19th Century Industry, op. cit.*

33. Harrison, R., *Before the Socialists*, p. 25.

34. Thompson, E. P., *The Making of the English Working Class*, pp. 270, 266.

35. Harrison, R., *Before the Socialists*, p. 5.

36. Perkin, H. J., *The Origins of Modern English Society*, p. 346.

37. Harrison, R., *Before the Socialists*, pp. 18-19.

38. Toynbee, A., *The Industrial Revolution*, p. 84.

39. Hobsbawm, E. J., *The Labour Aristocracy in 19th Century Britain, op. cit.*

40. Foster, J., 19th century Towns – A Class Dimension, in Dyos, H. J. ed., *A Study of Urban History*, pp. 284-292.

41. Checkland, S. G. in *Ibid.*, p. 348.

42. Marshall, J. D. in *Ibid.*, pp. 215-230.

43. Gaskell, P., *Artisans and Machinery*, p. 248.

44. Perkin, H. J., *The Origins of Modern English Society*, 1780–1880, pp. 305-6; Tames, R., *Economy and Society in 19th Century Britain*, p. 119.

45. Eliot, G., *Felix Holt*, 1907 edit., p. 66.

46. Cooper, T., *The Life of Thomas Cooper*, 1879, p. 393.

47. Harrison, R., *Before the Socialists*, pp. 114, 119, 6-10, 17-18, 57; Perkin, H. J., *The Origins of Modern English Society*, 1780–1880, pp. 381-407.

48. Harrison, R., *Before the Socialists*, pp. 190-1.

49. Hoggart, R., *The Uses of Literacy*, p. 16.

50. Thomis, M. I., *Politics and Society in Nottingham*, p. 28; Cooper, T., *The Life of Thomas Cooper*, p. 393.

51. Webb, B., *My Apprenticeship*, p. 191.

52. Harrison, R., *Before the Socialists*, p. 21.

53. Tawney, R. H., *Commonplace Book*, *op. cit.*, p. 80.

54. Harrison, R., *Before the Socialists*, p. 342.

55. Checkland, S. G., *The Rise of Industrial Society in England*, 1815–1885, pp. 265-9; Tames, R., *Economy and Society in 19th Century Britain*, pp. 141-2.

56. Anderson, M., *Family Structure in 19th Century Lancashire*, p. 178.

Select bibliography

Bibliographical Note

This is not a work of original research. I have consulted only a small selection of the most obvious primary sources, such as Parliamentary papers, contemporary political writings, and contemporary novels. These are referred to in footnotes and are not listed here; nor are the 'learned articles'. I have shirked the nigh-impossible task of trying to compile a comprehensive book-list on this subject and have instead listed the principal books which I found particularly helpful. Not all will agree with my selection.

ANDERSON, M. *Family Structure in Nineteenth Century Lancashire*, 1971.
ASPINALL, A. *The Early English Trade Unions*, 1949.
BARKER, T. C. and HARRIS, J. R. *A Merseyside Town in the Industrial Revolution: St Helens, 1750–1900*, 1959.
BODY, A. H. *John Wesley and Education*, 1936.
BRIGGS, A. *The Age of Improvement*, 1959.
—— *Victorian Cities*, 1968 edit., 1963.
—— ed. *Chartist Studies*, 1967 edit., 1959.
—— and SAVILLE, J. *Essays in Labour History*, 1967 edit., 1960.
BROWN, F. K. *Fathers of the Victorians*, 1961.
BYTHELL, D. *The Handloom Weavers*, 1969.
CARR, E. H. *What is History*, 1964 edit., 1961.
CHALONER, W. H. *The Social and Economic Development of Crewe*, 1950.
—— and HENDERSON, W. O. eds. *The Condition of the Working Class in England*, F. Engels, 1958.
CHAMBERS, J. D. *Modern Nottingham in the Making*, 1945.
—— and MINGAY, G. E. *The Agricultural Revolution, 1750–1880*, 1966.
CHAPMAN, S. D. *The Early Factory Masters*, 1967.
—— ed. *The History of Working Class Housing*, 1971.
CHECKLAND, S. G. *The Rise of Industrial Society in England, 1815–85*, 1964.
CHURCH, R. A. *Economic and Social Change in a Midland Town: Victorian Nottingham, 1815–1900*, 1966.

SELECT BIBLIOGRAPHY

CLAPHAM, J. H. *An Economic History of Modern Britain: The Railway Age*, 1963–1964 edit., 1926.

CLARK, G. KITSON *The Making of Victorian England*, 1965 edit., 1962.

—— *Churchmen and the Condition of England*, 1973.

COLE, G. D. H. *Attempts at General Union*, 1818–34, 1953.

—— and FILSON, R. W. *eds.* *British Working Class Movements, Select Documents, 1789–1875*, 1965 edit., 1951

—— and POSTGATE, R. *The Common People*, 1946 edit., 1938.

COURT, W. H. B. *The Rise of the Midland Industries, 1600–1838*, 1938.

COWHERD, R. G. *The Politics of Engish Dissent*, 1959.

CRITCHLEY, T. A. *A History of Police in England and Wales, 900–1966*, 1967.

CURRIE, R. *Methodism Divided*, 1968.

DARVALL, F. O. *Popular Disturbances and Public Order in Regency England*, 1934.

DRIVER, C. *Tory Radical: The Life of Richard Oastler*, 1946.

DYOS, H. J. ed. *The Study of Urban History*, 1968.

FLINN, M. W. Introduction to Chadwick's *Report on the Sanitary Condition of the Labouring Population of Great Britain, 1842*, 1965.

FORTESCUE, J. W. *A History of the British Army*, Vol. IV, 1906.

FRASER, D. *The Evolution of the British Welfare State*, 1973.

GATRELL, V. A. C. ed. *A New View of Society and Report to the County of Lanark*, R. Owen, 1970.

GILL, C. *History of Birmingham*, Vol. 1, 1952.

GOSDEN, P. H. J. H. *The Friendly Societies in England, 1815–75*, 1961.

HABAKKUK, H. J. *American and British Technology in the 19th Century*, 1962.

HALEVY, E. *England in 1815*, 1924.

HAMMOND, J. L. and B. *The Town Labourer*, 1966 edit., 1917.

—— *The Skilled Labourer, 1760–1832*, 1919.

—— *Lord Shaftesbury*, 1923.

—— *The Rise of Modern Industry*, 1966 edit., 1925.

—— *The Bleak Age*, 1934.

HARRISON, J. F. C. *Learning and Living, 1790–1960*, 1961.

—— *The Early Victorians*, 1971.

HARTWELL, R. M. *The Industrial Revolution and Economic Growth*, 1971.

—— ed. *The Industrial Revolution*, 1970.

HAYEK, F. A. ed. *Capitalism and the Historians*, 1954.

HENDERSON, W. O. ed. *Engels: Selected Writings*, 1967.

HENNOCK, E. P. *Fit and Proper Persons*, 1973.

HILL, C. *Reformation to Industrial Revolution*, 1969 edit., 1967.

HOBSBAWM, E. J. *The Age of Revolution*, 1962.

—— *Industry and Empire*, 1968.

—— *Labouring Men*, 1968 edit., 1964.

—— and RUDE, G. F. E. *Captain Swing*, 1969.

HOGGART, R. *The Uses of Literacy*, 1958 edit., 1957.

HOWSE, E. M. *Saints in Politics*, 1971 edit., 1953.

HUTCHINS, B. L. and HARRISON, A. *A History of Factory Legislation*, 1911.

INGLIS, B. *Poverty and the Industrial Revolution*, 1971.

INGLIS, K. S. *Churches and the Working Classes in Victorian England*, 1963.

JEFFERYS, J. B. *The Story of the Engineers, 1800–1945*, 1945.

JONES, E. and MINGAY, G. E. eds. *Land, Labour and Population, Essays in honour of J. D. Chambers*, 1967.

KELLETT, J. R. *The Impact of Railways on Victorian Cities*, 1969.

LANDES, D. M. *The Unbound Prometheus*, 1969.

LASLETT, P. *The World we have lost*, 1971 edit., 1965.

SELECT BIBLIOGRAPHY

MARWICK, A. *The Nature of History*, 1970.
MATHER, F. C. *Public Order in the Age of the Chartists*, 1959.
MATHIAS, P. M. *The First Industrial Nation*, 1969.
MUMFORD, L. *The City in History*, 1966 edit., 1961.
MUSSON, A. E. *British Trade Unions, 1800–1875*, 1972.
PATTERSON, A. T. *Radical Leicester*, 1954.
PELLING, H. *A History of British Trade Unionism*, 1963.
PERKIN, H. J. *The Origins of Modern English Society*, 1969.
PINCHBECK, I. *Women Workers and the Industrial Revolution, 1750–1850*, 1930.
POLLARD, S. *A History of Labour in Sheffield*, 1959.
—— *The Genesis of Modern Management*, 1968 edit., 1965.
POSTAN, M. M. *Fact and Relevance, Essays on Historical Method*, 1971.
POSTGATE, R. W. *The Builders' History*, 1923.
PREST, J. *The Industrial Revolution in Coventry*, 1960.
RADZINOWICZ, L. *A History of English criminal law and its administration from 1750*, Vol. 4, 1968.
READ, D. *Press and people, 1790–1850: opinion in 3 English cities*, 1961.
—— *The English provinces, 1760–1960*, 1964.
REITH, C. *Short History of the British Police*, 1948.
RUDE, G. F. E. *The Crowd in History*, 1964.
SMELSER, N. J. *Social Change in the Industrial Revolution*, 1959.
TAMES, R. *Economy and Society in 19th century Britain*, 1972.
TAWNEY, R. H. *Religion and the Rise of Capitalism*, 1938 edit., 1926.
—— *Equality*, 1931.
—— *Commonplace Book*, ed. Winter, J. M. and Joslin, D. M., 1972.
TAYLOR, A. J. *Laissez-faire and State Intervention in Nineteenth Century Britain*, 1972.
TAYLOR, E. R. *Methodism and Politics, 1791–1851*, 1935.
THOMAS, M. W. *The Early Factory Legislation*, 1948.
THOMIS, M. I. *Politics and Society in Nottingham, 1785–1835*, 1969.
—— *The Luddites*, 1970.
THOMPSON, D. M. ed. *Nonconformity in the Nineteenth Century*, 1972.
THOMPSON, E. P. *The Making of the English Working Class*, 1968 edit, 1963.
TOBIAS, J. J. *Crime and Industrial Society in the 19th century*, 1967.
WALMSLEY, R. *Peterloo: The Case Reopened*, 1969.
WARD, J. T. *The Factory Movement*, 1962.
—— ed. *The Factory System*, Vols. 1 and 2, 1970.
—— ed. *Popular Movements*, c. *1830–1850*, 1970.
WEARMOUTH, R. F. *Methodism and the Working Class Movements of England, 1800–50*, 1937.
WEBB, B. *My Apprenticeship*, 1971 edit., 1926.
WEBB, S. and B. *History of Trade Unionism*, 1920 edit., 1894.
WESTERN, J. R. *The English Militia in the Eighteenth Century*, 1965.
WHITE, R. J. *Waterloo to Peterloo*, 1963 edit., 1957.
—— ed. *Political Tracts of Wordsworth, Coleridge and Shelley*, 1953.
WILLIAMS, J. E. *The Derbyshire Miners*, 1962.
WILLIAMS, R. *Culture and Society*, 1961 edit., 1958.
WOODCOCK, G. *ed. Rural Rides*, W. Cobbett, 1967.

Index